SCOTT FORESMAN · ADDISON WESLEY

Mathematics

Authors

Randall I. Charles

Janet H. Caldwell
Mary Cavanagh
Dinah Chancellor
Alma B. Ramirez

Warren Crown

Jeanne F. Ramos
Kay Sammons
Jane F. Schielack

Francis (Skip) Fennell

William Tate
Mary Thompson
John A. Van de Walle

Consulting Mathematicians

Edward J. Barbeau
Professor of Mathematics
University of Toronto
Toronto, Ontario, Canada

David M. Bressoud
DeWitt Wallace Professor of
  Mathematics
Macalester College
Saint Paul, Minnesota

Gary Lippman
Professor of Mathematics and
  Computer Science
California State University
  Hayward
Hayward, California

D1500453

Editorial Offices: Glenview, Illinois • Parsippany, New Jersey • New York, New York

Sales Offices: Boston, Massachusetts • Duluth, Georgia • Glenview, Illinois
Coppell, Texas • Sacramento, California • Mesa, Arizona

Reading Consultants

Peter Afflerbach
Professor and Director of
   The Reading Center
University of Maryland
College Park, Maryland

Donald J. Leu
John and Maria Neag
   Endowed Chair in Literacy and Technology
University of Connecticut
Storrs, Connecticut

Reviewers

Donna McCollum Derby
Teacher
Kernersville Elementary School
Kernersville, North Carolina

Terri Geaudreau
Title I Math Facilitator
Bemiss Elementary
Spokane, Washington

Sister Helen Lucille Habig, RSM
Assistant Superintendent of
   Catholic Schools
Archdiocese of Cincinnati
Cincinnati, Ohio

Kim Hill
Teacher
Hayes Grade Center
Ada, Oklahoma

Martha Knight
Teacher
Oak Mountain Elementary
Birmingham, Alabama

Catherine Kuhns
Teacher
Country Hills Elementary
Coral Springs, Florida

Susan Mayberger
Supervisor of English as a Second
   Language/Director of Migrant Education
Omaha Public Schools
Omaha, Nebraska

Judy Peede
Elementary Lead Math Teacher
Wake County Schools
Raleigh, North Carolina

Lynda M. Penry
Teacher
Wright Elementary
Ft. Walton Beach, Florida

Jolyn D. Raleigh
District Math Curriculum Specialist K–2
Granite School District
Salt Lake City, Utah

Vickie H. Smith
Assistant Principal
Phoenix Academic Magnet
   Elementary School
Alexandria, Louisiana

Ann Watts
Mathematics Specialist
East Baton Rouge Parish School System
Baton Rouge, Louisiana

ISBN: 0-328-26365-6

13 14 15 16 V064 17 16 15

Instant Check System
- Check, daily
- Think About It, daily
- Diagnostic Checkpoint, 11, 21, 33

Test Prep
- Test Talk, 37
- Cumulative Review and Test Prep, 12, 22, 34

Reading For Math Success
- Math Story, 1A
- Reading for Math Success, 7

Writing in Math
- Writing in Math exercises, 8, 16, 20, 24, 32, 35

 Problem-Solving Applications, 31

Discovery CHANNEL SCHOOL Discover Math in Your World, 38

Additional Resources
- Home-School Connection, 1
- Practice Game, 2
- Enrichment, 35
- Learning with Technology, 36
- Chapter 1 Test, 39

© Pearson Education, Inc.

Instant Check System
- Check, daily
- Think About It, daily
- Diagnostic Checkpoint, 59, 71

Test Prep
- Test Talk, 75
- Cumulative Review and Test Prep, 60, 72, 78A

Reading For Math Success
- Math Story, 2A
- Reading for Math Success, 55

Writing in Math
- Writing in Math exercises, 48, 56, 62, 64, 70, 73, 78B

Problem-Solving Applications, 69

Discovery Discover Math in **SCHOOL** Your World, 76

Additional Resources
- Home-School Connection, 41
- Practice Game, 42
- Enrichment, 73
- Learning with Technology, 74
- Chapter 2 Test, 77

Place Value to 100 and Money

CHAPTER 4

Mental Math: Addition and Subtraction

© Pearson Education, Inc.

Instant Check System
- Check, daily
- Think About It, daily
- Diagnostic Checkpoint, 183, 201

 Test Prep
- Test Talk, 205
- Cumulative Review and Test Prep, 184, 202

 *Reading For Math Success*
- Math Story, 5A
- Reading for Math Success, 195

Writing in Math
- Writing in Math exercises, 176, 196, 200, 202, 203

Problem-Solving Applications, 199

Discovery Discover Math in Your World, 206

Additional Resources
- Home-School Connection, 173
- Practice Game, 174
- Enrichment, 203
- Learning with Technology, 204
- Chapter 5 Test, 207

Two-Digit Subtraction

CHAPTER 7 Geometry and Fractions

ix

Instant Check System
- Check, daily
- Think About It, daily
- Diagnostic Checkpoint, 307, 317, 331

Test Prep
- Test Talk, 335
- Cumulative Review and Test Prep, 308, 318, 332, 338A

- Math Story, 8A
- Reading for Math Success, 309

Writing in Math

- Writing in Math exercises, 296, 308, 316, 318, 322, 326, 330, 332, 333, 338B

Problem-Solving Applications, 329

Discovery Discover Math in Your World, 336

Additional Resources
- Home-School Connection, 289
- Practice Game, 290
- Enrichment, 333
- Learning with Technology, 334
- Chapter 8 Test, 337

Instant Check System
- Check, daily
- Think About It, daily
- Diagnostic Checkpoint, 361, 371, 381

Test Prep
- Test Talk, 385
- Cumulative Review and Test Prep, 362, 372, 382

Reading For Math Success

- Math Story, 9A
- Reading for Math Success, 349

Writing in Math

- Writing in Math exercises, 348, 352, 354, 362, 370, 372, 380, 382, 383

Problem-Solving Applications, 379

Discovery Discover Math in Your World, 386

Additional Resources

- Home-School Connection, 339
- Practice Game, 340
- Enrichment, 383
- Learning with Technology, 384
- Chapter 9 Test, 387

© Pearson Education, Inc.

xi

Numbers to 1,000

 Instant Check System
- Check, daily
- Think About It, daily
- Diagnostic Checkpoint, 403, 417

 Test Prep
- Test Talk, 421
- Cumulative Review and Test Prep, 404, 418, 424A

 **Reading For Math Success**
- Math Story, 10A
- Reading for Math Success, 411

Writing in Math
- Writing in Math exercises, 398, 404, 410, 416, 418, 419, 424, 424B

 Problem-Solving Applications, 415

DISCOVERY CHANNEL SCHOOL Discover Math in Your World, 422

Additional Resources
- Home-School Connection, 389
- Practice Game, 390
- Enrichment, 419
- Learning with Technology, 420
- Chapter 10 Test, 423

CHAPTER 11
Addition and Subtraction of Three-Digit Numbers

 Instant Check System
- Check, daily
- Think About It, daily
- Diagnostic Checkpoint, 441, 457

 Test Prep
- Test Talk, 461
- Cumulative Review and Test Prep, 442, 458

 **Reading For Math Success**
- Math Story, 11A
- Reading for Math Success, 437

Writing in Math
- Writing in Math exercises, 440, 442, 454, 456, 458, 459

 Problem-Solving Applications, 455

Discovery SCHOOL Discover Math in Your World, 462

Additional Resources
- Home-School Connection, 425
- Practice Game, 426
- Enrichment, 459
- Learning with Technology, 460
- Chapter 11 Test, 463

© Pearson Education, Inc.

Understanding Multiplication and Division

Ten in the Bed

An Old Rhyme Retold by Anne Miranda

Illustrated by Bridget Starr Taylor

This Math Storybook belongs to

_____

There were **10** in the bed,
and the little one said,
"Roll over. Roll over!"
So they all rolled over,
and **I** fell out.

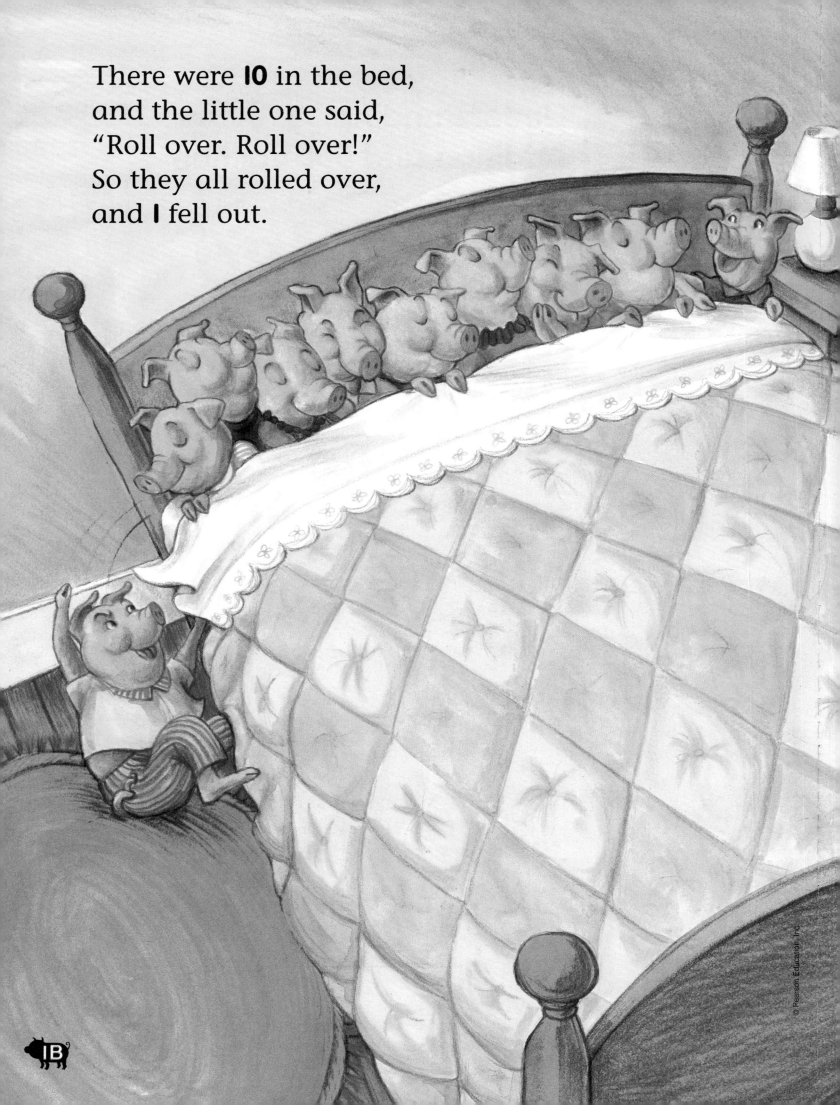

Then there were **9** in the bed,
and the little one said,
"Roll over. Roll over!"
So they all rolled over,
and **2** more fell out.

Then there were **7** in the bed,
and the little one said,
"Roll over. Roll over!"
So they all rolled over,
and **3** more fell out.

Then there were **4** in the bed,
and the little one said,
"Roll over. Roll over!"
So they all rolled over,
and all **4** fell out.

Then there were ZERO in the bed,
and the little one said,
"What happened?
What happened?"
So they all got up
and went back to bed.

There were **10** in the bed,
and the little one said,
"Roll over. Roll over!"

But the other **9** said,
"No! Go to sleep!"
And he did, without another peep!

Dear Family,

Today my class started Chapter 1, **Understanding Addition and Subtraction.** I will learn that adding means joining groups of things together, and that subtracting means taking things away from a group, or comparing two groups to see which one has more. Here are some of the math words I will be learning and some things we can do to help me with my math.

Love,

_____

Math Activity to Do at Home

Gather a collection of objects and help your child use them to make up and solve "joining" stories, "taking away" stories, and "comparing" stories. *A joining story:* "I have 8 books, and here are 4 more. So now how many books do I have? I have 12 books in all."

Books to Read Together

Reading math stories reinforces concepts. Look for these titles in your local library:

12 Ways to Get to 11
By Eve Merriam
(Simon & Schuster, 1993)

Rooster's Off to See the World
By Eric Carle
(Turtleback Books, 1999)

Take It to the NET
More Activities
www.scottforesman.com

My New Math Words

addend Each number that is being added to another number is called an addend.

addend
$$4 + 3 = 7 \longleftarrow \text{sum}$$

sum When numbers are added together, the answer is called the sum. (See above.)

difference When one number is subtracted from another number, the answer is called the difference.

$$8 - 3 = 5 \longleftarrow \text{difference}$$

$$\begin{array}{r} 8 \\ - 3 \\ \hline 5 \end{array}$$

fact family A fact family is a group of related facts. A fact family has either two members (e.g., $4 + 4 = 8$ and $8 - 4 = 4$) or four members (e.g., $4 + 8 = 12$, $8 + 4 = 12$, $12 - 4 = 8$, and $12 - 8 = 4$).

Name _____

Spin and Subtract

How to Play

1. Take turns spinning to find the number of pigs that have fallen out of bed.
2. Subtract that number from 10.
3. Place your marker on the answer. (Once an answer is covered, you may not use it again.)
4. Continue taking turns until you have covered all of the answers.

Name_____

How many muffins are there in the two groups?

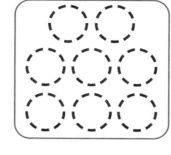

____5____ and ____3____ is ____8____ in all .

To add, join the two groups together.

Check ✓

Count the muffins in the two groups.
Draw and write how many there are in all.

1

_____ and _____ is _____ in all.

2

_____ and _____ is _____ in all.

Think About It   Reasoning

When you join two groups together, do
you get more or fewer objects? Explain.

Practice

Count the fruit in the two groups.
Draw and write how many there are in all.

3

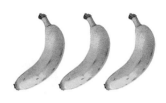

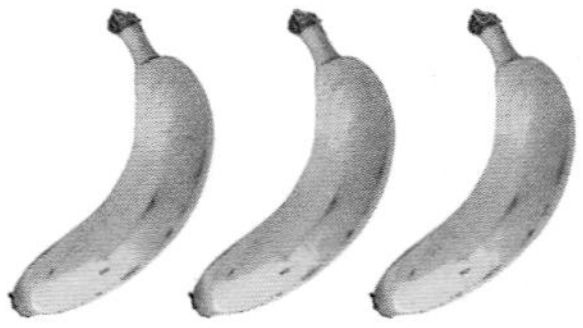

3 and 3 is 6 in all.

4

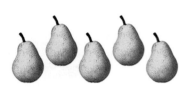

____ and ____ is ____ in all.

5

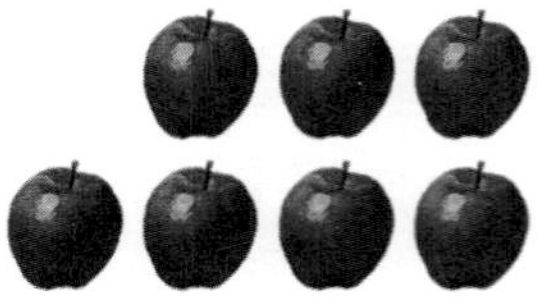

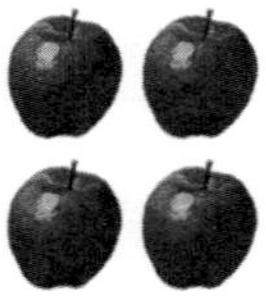

____ and ____ is ____ in all.

Problem Solving **Algebra**

6 Draw the missing oranges.
Then write the missing numbers.

9 and ____ is ____ in all.

Home Connection Your child joined groups of objects to find how many in all. **Home Activity** Give your child two groups of similar objects (e.g., a group of 3 spoons and a group of 5 spoons). Ask your child to join the groups to find how many there are in all.

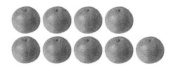

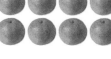

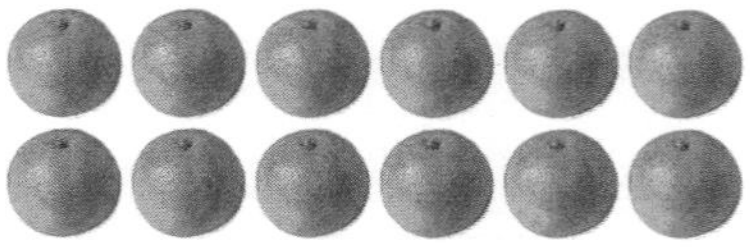

Name _____

 **Algebra**

How many balloons are there in all?

___7___ and ___2___ is ___9___ .

___7___ plus ___2___ equals ___9___ .

___7___ + ___2___ = ___9___ .

addend   **addend**   **sum**

The sum tells how many there are in all.

Word Bank

addend

sum

Check ✓

Write the addition sentence.
Use counters if you need to.

1 There are 6 blue cups.
There are 4 red cups.
How many cups are there in all?

___6___ + ___4___ = ___10___ cups

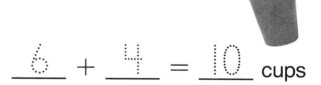

2 There are 9 large plates
and 3 small plates.
How many plates are there in all?

____ + ____ = ____ plates

3 There are 2 gifts with ribbons.
There are 2 gifts with bows.
How many gifts are there in all?

____ + ____ = ____ gifts

Think About It   Number Sense

Tell a number story to go with $8 + 3 = 11$.

Write an addition sentence.
Use counters if you need to.

4 5 flags are on the long pole.
3 flags are on the short pole.
How many flags are there in all?

_5_ + _3_ = _8_ flags

5 There are 3 blue chairs.
There are 2 red chairs.
How many chairs are there in all?

____ + ____ = ____ chairs

6 9 crackers are on a plate.
0 crackers are in a bowl.
How many crackers are there in all?

____ + ____ = ____ crackers

7 There is 1 red flower.
There are 5 yellow flowers.
How many flowers are there in all?

____ + ____ = ____ flowers

Problem Solving Visual Thinking

Complete the addition sentence.

8 There are 11 balls in all.
How many balls are in the bag?

____ + ____ = ____ balls

Home Connection Your child wrote addition sentences to tell how many in all. **Home Activity** Show your child two groups of objects. Have him or her add and write an addition sentence that tells how many objects there are in all.

Name _____

Identify the Main Idea

1 Kevin and Kelsey used puppets to tell this number story:

Once upon a time, there were three little pigs.
A wolf lived near the three little pigs.
The wolf was not very nice.
How many animals were there in all?

2 What is the main idea in this number story?
  a. Which animal was the nicest?
  b. How close to the pigs did the wolf live?
  c. How many animals were there in all?

3 Write a number sentence about the puppets shown below.

_____ + _____ = _____ puppets in all

4 If another wolf joined them, there would be
three little pigs and two wolves.
How many animals is that?
Write a number sentence.

_____ + _____ = _____ animals in all

Think About It   Reasoning

How do you find the main idea in a number story problem?

5 Read another number story:

Once upon a time, there was a farmer.
His name was Farmer Brown.
On Mr. Brown's farm, there were 7 cows and 4 horses.
How many cows and horses did he have in all?

6 What is the main idea of this number story?
  a. How big was Mr. Brown's farm?
  b. How many cows and horses were there on the farm?
  c. Did Mr. Brown have any chickens?

7 Write a number sentence about the cows and horses.

_____ + _____ = _____ animals in all

---

8 **Writing in Math**

Draw two kinds of farm animals.
Write a number sentence about your picture.

_____ + _____ = _____

Home Connection Your child identified the main ideas in two stories and wrote number sentences about those stories. **Home Activity** Talk with your child about the main idea of a number sentence: the numbers before the equal sign and the number after the equal sign are different ways of naming the same amount.

Name _____

  **Algebra**

How do we solve a story problem?

Read and Understand

Will has 3 gold fish.
He also has 4 red fish.
How many fish does he
have **altogether**?

Plan and Solve

You need to find out how many
fish Will has altogether.

This is a joining story, so you can
write an addition sentence.

$\underline{3} \oplus \underline{4} \ominus \underline{7}$ fish

Look Back and Check

Did you answer the question?

Word Bank

altogether

Check ✓

Write a number sentence. Use counters if you need to.

1 2 turtles are in one tank.
5 turtles are in another tank.
How many turtles are
there altogether?

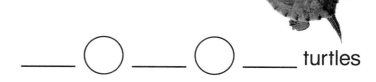

____ ◯ ____ ◯ ____ turtles

2 7 ducklings are sleeping.
1 other duckling begins to cheep.
How many ducklings are
there in all?

____ ◯ ____ ◯ ____ ducklings

Write a number sentence.
Use counters if you need to.

3 5 yellow birds are in one cage.
6 gray birds are in another cage.
How many birds are there in all?

__5__ ⊕ __6__ ⊜ __11__ birds

---

4 There are 4 kittens sleeping.
There are 8 kittens playing.
How many kittens are there?

____ ◯ ____ ◯ _____ kittens

---

5 Max is playing with 5 puppies.
Zoe is playing with 5 other puppies.
How many puppies in all are there?

____ ◯ ____ ◯ _____ puppies

---

6 9 rabbits are following butterflies.
3 rabbits are following grasshoppers.
How many rabbits are there?

____ ◯ ____ ◯ _____ rabbits

---

7 3 hamsters are eating.
No hamsters join them.
How many hamsters are
there altogether?

_____ ◯ ____ ◯ _____ hamsters

Home Connection Your child learned to write number sentences to solve problems. **Home Activity** Tell your child addition stories and have him or her write the addition sentences that solve the problems.

© Pearson Education, Inc.

Name ______________________________

Diagnostic Checkpoint

Count the fruit in the two groups.
Draw and write how many there are in all.

1

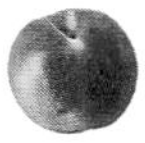

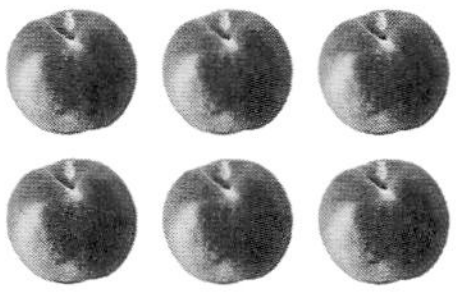

____ and ____ is ____ in all.

2

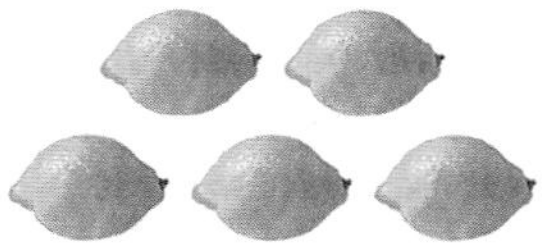

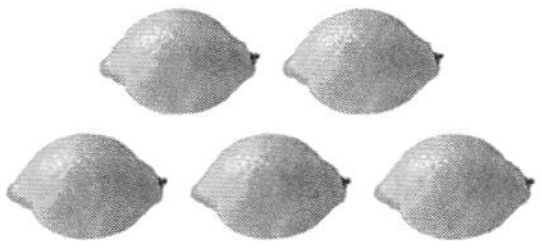

____ + ____ = ____ in all.

Write the addition sentence. Use counters if you need to.

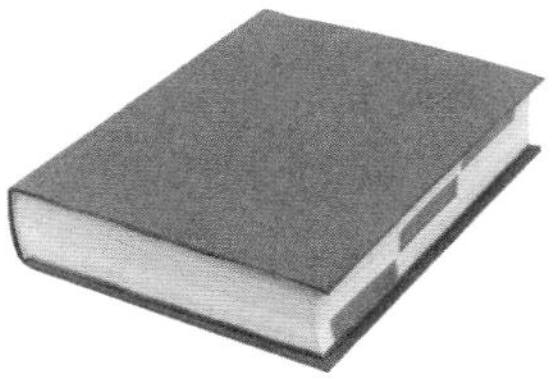

3 There are 5 books about dogs.
There are 7 books about cats.
How many books are there in all?

____ + ____ = ____ books

Write a number sentence. Use counters if you need to.

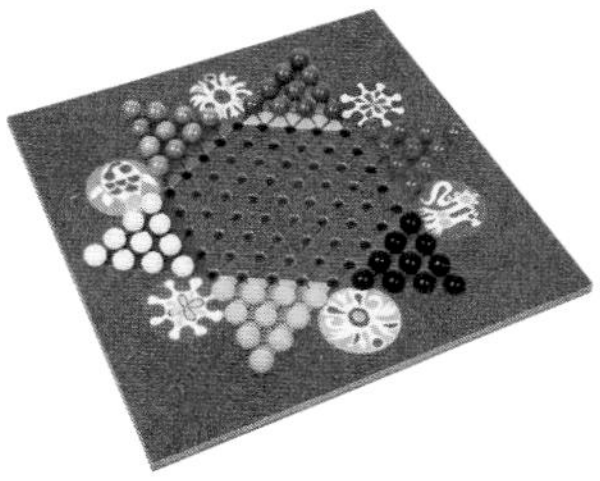

4 Hank has 3 games.
Mary has 6 games.
How many games are there in all?

____ ◯ ____ ◯ ____ games

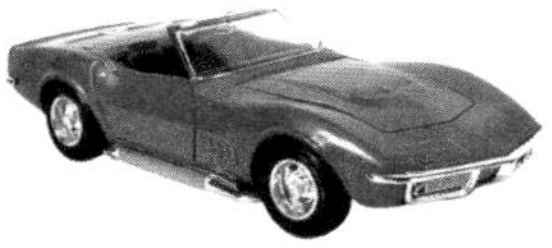

5 Jon has 8 car models
and no boat models.
How many models does Jon have?

____ ◯ ____ ◯ ____ models

Name_____

1 Mark the coin with the value of five cents.

Ⓐ   Ⓑ   Ⓒ   Ⓓ

2 Which number comes next?

55, 56, _____

54   56   57   58
Ⓐ   Ⓑ   Ⓒ   Ⓓ

3 Which drawing shows equal parts?

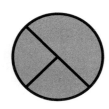   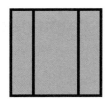      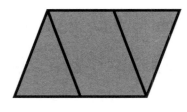

Ⓐ   Ⓑ   Ⓒ   Ⓓ

4 Which are in order from least to greatest?

7, 8, 6   0, 5, 3   9, 1, 4   0, 1, 2
Ⓐ   Ⓑ   Ⓒ   Ⓓ

5 Add or subtract.

$$\begin{array}{r} 0 \\ + 7 \\ \hline \end{array}$$

0   7   9   10
Ⓐ   Ⓑ   Ⓒ   Ⓓ

6 Add or subtract.

$$\begin{array}{r} 11 \\ - 0 \\ \hline \end{array}$$

11   10   0   1
Ⓐ   Ⓑ   Ⓒ   Ⓓ

Name _____

There are 7 cubes. Take away 2 cubes.
How many cubes are left?

___7___ take away ___2___ is ___5___.

___5___ cubes are left.

When we take away, we subtract.

Check ✓

Cross out to subtract.
Write how many are left.

1

8 take away 5 is _____.

2

11 take away 4 is _____.

3

9 take away 5 is _____.

4

6 take away 1 is _____.

Think About It   Reasoning

When you subtract, do you get more than or
less than the number of objects you started with? Explain.

Take away to subtract. Write the numbers.

5

_5_ take away _1_ is _4_.

6

____ take away ____ is ____.

7

____ take away ____ is ____.

8

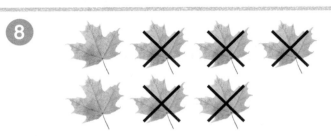

____ take away ____ is ____.

9

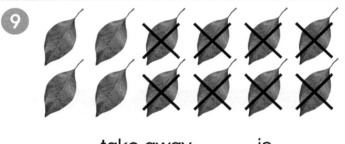

____ take away ____ is ____.

10

____ take away ____ is ____.

Problem Solving   Algebra

Circle the tray that answers the question.

11 Pam ate 1 strawberry.
She has 2 strawberries left.
How many strawberries did she start with?

 Home Connection Your child subtracted by taking away objects and then counting to find out how many objects were left. **Home Activity** Display a group of objects and then take some objects away. Have your child tell how many objects you started with, how many were taken away, and how many are left.

14   fourteen

© Pearson Education, Inc.

Learn!

How many more green cubes than yellow cubes are there?
Compare the number of cubes in each color.

There are ___9___ 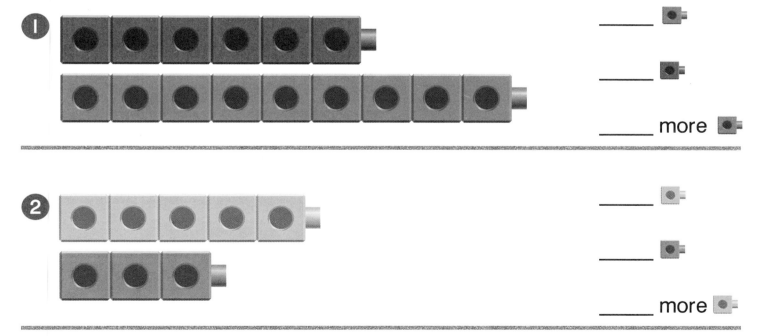.

There are ___5___ 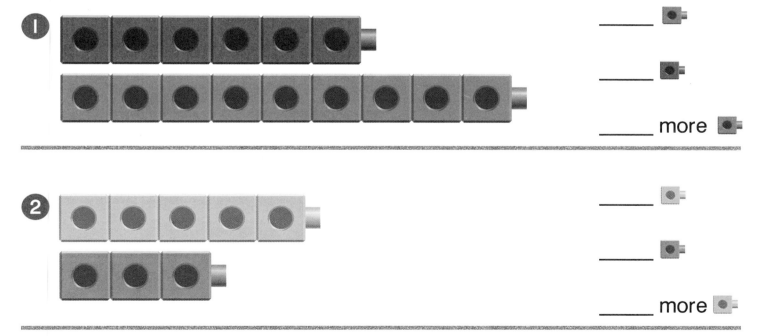.

There are ___4___ more 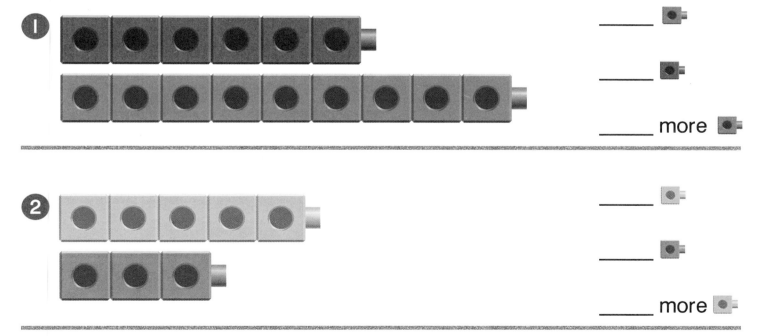.

When we compare
two groups, we subtract.

Check ✓

Compare. Write the numbers.
Use cubes if you need to.

1. _____

   _____

   _____ more

2. _____

   _____

   _____ more

Think About It   Reasoning

How can you decide how many more cubes there are?

Compare the number of objects in each group.
Write the numbers.

 3

How many more red cars are there?

_10_ red cars   _5_ blue cars   _5_ more red cars

How many more purple yo-yos are there?

_____ purple yo-yos   _____ orange yo-yos   _____ more purple yo-yos

5

How many more red frogs are there?

_____ red frogs   _____ blue frogs   _____ more red frogs

Reasoning *Writing in Math*

6 Write a math story to go with one of the exercises above.

_____

_____

_____

© Pearson Education, Inc.

Home Connection Your child counted objects in two groups and determined how many more objects one group had. **Home Activity** Show your child two groups of objects and have him or her tell you how many more objects are in the larger of the two groups.

Learn! Algebra

How many flowers are left in the pot?

__7__ take away __2__ is 5.

__7__ minus __2__ is 5.

__7__ − __2__ = __5__ flowers left

How many more purple flowers are there?

Compare 7 with 4.

__7__ minus __4__ is 3.

__7__ − __4__ = __3__ more flowers

In a subtraction sentence, the answer is the **difference**.

Word Bank

difference

Check ✓

Write the subtraction sentence.
Use counters if you need to.

1 There are 4 bees on a flower.
2 bees fly away.
How many bees are left?

_____ − _____ = _____ bees

2 There are 10 ladybugs on the leaves.
There are 7 ladybugs on the ground.
How many more ladybugs
are on the leaves?

_____ − _____ = _____ ladybugs

Think About It   Number Sense

Tell a subtraction story for 11 − 8 = 3.

Write the subtraction sentence.
Use counters if you need to.

3 There were 10 butterflies.
Then 2 butterflies flew away.
How many butterflies are left?

_10_ – _2_ = _8_ butterflies

4 There were 12 flowers in the garden.
Juan picked 8 of them.
How many flowers are left?

____ – ____ = ____ flowers

5 9 birds are eating.
7 birds are flying.
How many more birds are eating?

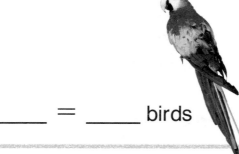

____ – ____ = ____ birds

Problem Solving   Reasonableness

Circle the answer to the question.

6 Molly had 8 bug books.
She gave some to Ned.
Which answer tells how many books
she might have left? Explain.

8 books   10 books   4 books

Home Connection Your child wrote subtraction sentences to solve
problems. **Home Activity** Change the numbers in Exercises 3–6. Together
with your child, read each new problem and write the subtraction sentence
that solves that problem.

Learn! Algebra

Two groups of children join together. Add.

Some children separate from the group. Subtract.

6 children are dancing.
2 more children join them.
How many children in all are dancing?

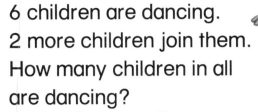

__6__ ⊕ __2__ ⊜ __8__ children

addition

5 children are riding bikes.
3 children stop riding.
How many children are left riding bikes?

__5__ ⊖ __3__ ⊜ __2__ children

subtraction

Check ✓

Circle **add** or **subtract**. Use counters if you need to.
Then write the number sentence.

1 There are 4 blue footballs
and 4 red footballs.
How many footballs
are there in all?

add   subtract

____ ◯ ____ ◯ ____ footballs

2 Mia had 7 golf balls.
She hit 6 of them away.
How many golf balls does
she have left?

add   subtract

____ ◯ ____ ◯ ____ golf ball

Think About It   Reasoning

How do you know whether you should add or subtract?

Circle **add** or **subtract**.
Then write the number sentence. Use counters if you need to.

3 Jana has 12 markers.
Maddie has 9 markers.
How many more markers
does Jana have?

add ⟨subtract⟩

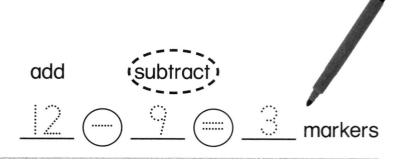

_12_ ⊖ _9_ ⊜ _3_ markers

4 Trevor has 7 erasers.
He buys 2 more.
How many erasers does
he have?

add   subtract

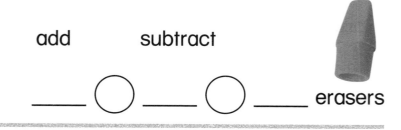

___ ◯ ___ ◯ ___ erasers

5 Jesse read 3 books last week.
This week he read 4 books.
How many books did he
read in all?

add   subtract

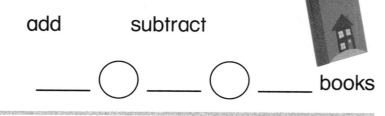

___ ◯ ___ ◯ ___ books

Reasoning Writing in Math

6 Write a math story. Have a friend write
a number sentence to solve it.

_____

_____

_____

Home Connection Your child chose whether to add or subtract to solve
each problem. **Home Activity** Have your child tell two math stories: one
that involves addition and one that involves subtraction.

Name _____

Write the numbers.

1

_____ take away _____ is _____.

2

_____ take away _____ is _____.

Compare the number of objects in each group.
Write the numbers.

3

How many more blue clips are there?

_____ blue clips   _____ red clips   _____ more blue clips

Circle **add** or **subtract**.
Write the number sentence.
Use counters if you need to.

4 There are 3 girls and
9 boys playing soccer.
How many children are
playing soccer in all?

add   subtract

____ ◯ ____ ◯ _____ children

Write the subtraction sentence.
Use counters if you need to.

5 Emma has 8 cows and 4 horses.
How many more cows than horses
does Emma have?

_____ − _____ = _____ cows

1 Count by twos.
Which number comes next?

10, 12, 14, _____

15	16	17	18
Ⓐ	Ⓑ	Ⓒ	Ⓓ

2 How much money is shown?

40¢	35¢	30¢	25¢
Ⓐ	Ⓑ	Ⓒ	Ⓓ

3 How many scissors are there in all?

Ⓐ 8 in all

Ⓑ 9 in all

Ⓒ 10 in all

Ⓓ 3 in all

4 Add.

4 + 4 = _____

8	9	10	0
Ⓐ	Ⓑ	Ⓒ	Ⓓ

5 Add.

5 + 6 = _____

9	10	11	1
Ⓐ	Ⓑ	Ⓒ	Ⓓ

Name _____

 **Algebra**

What happens to the sum when we change the order of the addends?

The sums are the same when two numbers are added in a different order.

$$3 + 5 = 8$$

$$5 + 3 = 8$$

These are **related addition facts**.

Word Bank

related fact

Check

Write the numbers for each picture.

1

$$\underline{6} + \underline{1} = \underline{7}$$

$$\underline{1} + \underline{6} = \underline{7}$$

2

$$\underline{} + \underline{} = \underline{}$$

$$\underline{} + \underline{} = \underline{}$$

3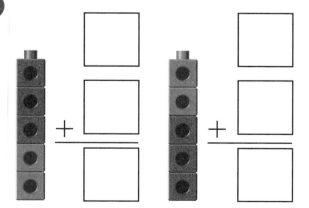

4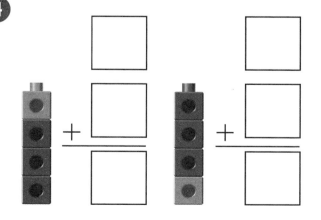

Think About It Reasoning

Does this picture have a related addition fact? Explain.

Write the sum.
Then write the related addition fact.

5   5 + 6 = __11__

        __6 + 5 = 11__

6   4 + 5 = ___

        _____

7   2 + 8 = ___

        _____

8   3 + 9 = ___

        _____

9

      4   ☐

+   3   + ☐
    ☐   ☐

10

      2   ☐

+   6   + ☐
    ☐   ☐

Reasoning   Writing in Math

11   Write a math story to go with the picture.

_____

_____

_____

_____

Home Connection Your child learned that we can add numbers in any order and the sum will be the same. **Home Activity** Write addition sentences such as 6 + 1 = 7, 4 + 8 = 12, and 2 + 3 = 5. Have your child switch the order of the addends and write the related addition facts. *(1 + 6 = 7, 8 + 4 = 12, 3 + 2 = 5)*

Name_____

Algebra

How can we make 10?

$8 + \underline{2} = 10$ $10 = 8 + \underline{2}$

Check ✓

Use counters and Workmat 2 to find
different ways to make 10.
Complete each number sentence.

1 $3 + \underline{7} = 10$

2 $\underline{\quad} + 6 = 10$

3 $10 = 1 + \underline{\quad}$

4 $10 = \underline{\quad} + 2$

5 $\underline{\quad} + \underline{\quad} = 10$

6 $10 = \underline{\quad} + \underline{\quad}$

7 $10 = \underline{\quad} + \underline{\quad}$

8 $\underline{\quad} + \underline{\quad} = 10$

Think About It   Number Sense

Did you write all of the number sentences
with sums of 10? Explain.

Find different ways to make 10. Use counters and Workmat 2
if you need to. Complete each number sentence.

9 2 + __8__ = 10

10 10 = 6 + ____

11 10 = ____ + 10

12 ____ + 9 = 10

13 10 = 7 + ____

14 ____ + 5 = 10

Write four more ways to make 10. Use different
number sentences from those in Exercises 9–14.

15 ____ + ____ = 10

16 ____ + ____ = 10

17 ____ + ____ = 10

18 ____ + ____ = 10

Problem Solving Mental Math

Look at the pattern.
Find the missing numbers.

What patterns can you find?

| 10 | + | 0 | = | 9 | + | 1 |

| 10 | + | 1 | = | 9 | + | 2 |

19 | 10 | + | 2 | = | ☐ | + | 3 |

20 | 10 | + | ☐ | = | ☐ | + | ☐ |

Home Connection Your child learned different ways to make ten.
Home Activity Ask your child to write three ways to make ten using
addition.

$$\underline{2} + \underline{6} = \underline{8} \qquad \underline{8} - \underline{6} = \underline{2}$$

What four facts do these cubes show?

Wow! All the facts have the same three numbers.

These related facts make up a **fact family**.

Word Bank

fact family

Check ✓

Write the fact family to match the cubes.

1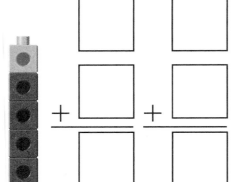

___ + ___ = ___   ___ − ___ = ___

___ + ___ = ___   ___ − ___ = ___

2
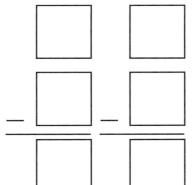

Think About It   Reasoning

Give an example of a fact family that has only
two facts. Explain why it does not have four facts.

Fact Families

Algebra

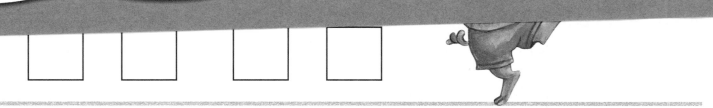

6 + 2 = ___

8 − 2 = ___

8 = 2 + ___

6 = 2 + ___

Problem Solving Algebra

Write your own fact families.

6 ___ + ___ = ___

___ + ___ = ___

___ − ___ = ___

___ − ___ = ___

7

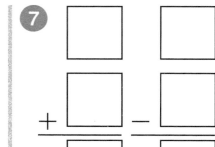

28   twenty-eight

 **Algebra**

There are 9 footballs in all. I see 3 footballs outside the bag. How many footballs are in the bag?

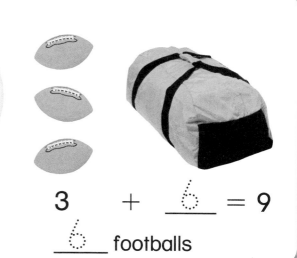

3 + _6_ = 9

_6_ footballs

Check ✓

Use counters. Find out how many objects are in the bag.

1 There are 12 books in all.
How many of them are in the bag?

8 + ___ = 12

_____ books

2 There are 6 cans in all.
How many of them are in the bag?

3 + ___ = 6

_____ cans

Think About It   Reasoning

What subtraction sentence could help you solve Exercise 1? Explain.

Practice

Find out how many objects are in the chest.
Use counters if you need to.

3 There are 5 trucks in all.
How many of them are
in the chest?

$1 + \underline{4} = 5$

$\underline{4}$ trucks

4 There are 11 frogs in all.
How many of them are
in the chest?

$2 + \underline{} = 11$

_____ frogs

5 There are 7 golf balls in all.
How many of them are
in the chest?

$5 + \underline{} = 7$

_____ golf balls

6 There are 9 jacks in all.
How many of them are
in the chest?

$9 + \underline{} = 9$

_____ jacks

Problem Solving **Algebra**

Solve.

7 What number is ?

 $= 4$

 $=$ _____

 $= 6$

 $+$ $=$

_____ $+$ _____ $=$ $\underline{6}$

30 thirty

Home Connection Your child used counters to find the missing part, or addend, in each addition sentence. **Home Activity** Gather a group of small objects. Place some in a closed container and place the remaining objects outside the container. Tell your child how many objects there are in all. Ask him or her to figure out how many objects are in the container.

© Pearson Education, Inc.

Name _____

Dorling Kindersley

Do You Know...
that a group of frogs is called an **army** and a group of toads is called a **knot**?

1 Here is an African bullfrog.
4 other frogs are coming to join him.
How many frogs will there be in all?

_____ ◯ _____ = _____ frogs in all

2 There were 7 toads in a knot.
Then 2 of them hopped away.
How many toads were left in the knot?

_____ − _____ = _____ toads

Fun Fact!
Frogs and toads swallow their food without chewing it first. It is not a good idea for people to do this!

3 The 2 toads that left the knot joined a new knot of 5 toads. How many toads are in the new knot now?

_____ ◯ _____ = _____ toads

These are poison-dart frogs. They have skin that is bright in color and poisonous!

4 A female toad might weigh 4 pounds.
A male might weigh only 2 pounds.
How many more pounds
does the female weigh?

_____ – _____ = _____ more pounds

Poison-dart frogs live in small groups, called armies.

5 There are 2 tree frogs up in the tree.
4 more tree frogs climb up to join them.
How many tree frogs are up there now?

_____ ◯ _____ = _____ tree frogs

Poison-dart frogs carry their tadpoles to small pools so that their skin can become colorful and they can grow.

6 **Writing in Math**

 Write a number story about frogs and toads.

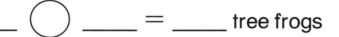

_____

Home Connection Your child learned to solve problems by applying his or her math skills. **Home Activity** Talk to your child about how he or she solved the problems on these two pages.

Diagnostic Checkpoint

Write the sum. Then write the related fact.

1 7 + 4 = ____

_____

2

$$
\begin{array}{r}
2 \\
+\ 6 \\
\hline
\square
\end{array}
$$

$$
\begin{array}{r}
\square \\
+\ \square \\
\hline
\square
\end{array}
$$

Complete each fact family.

3 3 + 6 = ____

____ + ____ = ____

____ − ____ = ____

____ − ____ = ____

4 ____ + ____ = ____

____ + ____ = ____

8 − 1 = ____

____ − ____ = ____

Complete each number sentence.
Use counters and Workmat 2 if you need to.

5 5 + ____ = 10

6 ____ + 7 = 10

Find out how many objects are in the bag.
Use counters if you need to.

7 There are 6 gifts in all.
How many of them are in the bag?

2 + ____ = 6

_____ gifts

1 How many more blue marbles than yellow marbles are there?

Ⓐ 3 more blue marbles
Ⓑ 2 more blue marbles
Ⓒ 8 more blue marbles
Ⓓ 12 more blue marbles

2 Mark the fifth balloon.

first
Ⓐ   Ⓑ   Ⓒ   Ⓓ

3 Mark the clock that shows 3:00.

Ⓐ   Ⓑ   Ⓒ   Ⓓ

4 Add or subtract.

$$\begin{array}{r} 12 \\ -\ 3 \\ \hline \end{array}$$

9   3   8   15
Ⓐ   Ⓑ   Ⓒ   Ⓓ

5 Add or subtract.

$$\begin{array}{r} 9 \\ +\ 6 \\ \hline \end{array}$$

15   13   10   3
Ⓐ   Ⓑ   Ⓒ   Ⓓ

6 Add or subtract.

8 + 4 = ____

11   4   12   13
Ⓐ   Ⓑ   Ⓒ   Ⓓ

7 Add or subtract.

9 − 1 = ____

1   9   7   8
Ⓐ   Ⓑ   Ⓒ   Ⓓ

Enrichment

Equivalent Expressions **Algebra**

There are different names for the same number.

$5 + 1 = 6$ $2 + 4 = 6$ $5 + 1 = 6$ $3 + \underline{3} = 6$

$5 + 1 = 2 + 4$ $5 + 1 = 3 + \underline{3}$

$\underline{6} = \underline{6}$ $\underline{6} = \underline{6}$

Write the missing numbers.

1 $6 + 3 = 2 + \underline{\quad}$

     $\underline{\quad} = \underline{\quad}$

2 $3 + 5 = 6 + \underline{\quad}$

     $\underline{\quad} = \underline{\quad}$

3 $1 + 9 = 5 + \underline{\quad}$

4 $7 + 0 = 5 + \underline{\quad}$

5 $12 - 2 = 3 + \underline{\quad}$

     $\underline{\quad} = \underline{\quad}$

6 $8 - 4 = 0 + \underline{\quad}$

     $\underline{\quad} = \underline{\quad}$

7 $11 - 5 = 8 - \underline{\quad}$

8 $10 - 5 = 2 + \underline{\quad}$

9 **Writing in Math**

If $6 + \triangle = 6 + \hexagon$, what do you know about $\triangle$ and $\hexagon$? Explain.

Home Connection Your child learned how to write equivalent expressions. **Home Activity** Ask your child to find the missing number for each of the following problems: $1 + 2 = 3 + \underline{\quad}$; $5 + 2 = 3 + \underline{\quad}$; $10 - 1 = 7 + \underline{\quad}$; and $9 - 3 = 2 + \underline{\quad}$.

Learning with Technology

Make Fact Families Using a Calculator

Use a calculator to make fact families.

Write the numbers you press for each fact.

Write the number in the display for each fact.

Press ON/C each time you begin.

1 Make a fact family.

2 Make another fact family.

3 Make a fact family using greater numbers.

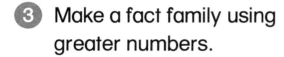

4 Make your own fact family.

Think About It   Number Sense

How could you use a calculator to find the missing number in this addition sentence? $4 + \boxed{} = 11$

Home Connection Your child used a calculator to make fact families.
Home Activity Ask your child to explain how he or she would make a fact family for 10 on a calculator. *(Sample response: I would press 6 + 4 =, 4 + 6 =, 10 − 4 =, and 10 − 6 =.)*

© Pearson Education, Inc.

CHAPTER 1
Test Talk

Understand the Question

Some words in a math problem are more important than others.

These words can help you understand the problem.

1. A toy set has 6 cars and 2 trucks. How many more cars than trucks are there?

    A   4 more cars

    B   8 more cars

    C   6 more cars

    D   9 more cars

The words **how many more** tell you to compare the number of cars with the number of trucks. Compare 6 and 2. Fill in the answer bubble.

Your Turn

Find the most important words in this math problem. Then solve the problem and fill in the answer bubble.

I have to read carefully!

2. Nick had 5 puppets. He gave away 3 of them. How many puppets does Nick have left?

    A   2 puppets

    B   5 puppets

    C   3 puppets

    D   8 puppets

Home Connection Your child prepared for standardized tests by identifying the most important words in a math problem. **Home Activity** Ask your child which words he or she identified as being the most important words in Exercise 2. *(Gave away, have left)*

Name _____

Discover Math in Your World

 Read Together

Using Your Eyes
We use our eyes to learn about the world around us.

Eyeing Your Classroom
Look around your classroom.

1. How many colors can you see? _____

2. Find some things in your classroom
that are **red** or **yellow** or **blue.**
These colors are called the primary colors.
They can be used to make all of the
other colors. Use a tally mark to record
each thing you find. Then count the things
in each group and record the totals.

Red Things	Yellow Things	Blue Things
Total: _____	Total: _____	Total: _____

3. Now write a number sentence that tells how many
things you found in all.

_____ + _____ + _____ = _____ things in all

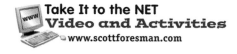 **Take It to the NET**
Video and Activities
www.scottforesman.com

 Home Connection Your child counted objects of different colors in
the classroom and wrote a number sentence to tell how many objects
he or she found in all. **Home Activity** Ask your child to go on a similar
"color hunt," perhaps limiting the search area to one room.

© Pearson Education, Inc.

Chapter Test

Count the bagels in each group.
Draw and write how many there are in all.

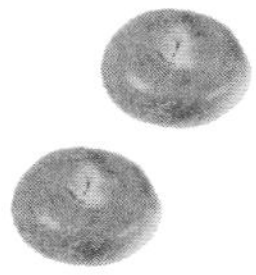

_____ and _____ is _____ in all.

Compare to find how many more there are. Write the numbers.

_____ blue whistles   _____ green whistles   _____ more blue whistles

Write the addition sentence.

❸ Josh has 2 toy sailboats
and 7 toy speedboats.
How many toy boats
in all does Josh have?

____ + ____ = _____ boats

Write the sum.
Then write the related addition fact.

❹ 7 + 4 = ____

_____

❺
$$\begin{array}{r} 2 \\ + 5 \\ \hline \square \end{array}$$

$$\begin{array}{r} \square \\ + \square \\ \hline \square \end{array}$$

6 Take away to subtract.
Write the numbers.

_____ take away _____ is _____.

Write the subtraction sentence.

7 5 squirrels are eating.
3 squirrels stop eating.
How many squirrels are left eating?

_____ − _____ = _____ squirrels

Complete the fact family.

8

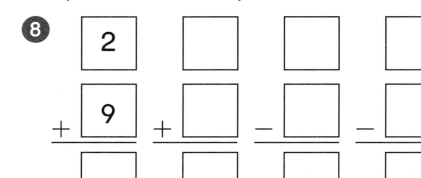

Circle **add** or **subtract**.
Write the number sentence.

9 6 children are riding bikes.
5 more children join them.
How many children are
riding bikes?

add   subtract

____ ◯ ____ ◯ _____ children

Find out how many objects are in the bag.
Use counters if you need to.

10 There are 12 balls in all.
How many of them
are in the bag?

5 + ____ = 12

_____ balls

My Wild and Crazy Dream

Written by Gene Howard   **Illustrated by Laura Ovresat**

$2 + 1 = 3$
$2 + 2 = 4$
$3 + 2 = 5$
$4 + 2 = 6$
$4 + 3 = 7$

Bird

This Math Storybook belongs to

_____

2A

In my dream I saw **2** flying pigs.
And then **1** more flying pig.
And all **3** were wearing wigs!

"**3** pigs? Wearing wigs?
What is going on?" I asked.

But they just smiled and flew away.

In my dream I saw **2** flying cats.
And then **2** more flying cats.
And all **4** were wearing hats!

"**4** cats? Wearing hats?
What is going on?" I asked.

But they just smiled and flew away.

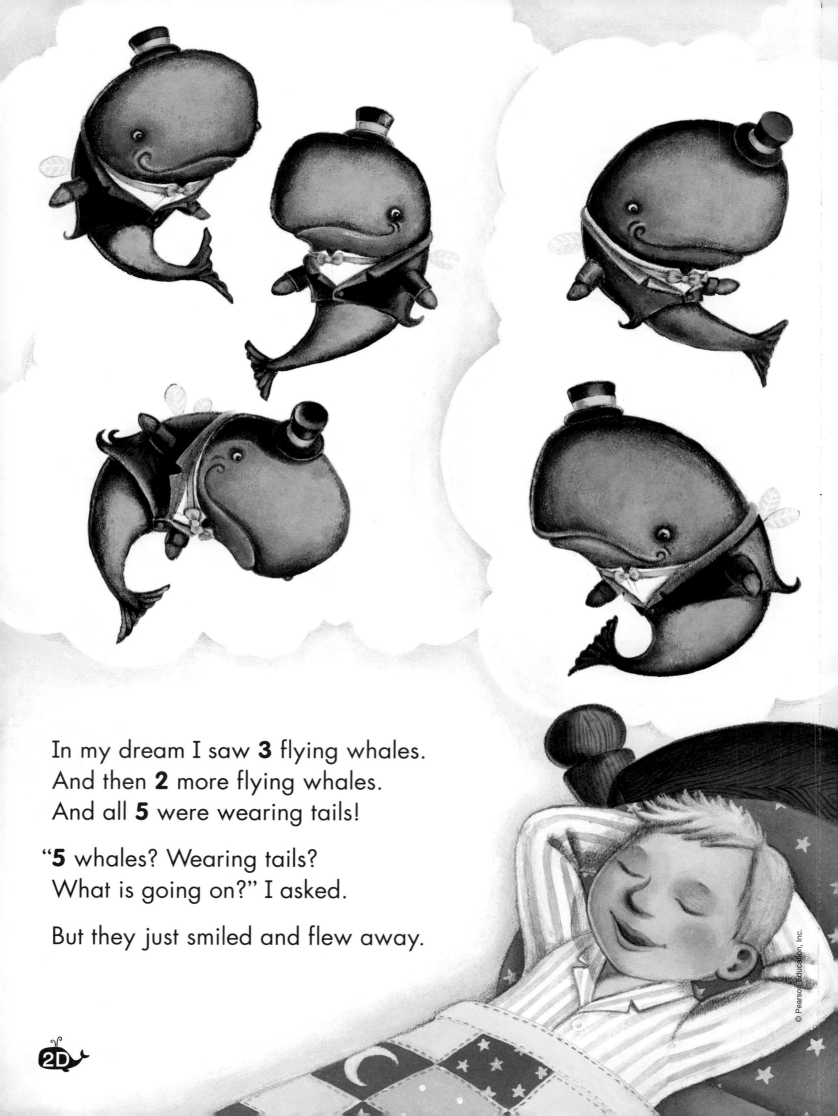

In my dream I saw **3** flying whales.
And then **2** more flying whales.
And all **5** were wearing tails!

"**5** whales? Wearing tails?
What is going on?" I asked.

But they just smiled and flew away.

2D

invited

wedding

are

you

to

the

In my dream I saw **4** flying birds.
And then **2** more flying birds.
And all **6** were wearing words!

"**6** birds? Wearing words?
What is going on?" I asked.

But they just smiled and flew away.

2E

In my dream I saw **4** flying mice.
And then **3** more flying mice.
And all **7** were throwing rice!

3 pigs wearing wigs.
4 cats wearing hats.
5 whales wearing tails.
6 birds wearing words.
7 mice throwing rice…

Now I know what's going on!

2F

Home-School Connection

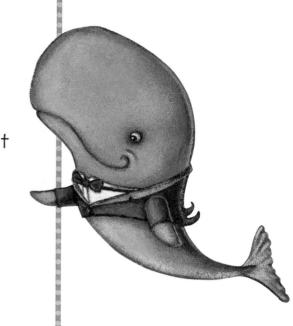

Dear Family,

Today my class started Chapter 2, **Fact Strategies for Addition and Subtraction.** I will learn different ways to add numbers that have sums all the way up to 18, and I will learn different ways to subtract from numbers all the way up to 18. Here are some of the math words I will be learning and some things we can do to help me with my math.

Love,

_____

Math Activity to Do at Home

Play "Doubles" with 18 pennies. Count out 7 pennies and say, "Double it!" Your child then counts out an additional 7 pennies, and together you say, "7 plus 7 equals 14 in all. 7 cents plus 7 cents equals 14 cents." Take turns, using other numbers.

Books to Read Together

Reading math stories reinforces concepts. Look for these titles in your local library:

Seven Blind Mice
By Ed Young
(Penguin Putnam, 1992)

Animals on Board
By Stuart J. Murphy
(HarperCollins, 1998)

Take It to the NET
More Activities
www.scottforesman.com

My New Math Words

count on An addition strategy: children count on 1, 2, or 3 from the greater addend.

Start at 7 and then count on 8, 9, 10.

count back A subtraction strategy: children count back 1 or 2 from the greater number.

Start at 10 and then count back 9, 8.

doubles A doubles fact is one in which the two addends are the same (e.g., $4 + 4 = 8$).

doubles plus 1 A doubles-plus-1 fact is one in which one addend is only one more than the other addend (e.g., $4 + 5 = 9$).

Name _____

Race to the Wedding

How to Play

1. Place your markers on START.
2. Take turns tossing the cubes.
3. Add the 2 numbers together and move that number of spaces.
4. If you land on a space with a word, go back to START!
5. The first person to get to the wedding wins the game!

Wedding

17
to
16
15
14
18
19
20
the
13
12 invited
11
10
9
8 are
7
START
1
2
3
4 you
5
6

Name _____

 **Learn!**

You can **count on** to **add** 1, 2, or 3 to the greater number.

Start at 7.
Count on 8, 9.
7 + 2 = 9

 7    _8_    _9_

7   +   2   =   _9_

Word Bank

count on
add
sum

Check ✓

Count on to find each **sum**.

1
 4

4   +   3   =   ____

2
 3

3   +   2   =   ____

3
 7

7   +   1   =   ____

4
 5

5   +   3   =   ____

Think About It   Reasoning

Do you need to count on to add zero to another number? Explain.

Count on to find each sum.

5 9 + 1 = __10__   3 + 5 = ___   1 + 5 = ___

6 8 + 1 = ___   ___ = 2 + 6   1 + 7 = ___

7 ___ = 4 + 2   3 + 3 = ___   3 + 4 = ___

8 2 + 9 = ___   3 + 7 = ___   ___ = 2 + 3

9
8	7	3	1	9	1
+ 3	+ 2	+ 9	+ 3	+ 1	+ 8

10
3	4	7	2	2	3
+ 6	+ 1	+ 3	+ 9	+ 6	+ 8

Problem Solving   Number Sense

Complete each list of number pairs.

11

Number of Tricycles	Number of Wheels
1	3
2	___
___	___

12

Number of Dogs	Number of Legs
0	0
2	___
___	___

Home Connection Your child learned that *counting on* is a strategy for adding 1, 2, or 3 to a greater number. **Home Activity** Say a number less than 18 and have your child count on 1, 2, or 3 from that number.

Name _____

Doubles facts are addition facts with two addends that are the same.

$$\underline{}\,7\,\underline{} + \underline{}\,7\,\underline{} = \underline{}\,14\,\underline{}$$

Word Bank

doubles fact
addition fact
addend

Check ✓

Draw to show the double.
Then write the addition sentence.

1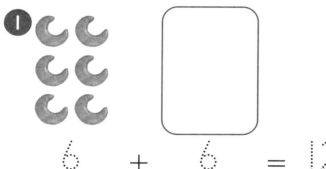

$$\underline{}\,6\,\underline{} + \underline{}\,6\,\underline{} = \underline{}\,12\,\underline{}$$

2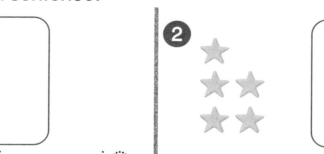

$$\underline{} + \underline{} = \underline{}$$

3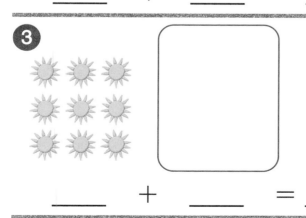

$$\underline{} + \underline{} = \underline{}$$

4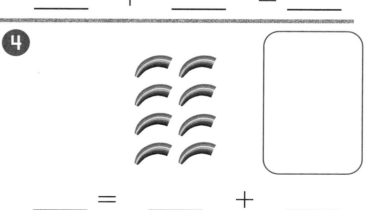

$$\underline{} = \underline{} + \underline{}$$

Think About It   Reasoning

Write all 5 of the sums on this page in order from least to greatest.
What pattern do you see in the sums?

Solve. Circle the doubles facts.

5 $\underline{14} = 7 + 7$ $1 + 7 = \underline{\hspace{1cm}}$ $\underline{\hspace{1cm}} = 3 + 6$

6 $9 + 3 = \underline{\hspace{1cm}}$ $\underline{\hspace{1cm}} = 4 + 4$ $1 + 8 = \underline{\hspace{1cm}}$

7 $1 + 1 = \underline{\hspace{1cm}}$ $\underline{\hspace{1cm}} = 2 + 3$ $0 + 0 = \underline{\hspace{1cm}}$

8
$\begin{array}{r} 9 \\ +9 \\ \hline \end{array}$
$\begin{array}{r} 5 \\ +2 \\ \hline \end{array}$
$\begin{array}{r} 2 \\ +2 \\ \hline \end{array}$
$\begin{array}{r} 7 \\ +1 \\ \hline \end{array}$
$\begin{array}{r} 6 \\ +6 \\ \hline \end{array}$
$\begin{array}{r} 2 \\ +8 \\ \hline \end{array}$

9
$\begin{array}{r} 6 \\ +8 \\ \hline \end{array}$
$\begin{array}{r} 9 \\ +1 \\ \hline \end{array}$
$\begin{array}{r} 5 \\ +5 \\ \hline \end{array}$
$\begin{array}{r} 7 \\ +7 \\ \hline \end{array}$
$\begin{array}{r} 8 \\ +4 \\ \hline \end{array}$
$\begin{array}{r} 5 \\ +3 \\ \hline \end{array}$

10
$\begin{array}{r} 8 \\ +8 \\ \hline \end{array}$
$\begin{array}{r} 4 \\ +2 \\ \hline \end{array}$
$\begin{array}{r} 2 \\ +6 \\ \hline \end{array}$
$\begin{array}{r} 9 \\ +9 \\ \hline \end{array}$
$\begin{array}{r} 6 \\ +3 \\ \hline \end{array}$
$\begin{array}{r} 3 \\ +3 \\ \hline \end{array}$

Problem Solving   Visual Thinking

Draw a picture to solve the problem.
Write the number sentence.

11 Dale bought 8 lemons.
Myra bought the same number
of limes. How many pieces
of fruit did they buy in all?

$\underline{\hspace{1cm}} + \underline{\hspace{1cm}} = \underline{\hspace{1cm}}$

Home Connection Your child learned that facts such as 7 + 7 and 9 + 9 are called *doubles facts*. **Home Activity** Have your child use small objects to make doubles and write an addition sentence for each double that he or she makes.

Name _____

You can use doubles facts to find other sums.

Think 7 + 7 and 1 more.

__7__ + __7__ = __14__

doubles fact

__7__ + __8__ = __15__

doubles plus 1

Check ✓

Write each addition sentence.

 1

__5__ + __5__ = __10__

___ + ___ = ___

2

___ + ___ = ___

___ + ___ = ___

3

___ = ___ + ___

___ = ___ + ___

Think About It   Reasoning

How does knowing 8 + 8 = 16 help you find 8 + 7?

Add. Use doubles facts to help you.

4
$$\begin{array}{r} 5 \\ + 6 \\ \hline \end{array} \qquad \begin{array}{r} 6 \\ + 7 \\ \hline \end{array} \qquad \begin{array}{r} 4 \\ + 5 \\ \hline \end{array} \qquad \begin{array}{r} 6 \\ + 6 \\ \hline \end{array} \qquad \begin{array}{r} 3 \\ + 4 \\ \hline \end{array} \qquad \begin{array}{r} 2 \\ + 2 \\ \hline \end{array}$$

5
$$\begin{array}{r} 9 \\ + 9 \\ \hline \end{array} \qquad \begin{array}{r} 2 \\ + 3 \\ \hline \end{array} \qquad \begin{array}{r} 8 \\ + 9 \\ \hline \end{array} \qquad \begin{array}{r} 7 \\ + 7 \\ \hline \end{array} \qquad \begin{array}{r} 8 \\ + 7 \\ \hline \end{array} \qquad \begin{array}{r} 5 \\ + 4 \\ \hline \end{array}$$

6
$$\begin{array}{r} 3 \\ + 3 \\ \hline \end{array} \qquad \begin{array}{r} 8 \\ + 8 \\ \hline \end{array} \qquad \begin{array}{r} 1 \\ + 1 \\ \hline \end{array} \qquad \begin{array}{r} 6 \\ + 5 \\ \hline \end{array} \qquad \begin{array}{r} 9 \\ + 8 \\ \hline \end{array} \qquad \begin{array}{r} 4 \\ + 3 \\ \hline \end{array}$$

7 $1 + 2 =$ _____ $\qquad 3 + 2 =$ _____ $\qquad$ _____ $= 5 + 5$

8 $9 + 9 =$ _____ $\qquad$ _____ $= 7 + 6 \qquad 8 + 9 =$ _____

Problem Solving   Writing in Math

9 Use pictures, numbers, or words to tell how
7 + 9 and 7 + 7 are related.

© Pearson Education, Inc.

Home Connection Your child learned that doubles-plus-1 facts are one more than doubles facts. **Home Activity** Name a doubles fact (e.g., 6 + 6 = 12) and ask your child to tell you its doubles-plus-1 fact (in this case, 6 + 7 = 13).

Name _____

 **Algebra**

You can group numbers in any order and get the same sum.

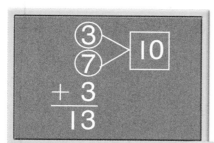

I counted on 2 from 7 and then added 4 more.

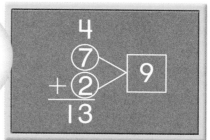

I made 10 and then added 3 more.

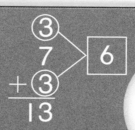

I used a doubles fact and then a doubles-plus-1 fact.

Check ✓

Find each sum in two different ways.
Circle the numbers you added first
and write their sum in the box.

1.
```
 (6)
 (6)  [12]
+ 3
 15
```
```
  6
 (6)  [9]
+(3)
 15
```

2.
```
  5
  4  [ ]
+ 3
```
```
  5
  4  [ ]
+ 3
```

3.
```
  8
  3  [ ]
+ 7
```
```
  8
  3  [ ]
+ 7
```

4.
```
  7
  3  [ ]
+ 5
```
```
  7
  3  [ ]
+ 5
```

Think About It   Reasoning

Tell two different ways you could add $2 + 8 + 2$.

Add. Try different ways.

5 $8 + 2 + 8 = \underline{18}$

6 $\underline{} = 4 + 1 + 6$

7 $8 + 3 + 0 = \underline{}$

8 $\underline{} = 9 + 3 + 2$

9

4	7	3	2	8	2
4	6	9	3	0	7
+4	+5	+3	+4	+9	+3

10

6	9	2	9	8	6
4	7	7	9	2	1
+6	+2	+7	+0	+7	+1

11

7	1	9	5	5	8
7	8	0	3	5	4
+4	+8	+3	+5	+5	+6

Problem Solving **Algebra**

Find the missing numbers. The same shapes are
the same numbers. The numbers in are sums.
Add across and down.

12

9	1	■	(15)
6	■	4	(15)
⬡	9	6	(15)
(15)	(15)	(15)	

■ = _____   ⬡ = _____

13

6	▲	6	(18)
6	5	▱	(18)
▲	7	5	(18)
(18)	(18)	(18)	

▲ = _____   ▱ = _____

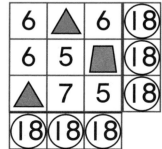

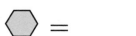

Home Connection Your child used different addition strategies to add
three numbers. **Home Activity** Give your child a set of 3 numbers. Have
your child explain the strategy he or she will use to add the numbers.

Name _____

Learn!

You can make 10 to help you add 9.

Find the sum.

9
+ 5
?

Make 10.

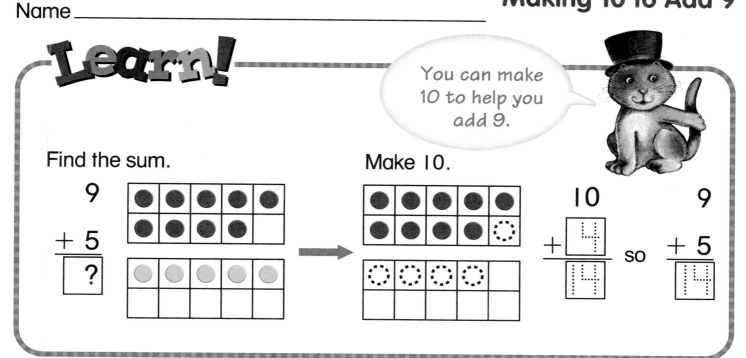

10
+ 4
14

so

9
+ 5
14

Check ✓

Make 10 to add 9.
Use counters and Workmat 3.

❶   9
    + 7
    ?

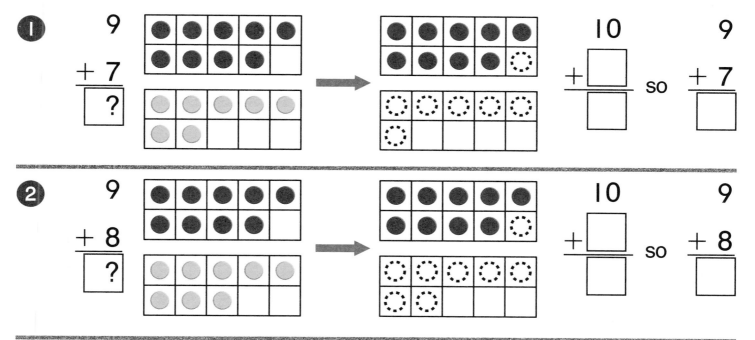

10
+ ☐
☐

so

9
+ 7
☐

❷   9
    + 8
    ?

10
+ ☐
☐

so

9
+ 8
☐

Think About It   Number Sense

Compare adding 9 to any number and adding 10
to that same number. What is different?

Practice

Add. Use counters and Workmat 3 if you need to.

3

9	6	0	9	3	9
+ 2	+ 9	+ 9	+ 8	+ 9	+ 1

4

7	9	8	4	9	2
+ 9	+ 3	+ 9	+ 9	+ 9	+ 9

5

9	5	9	9	1	4
+ 0	+ 9	+ 4	+ 7	+ 9	+ 9

6 9 + 6 = ____   9 + 7 = ____   8 + 9 = ____

7 5 + 9 = ____   4 + 9 = ____   3 + 9 = ____

Problem Solving Reasoning

Solve by using pictures, numbers, or words.

8 Harriet had 7 trees in her yard. She planted some more. Now she has 16 trees. How many new trees did Harriet plant?

Home Connection Your child learned that it is helpful to make 10 when adding 9. **Home Activity** Ask your child to explain how to add 9 + 7 by first making 10.

Name _____

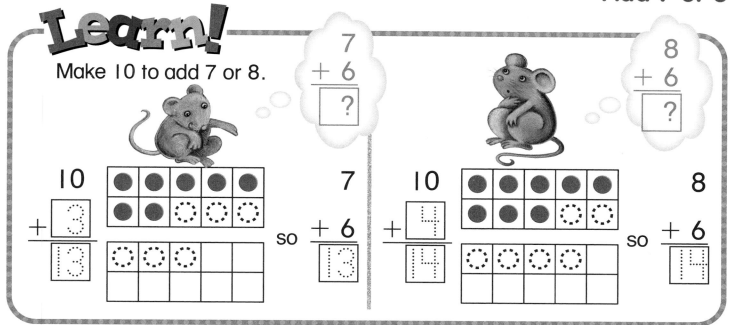

Learn!

Make 10 to add 7 or 8.

$$7 + 6 = \boxed{?}$$

10
+ 3
13

7
+ 6
13

so

$$8 + 6 = \boxed{?}$$

10
+ 4
14

8
+ 6
14

so

Check ✓

Make 10 to add 7 or 8.

Use counters and Workmat 3.

1 8
+ 5
?

10
+ ☐
☐

so

8
+ 5
☐

2 7
+ 4
?

10
+ ☐
☐

so

7
+ 4
☐

Think About It   Number Sense

How would you make 10 to find the sum of 7 + 8?

Add. Use counters and Workmat 3 if you need to.

3
$$7 + 3$$ $$8 + 4$$ $$6 + 9$$ $$3 + 8$$ $$10 + 2$$ $$9 + 5$$

4
$$8 + 9$$ $$2 + 8$$ $$7 + 5$$ $$9 + 4$$ $$7 + 7$$ $$5 + 8$$

5 $0 + 7 =$ _____ $9 + 0 =$ _____   _____ $= 7 + 9$

6 _____ $= 6 + 7$ _____ $= 10 + 7$ _____ $= 9 + 8$

Problem Solving **Algebra**

Find the pattern. Write the missing numbers.

7 $\boxed{9} + \boxed{9} = \boxed{10} + \boxed{8}$

$\boxed{9} + \boxed{8} = \boxed{10} + \boxed{}$

$\boxed{9} + \boxed{7} = \boxed{10} + \boxed{}$

$\boxed{9} + \boxed{} = \boxed{10} + \boxed{5}$

$\boxed{9} + \boxed{} = \boxed{10} + \boxed{}$

8 $\boxed{8} + \boxed{9} = \boxed{10} + \boxed{7}$

$\boxed{8} + \boxed{8} = \boxed{10} + \boxed{}$

$\boxed{8} + \boxed{} = \boxed{10} + \boxed{5}$

$\boxed{8} + \boxed{} = \boxed{10} + \boxed{}$

$\boxed{} + \boxed{} = \boxed{} + \boxed{}$

Home Connection Your child learned that it is helpful to make 10 when adding 7 or 8. **Home Activity** Give your child a number less than 11. Have him or her add that number to 7, 8, and then 9. Ask your child to tell you how he or she found each of the sums.

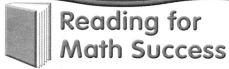

Reading for Math Success

Identify the Main Idea

1 Read and solve this number riddle:

Red Run ←

As I was going to Red Run,

I met a man with seven sons.

Every son had seven sacks.

Every sack had seven cats.

Every cat had seven kits.

Kits, cats, sacks, sons,

How many were going to Red Run?

2 Write your answer. _____

3 Explain your thinking.

_____

_____

_____

Think About It   Number Sense

Suppose you had seven cats.
Some are gray. Some are orange.
How many of each color might you have?

See if you can solve these three number riddles:

4 I am the number of hours in the day.
I am what you get if you add 12 + 12.
I am made of two tens and four ones.

What number am I? _____

5 I am the number of senses you have.
I am one more than four. I am one less than six.

What number am I? _____

6 I am the number of states in the United States of America.
I am half of 100.
I am ten more than 40.

What number am I? _____

United States

---

7 **Writing in Math**

Write your own number riddle.

I am _____.

I am _____.

I am _____.

What number am I? _____

© Pearson Education, Inc.

Name _____

Write a Number Sentence

 **Algebra**

Read and Understand

Juan and Elisa played a bean bag tossing game. Here are their scores.

How many points did Juan score in all three games?

Bean Bag Toss			
	Game 1	Game 2	Game 3
Juan	5	6	4
Elisa	7	3	7

Plan and Solve

You need to find out how many points Juan scored in all. Write a **number sentence** using Juan's points from the chart.

$5 + 6 + 4 = 15$ points

Look Back and Check

Which fact strategies did you use to solve this problem? Does your answer make sense?

Word Bank

number sentence

Check ✓

Write a number sentence to solve the problem. Use the table to help you.

1. How many points did Elisa score in all?

_____ = _____ points

Think About It   Reasoning

In Exercise 1, explain two ways to add. Which way is easier? Tell why.

Write a number sentence
to solve the problem.
Use the table to help you.

Game Scores			
	Game 1	Game 2	Game 3
Golds	8	2	8
Blues	6	7	3

2 How many points did the Golds
score altogether in Games 1 and 2?

_____ = _____ points

3 How many points did the Blues score
altogether in Games 1 and 2?

_____ = _____ points

4 Which team had scored more points
after Game 2?

_____

5 How many points did the Blues score
altogether?

_____ = _____ points

6 How many points did the Golds
score altogether?

_____ = _____ points

7 Which team, the Golds or the Blues,
scored more points altogether?

_____

How many more? _____ more points

Home Connection Your child wrote number sentences, with two or three
addends, to solve problems. **Home Activity** Give your child three scores
using 1 to 9 points. Ask your child to find the total number of points.

Name _____

Count on to find each sum.

1 3 + 2 = ___   7 + 3 = ___   2 + 9 = ___

2 ___ = 1 + 5   ___ = 3 + 8   ___ = 6 + 3

Add. Circle the doubles facts.

3
```
   8        7        8        5        5        9
 + 9      + 7      + 8      + 6      + 5      + 7
```

Add. Try different ways.

4 5 + 6 + 4 = ___   9 + 1 + 8 = ___

Add. Make 10 to help you.

5
```
   9        4        6        7        8        9
 + 5      + 7      + 8      + 9      + 5      + 4
```

Write the number sentence to solve the problem.
Use the table to help you.

6 How many points did Adam score in all?

Game Points			
	Game 1	Game 2	Game 3
Emma	2	7	3
Adam	8	5	2

_____ points

1 Count the pineapples in the two groups.
Draw and write how many there are in all.

4	and	2	is	_____ in all.
2		5		6		8
Ⓐ		Ⓑ		Ⓒ		Ⓓ

2 There are 8 tulips. Amanda picks 5.
Which number sentence tells how many tulips are left?

8   5

| $8 + 5 = 13$ | $8 - 5 = 3$ | $5 + 3 = 8$ | $13 - 5 = 8$ |
| Ⓐ | Ⓑ | Ⓒ | Ⓓ |

3 Which number sentence does not tell about the picture?

| $8 + 1 = 9$ | $4 + 5 = 9$ | $5 + 4 = 9$ | $9 = 5 + 4$ |
| Ⓐ | Ⓑ | Ⓒ | Ⓓ |

4 Mark the number sentence that is true.

| $3 + 3 + 4 = 12$ | $8 + 8 = 17$ | $7 + 3 + 7 = 17$ | $5 + 4 = 12$ |
| Ⓐ | Ⓑ | Ⓒ | Ⓓ |

5 Which doubles fact helps you solve the problem?

$$\begin{array}{r} 7 \\ + 8 \\ \hline \end{array}$$

| $\begin{array}{r} 5 \\ + 5 \\ \hline 10 \end{array}$ | $\begin{array}{r} 9 \\ + 9 \\ \hline 18 \end{array}$ | $\begin{array}{r} 6 \\ + 5 \\ \hline 11 \end{array}$ | $\begin{array}{r} 7 \\ + 7 \\ \hline 14 \end{array}$ |
| Ⓐ | Ⓑ | Ⓒ | Ⓓ |

Name_____

You can **count back** to **subtract** 1 or 2.

Start at 8.
Then count back 2:
8, 7, 6.

$8 - 2 = \underline{6}$

0 1 2 3 4 5 (6) 7 8 9 10 11 12 13 14 15 16 17 18 19 20

Check ✓

Subtract. Use the number line to help you.

Word Bank

count back
subtract

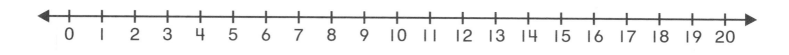

0 1 2 3 4 5 6 7 8 9 10 11 12 13 14 15 16 17 18 19 20

①

4	9	5	10	11	6
-1	-2	-2	-1	-2	-2

②

3	8	1	7	2	9
-1	-1	-1	-2	-1	-1

Think About It   Number Sense

Should you count back to solve $7 - 0$? Explain.

Subtract. Use the number line if you need to.

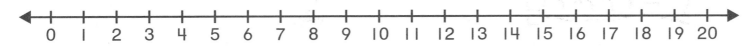

3 $6 - 2 = $ ____ $12 - 6 = $ ____   ____ $= 8 - 1$

4 $7 - 1 = $ ____   ____ $= 17 - 9$ $13 - 5 = $ ____

5
$$\begin{array}{r} 9 \\ -2 \\ \hline \end{array}$$
$$\begin{array}{r} 10 \\ -2 \\ \hline \end{array}$$
$$\begin{array}{r} 15 \\ -8 \\ \hline \end{array}$$
$$\begin{array}{r} 1 \\ -1 \\ \hline \end{array}$$
$$\begin{array}{r} 4 \\ -2 \\ \hline \end{array}$$
$$\begin{array}{r} 12 \\ -3 \\ \hline \end{array}$$

6
$$\begin{array}{r} 6 \\ -5 \\ \hline \end{array}$$
$$\begin{array}{r} 14 \\ -7 \\ \hline \end{array}$$
$$\begin{array}{r} 10 \\ -1 \\ \hline \end{array}$$
$$\begin{array}{r} 7 \\ -1 \\ \hline \end{array}$$
$$\begin{array}{r} 5 \\ -2 \\ \hline \end{array}$$
$$\begin{array}{r} 13 \\ -6 \\ \hline \end{array}$$

7
$$\begin{array}{r} 11 \\ -6 \\ \hline \end{array}$$
$$\begin{array}{r} 9 \\ -1 \\ \hline \end{array}$$
$$\begin{array}{r} 4 \\ -0 \\ \hline \end{array}$$
$$\begin{array}{r} 3 \\ -1 \\ \hline \end{array}$$
$$\begin{array}{r} 11 \\ -2 \\ \hline \end{array}$$
$$\begin{array}{r} 16 \\ -8 \\ \hline \end{array}$$

Problem Solving   Writing in Math

Write a story or draw a picture to go with the problem. Then solve.

8 $10 - 2 = $ ____

Home Connection Your child used the counting-back strategy for subtracting 1 or 2 from a greater number. **Home Activity** Say a number less than 18. Ask your child to count back 1 or 2 from that number.

 **Algebra**

Find the difference.

$16 - 8 = ?$

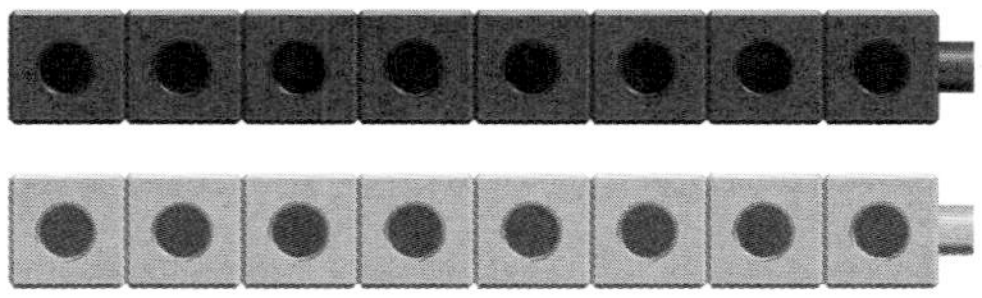

Think $8 + \underset{8}{\underline{}} = 16$

so $16 - 8 = \underset{8}{\underline{}}$

Another way to think of this is shown here.

whole	
16	
8	8
part	part

Check ✓

Use doubles facts to help you subtract.

1) $10 - 5 = ?$

Think $5 + \underline{} = 10$

so $10 - 5 = \underline{}$

2) $? = 18 - 9$

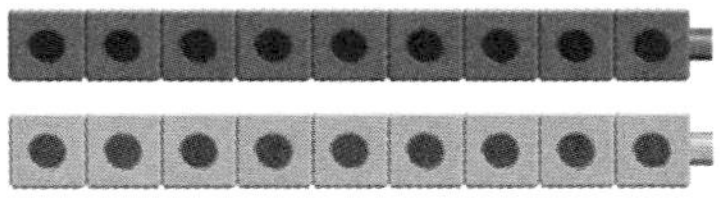

Think $18 = 9 + \underline{}$

so $\underline{} = 18 - 9$

3)

$\begin{array}{r} 14 \\ -\ 7 \\ \hline \boxed{?} \end{array}$

Think

$\begin{array}{r} 7 \\ +\ \boxed{} \\ \hline 14 \end{array}$ so $\begin{array}{r} 14 \\ -\ 7 \\ \hline \boxed{} \end{array}$

4)

$\begin{array}{r} 12 \\ -\ 6 \\ \hline \boxed{?} \end{array}$

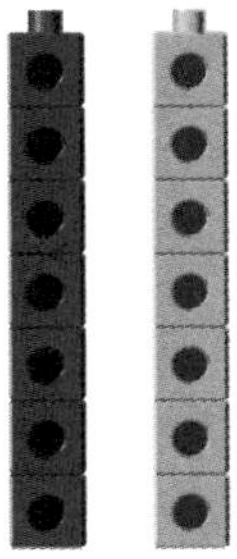

Think

$\begin{array}{r} 6 \\ +\ \boxed{} \\ \hline 12 \end{array}$ so $\begin{array}{r} 12 \\ -\ 6 \\ \hline \boxed{} \end{array}$

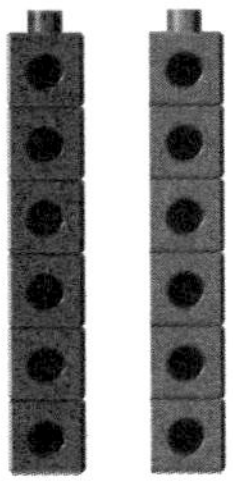

Think About It Reasoning

Can you use doubles to solve $17 - 8$? Explain.

Subtract. Write the doubles fact that helps you.

If $4 + 4 = 8$,
then $8 - 4 = 4$.

5 $8 - 4 =$ _____

_____ $+$ _____ $=$ _____

6 $18 - 9 =$ _____

_____ $+$ _____ $=$ _____

7   _____ $= 6 - 3$

_____ $=$ _____ $+$ _____

8 $14 - 7 =$ _____

_____ $+$ _____ $=$ _____

9   _____ $= 16 - 8$

_____ $=$ _____ $+$ _____

10
$$\begin{array}{r} 12 \\ -\ 6 \\ \hline \square \end{array} \qquad \begin{array}{r} \square \\ +\ \square \\ \hline \square \end{array}$$

11
$$\begin{array}{r} 10 \\ -\ 5 \\ \hline \square \end{array} \qquad \begin{array}{r} \square \\ +\ \square \\ \hline \square \end{array}$$

Problem Solving   Writing in Math

12   Lou's grandma gave him 18 sports cards to
share equally with his brother. If Lou gives his
brother 8 cards, is he being fair? Explain.

_____

_____

_____

Home Connection Your child used doubles facts to subtract.
Home Activity Ask your child to tell you which doubles fact he or
she would use to solve $14 - 7$. $(7 + 7 = 14)$

 **Algebra**

Find the difference.

$13 - 6 = ?$

I know that
$6 + 7 = 13$,
so $13 - 6 = 7$.

Think $6 + \underline{7} = 13$

so $13 - 6 = \underline{7}$

13	
6	7

Check ✓

Use addition facts to help you subtract.

1 $17 - 9 = ?$

Think $9 + \underline{} = 17$

so $17 - 9 = \underline{}$

2 $? = 16 - 7$

Think $16 = 7 + \underline{}$

so $\underline{} = 16 - 7$

3

$\begin{array}{r} 12 \\ -5 \\ \hline \boxed{?} \end{array}$

Think

$\begin{array}{r} 5 \\ +\ \boxed{} \\ \hline 12 \end{array}$

so

$\begin{array}{r} 12 \\ -5 \\ \hline \boxed{} \end{array}$

4

$\begin{array}{r} 13 \\ -8 \\ \hline \boxed{?} \end{array}$

Think

$\begin{array}{r} 8 \\ +\ \boxed{} \\ \hline 13 \end{array}$

so

$\begin{array}{r} 13 \\ -8 \\ \hline \boxed{} \end{array}$

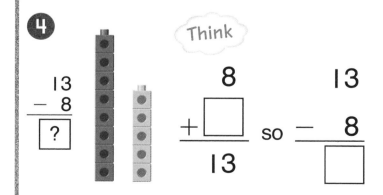

Think About It   Number Sense

What pair of addition facts helps you solve $14 - 8$?

Solve. Draw a line to match each subtraction fact
with its related addition fact.

5   15 − 8 = __7__

12 − 7 = ___

14 − 9 = ___

11 − 7 = ___

13 − 8 = ___

7 + ___ = 12

8 + ___ = 13

8 + __7__ = 15

9 + ___ = 14

7 + ___ = 11

---

6   __9__ = 12 − 3

___ = 11 − 6

___ = 18 − 9

___ = 16 − 9

16 = 9 + ___

12 = 3 + __9__

11 = 6 + ___

18 = 9 + ___

Problem Solving   Mental Math

7   Chen got 15¢. He bought a used book for 8¢.
Circle the used toy that he has enough money
left to buy.

8¢

10¢

5¢

Home Connection Your child used addition to help with subtraction.
Home Activity Ask your child to tell which addition facts could help
solve problems like 17 − 8. (8 + 9 = 17 or 9 + 8 = 17)

 **Algebra**

What does weigh?

If   7   +   _8_   =   15,

then   15   −   7   =   _8_.

 weighs _8_ pounds.

Complete the number sentence.

Check ✓

Find and write the missing numbers.

1 What does weigh?

If   9   +   ___   =   16,

then   16   −   9   =   ___.

 weighs _____ pounds.

---

2 What does weigh?

If   ___   +   7   =   13,

then   13   −   ___   =   7.

 weighs _____ pounds.

Think About It   Reasoning

If 16 + 2 = 18, then 16 + _____ = 20.
Explain.

Find and write the missing numbers.

3 What does weigh?

If _____ + 9 = 17,

then 17 − _____ = 9.

 weighs _____ pounds.

---

4 What does weigh?

If _____ + 8 = 14,

then 14 − _____ = 8.

 weighs _____ pounds.

---

5 What does weigh?

If 10 = 8 + _____,

then _____ = 10 − 8.

 weighs _____ pounds.

Reasoning

Write the missing number for each number sentence.

6 7 + _____ = 15

14 = 6 + _____

18 = _____ + 9

7 7 + 7 + _____ = 16

4 + _____ + 6 = 13

17 = 8 + _____ + 1

Home Connection Your child found the missing number in addition and subtraction sentences. **Home Activity** Write some addition and subtraction facts with missing numbers. Have your child write the missing numbers.

Name _____

 Dorling Kindersley

Do You Know...

that a baby bird hatched in a nest in a tree is called a *nestling*?

1 These 3 birds are old enough to be out of their nest. If 3 birds are on one branch and 3 birds are on another branch, how many birds are there in all?

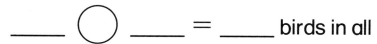

____ ◯ ____ = ____ birds in all

Fun Fact!

Here are three different kinds of outer wing feathers. They are called the flight feathers. Aren't they beautiful?

2 Many kinds of mother and father birds go hunting for food for their nestlings. They hunt hour after hour. A father bird made 20 hunting trips in 2 hours. He made 10 trips in the first hour. How many trips did he make in the second hour?

10 + ____ = 20 trips

He made ____ trips in the second hour.

3 A group of nestlings is 13 days old. In 5 more days they will be ready to leave the nest. How old will they be then?

Carrying a nestling to safety

_____ ◯ _____ = _____ days old

4 Many kinds of nestlings are cared for by their parents. If there were 8 eggs, and 2 nestlings hatched, how many eggs would still be in the nest?

_____ − _____ = _____ eggs

5 Not all birds are hatched in nests in trees. Flamingos are hatched in nests on the ground. If there are 13 parrots and 20 flamingos at the zoo, how many parrots and flamingos are there in all?

_____ parrots and flamingos

6 **Writing in Math**

Write a story about flamingos at a zoo. Try to use both addition and subtraction in your story.

Home Connection Your child learned to solve problems by applying his or her math skills. **Home Activity** Talk to your child about how he or she solved the problems on these two pages.

Diagnostic Checkpoint

Subtract.

1

7	10	5	12	11	16
− 2	− 2	− 0	− 6	− 2	− 9

Subtract. Write the doubles fact that helps you.

2 14 − 7 = ____

____ + ____ = ____

3

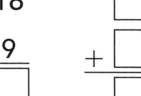

Solve. Draw a line to match each subtraction fact
with its related addition fact.

4 16 − 8 = ____   9 + ____ = 14

14 − 9 = ____   7 + ____ = 13

13 − 7 = ____   8 + ____ = 16

Find and write the missing number.
Complete the number sentence.

5 What does weigh?

If   5   + ____ = 7,

then   7 − 5 = ____.

 weighs ____ pounds.

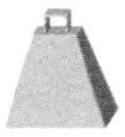

1 There are 6 purple forks. 2 yellow forks are added. Mark the number sentence that tells how many forks there are in all.

6   2

$6 + 2 = 8$ forks $8 + 6 = 14$ forks $8 + 2 = 10$ forks $6 - 2 = 4$ forks

Ⓐ   Ⓑ   Ⓒ   Ⓓ

2 How many more blue bowls than orange bowls are there?

Ⓐ   1 more blue bowl

Ⓑ   2 more orange bowls

Ⓒ   2 more blue bowls

Ⓓ   3 more blue bowls

3 There are 9 cups in all. How many cups are inside the basket?

6   +   ___   = 9

Ⓐ   7

Ⓑ   3

Ⓒ   11

Ⓓ   14

4 Subtract. Mark the difference.

$$\begin{array}{r} 8 \\ -\ 2 \\ \hline \end{array}$$

18   17   9   6

Ⓐ   Ⓑ   Ⓒ   Ⓓ

5 Mark the related fact.

$15 - 8$ $9 + 6 = 15$ $8 + 4 = 12$ $8 + 7 = 15$ $6 + 8 = 14$

          Ⓐ   Ⓑ   Ⓒ   Ⓓ

Adding Doubles Plus 2

You can use doubles facts to find doubles-plus-2 facts.

5 + 5 = 10 is a doubles fact.

$$\begin{array}{r} 5 \\ + 5 \\ \hline 10 \end{array}$$

5 + 7 is a doubles-plus-2 fact.

$$\begin{array}{r} 5 \\ + 7 \\ \hline 12 \end{array}$$

5, 10, 11, 12

Add the double.

Then count on 2.

Write each sum. Use cubes if you need to.

1
$$\begin{array}{r} 3 \\ + 3 \\ \hline \end{array} \qquad \begin{array}{r} 3 \\ + 5 \\ \hline \end{array}$$

2
$$\begin{array}{r} 4 \\ + 4 \\ \hline \end{array} \qquad \begin{array}{r} 6 \\ + 4 \\ \hline \end{array}$$

3
$$\begin{array}{r} 7 \\ + 7 \\ \hline \end{array} \qquad \begin{array}{r} 9 \\ + 7 \\ \hline \end{array}$$

4
$$\begin{array}{r} 6 \\ + 6 \\ \hline \end{array} \qquad \begin{array}{r} 8 \\ + 6 \\ \hline \end{array}$$

5
$$\begin{array}{r} 8 \\ + 8 \\ \hline \end{array} \qquad \begin{array}{r} 8 \\ + 10 \\ \hline \end{array}$$

6
$$\begin{array}{r} 2 \\ + 4 \\ \hline \end{array} \qquad \begin{array}{r} 6 \\ + 4 \\ \hline \end{array} \qquad \begin{array}{r} 5 \\ + 3 \\ \hline \end{array} \qquad \begin{array}{r} 10 \\ + 8 \\ \hline \end{array} \qquad \begin{array}{r} 7 \\ + 9 \\ \hline \end{array} \qquad \begin{array}{r} 6 \\ + 8 \\ \hline \end{array}$$

7 **Writing in Math** ✏️ ✏️

Find the missing numbers.

What pattern do you see?

$3 + 5 = 4 + \boxed{}$

$6 + 8 = 7 + \boxed{}$

$9 + 7 = 8 + \boxed{}$

Home Connection Your child learned how to solve doubles-plus-two facts. **Home Activity** Ask your child which doubles fact he or she used to solve each problem.

Name _____

Learn Doubles Facts Using a Calculator

Press ON/C each time you begin.

1. | 3 | + | 3 | = | __6__

2. | 7 | + | 7 | = | ____

3. | 5 | + | 5 | = | ____

4. | ☐ | + | 8 | = | __16__

5. | 8 | − | ☐ | = | __4__

6. | ☐ | − | 2 | = | __2__

7. | 1 | 2 | − | ☐ | = | __6__

8. | ☐ | ☐ | − | 9 | = | __9__

Complete each number sentence. Find the pattern.

9. | 2 | + | 2 | = | ____

10. | 4 | + | 4 | = | ____

11. | 8 | + | 8 | = | ____

12. | 1 | 6 | + | ☐ | ☐ | = | ____

13. | ☐ | ☐ | + | 3 | 2 | = | ____

14. | ☐ | ☐ | + | ☐ | ☐ | = | ____

Think About It   Reasoning

What pattern do you notice in Exercises 9–14?

Home Connection Your child used a calculator to complete number sentences involving doubles. **Home Activity** Ask your child to explain how he or she solved Exercise 5. (Sample answer: Since I know 4 + 4 = 8, I pressed 8 − 4 = on my calculator.)

Get Information for the Answer

Many math problems have tables. You can get information from these tables to help you solve the problems.

Test-Taking Strategies

Understand the Question

Get Information for the Answer

Plan How to Find the Answer

Make Smart Choices

Use Writing in Math

The table below shows scores for three card games. Use the information in the table to answer the question below the table. Then fill in the answer bubble.

Card Game Points			
	David	**Chris**	**Ann**
Game 1	8	6	3
Game 2	4	9	6
Game 3	5	3	7

1 Which addition sentence tells how many points Ann scored in all three games?

Ⓐ $3 + 6 + 7 = 16$ 　　Ⓒ $6 + 9 + 3 = 18$

Ⓑ $8 + 6 + 3 = 17$ 　　Ⓓ $5 + 3 + 7 = 15$

Your Turn

Use information from the same table to answer this question:

2 How many points did all three players score in Game 2?

Ⓐ $8 + 4 + 5 = 17$ 　　Ⓒ $5 + 3 + 7 = 15$

Ⓑ $6 + 9 + 3 = 18$ 　　Ⓓ $4 + 9 + 6 = 19$

Home Connection Your child prepared for standardized tests by using information from a table to solve math problems. **Home Activity** Ask your child to explain how he or she used the table to answer the question in Exercise 2.

Name _____

What's the Buzz?

Have you ever heard a bee buzzing around your ear?
Sometimes people are afraid of bees,
but bees help flowers and plants form seeds.
Then the seeds can grow into new plants.

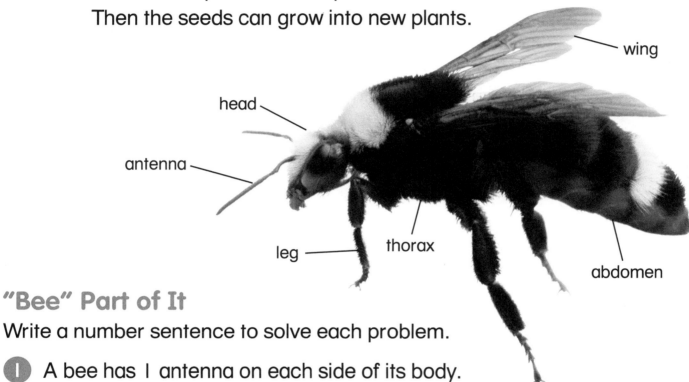

wing

head

antenna

leg

thorax

abdomen

"Bee" Part of It

Write a number sentence to solve each problem.

1 A bee has 1 antenna on each side of its body.
How many antennae does it have in all?

_____ + _____ = _____ antennae in all

2 A bee has 3 legs on each side of its body.
How many legs does it have in all?

_____ + _____ = _____ legs in all

3 How many legs do 3 bees have?

_____ + _____ + _____ = _____ legs

Take It to the NET
Video and Activities
www.scottforesman.com

Home Connection Your child wrote number sentences to solve problems about bees. **Home Activity** Ask your child to write a number sentence that shows how many wings a bee has and then a number sentence to show how many wings 2 bees have.

Name _____

Count on to find each sum.

1 4 + 3 = ____   1 + 7 = ____   ____ = 9 + 2

Add. Circle the doubles facts.

2
```
   5       6       7       9       5       9
 + 5     + 7     + 7     + 8     + 4     + 9
```

Add. Try different ways.

3
```
   8       6       4       8       5       1
   2       4       4       3       5       7
 + 8     + 3     + 2     + 7     + 5     + 8
```

Use the table to solve.
Write the number sentence.

4 How many lions are there
in all three zoos?

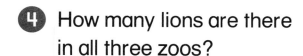 = ____ lions

Zoo Animals			
	Zoo A	Zoo B	Zoo C
Monkeys	1	9	9
Lions	8	2	7

Subtract.

5
```
  14       9      16      18       7      15
 - 8     - 2     - 9     - 9     - 1     - 7
```

Subtract. Write the doubles fact that helps you.

6 14 − 7 = ___

___ + ___ = ___

12 − 6 = ___

___ + ___ = ___

7

18
− 9
⬚

+ ⬚
⬚

16
− 8
⬚

+ ⬚
⬚

Solve. Draw a line to match each subtraction fact
with its related addition fact.

8 11 − 2 = ___

9 16 − 9 = ___

10 15 − 7 = ___

11 18 − 9 = ___

12 4 − 1 = ___

2 + ___ = 11

1 + ___ = 4

9 + ___ = 18

9 + ___ = 16

7 + ___ = 15

Find and write the missing number. Complete the number sentence.

13 What does weigh?

If 6 + ___ = 9,

then 9 − 6 = ___.

 weighs ___ pounds.

Write the missing number for each number sentence.

14 13 − ___ = 7

9 + ___ = 14

Name_____

Mark the addition sentence that
tells how many people there are in all.

1 There are 6 people on the bus.
3 more people get on the bus.

    Ⓐ 6 − 3 = 3 people
    Ⓑ 6 + 3 = 9 people
    Ⓒ 3 + 3 = 6 people
    Ⓓ 5 + 5 = 10 people

Mark the correct number sentence.

2
9 + 9 = 18	9 + 9 = 17	9 + 9 = 20	9 + 9 = 0
Ⓐ	Ⓑ	Ⓒ	Ⓓ

Add. Mark the sum.

3

3 + 2 = _____

  Ⓐ 1
  Ⓑ 6
  Ⓒ 2
  Ⓓ 5

4

$$\begin{array}{r} 8 \\ + 7 \\ \hline \end{array}$$

  Ⓐ 14
  Ⓑ 1
  Ⓒ 8
  Ⓓ 15

Subtract. Mark the difference.

5

5 − 1 = _____

  Ⓐ 1
  Ⓑ 6
  Ⓒ 5
  Ⓓ 4

6

$$\begin{array}{r} 13 \\ - 6 \\ \hline \end{array}$$

  Ⓐ 2
  Ⓑ 19
  Ⓒ 7
  Ⓓ 8

Mark the number of shells that are in the bucket.

7 There are 12 shells in all.

8 + _____ = 12
_____ shells

  Ⓐ 4 shells
  Ⓑ 2 shells
  Ⓒ 5 shells
  Ⓓ 3 shells

Count the cups in each group.
Draw and write how many there are in all.

 8

_____ and _____ is _____ in all.

Compare to find how many more blue spoons there are.
Write the numbers.

 9

_____ blue spoons   _____ orange spoons   _____ more blue spoons

Write a number sentence to solve.
Use the table to help you.

10 How many points did Molly
score in all?

_____ = _____ points

	Game 1	Game 2	Game 3
Game Points			
Jack	6	5	4
Molly	7	7	3

Find and write the missing number.
Complete the number sentence.

11 What does weigh?

If $9 + \underline{\quad} = 14$,

then $14 - 9 = \underline{\quad}$.

Writing in Math

12 Find the difference. Then write a
number story or draw a picture
for this number sentence.

$12 - 3 = \underline{\quad}$

CHAPTER 3

Place Value to 100 and Money

Read Together

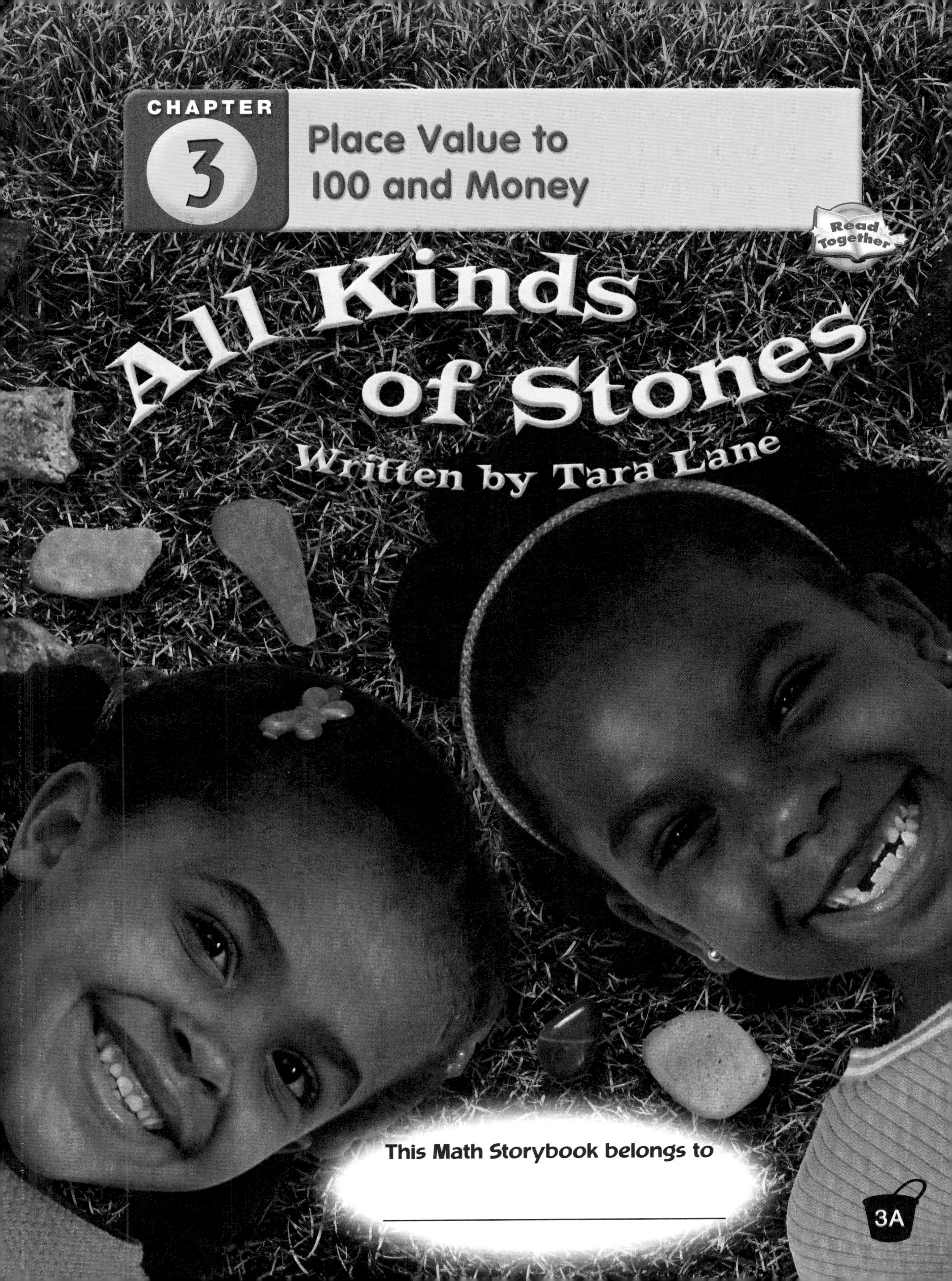

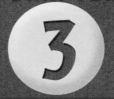

All Kinds of Stones

Written by Tara Lane

This Math Storybook belongs to

____

3A

Collecting stones is what we like.
We think it's so much fun!
We like them big.
We like them small.
Let's count them, everyone.

We gathered all the shiny stones.
They look so smooth and round.
We filled **1** box of **10**, and
5 more are on the ground.

How many do we have in all?

3C

Look at all the thin, flat stones! We found some at the shore. We filled **3** buckets of **10**, and here we have **2** more.

How many do we have in all?

Shiny, flat, or bumpy stones—
which kind do you like best?
Let's count the groups of 10 we have
and then count all the rest.

Home-School Connection

Dear Family,

Today my class started Chapter 3, **Place Value to 100 and Money.** I will learn about tens and ones, even numbers and odd numbers, and how the numbers from 1 through 100 fit together. I will also learn how to count different combinations of coins. Here are some of the math words I will be learning and some things we can do to help me with my math.

Love,

_____

Math Activity to Do at Home

Collect 100 buttons or bottle caps. Count them by 1s. Group them by 10s. Count the sets by 10s. Break apart one of the sets and count the entire 100 by 10s and then by 1s (when you get to the broken-apart set). Count by 2s and 5s; count forward and backward. Have fun!

Books to Read Together

Reading math stories reinforces concepts. Look for these books in your local library:

From One to One Hundred
by Teri Sloat
(Puffin, 1995)

The King's Commissioners
by Aileen Friedman
Scholastic, 1994)

Take It to the NET
More Activities
www.scottforesman.com

My New Math Words

even numbers If every part has a match, the number is even.

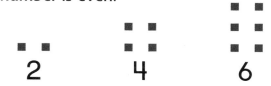

2   4   6

odd numbers If one part has no match, the number is odd.

1   3   5

ordinal numbers Ordinal numbers (e.g., *first, second, third, fourth*) show the order of things.

dollar A bill or coin worth 100 cents (100¢).

100 cents *or* 100¢ *or* $1.00

How Many in All?

What You Need

1 dot cube

2 kinds of game markers ● ♟

How to Play

1. Place your marker on a pile of stones marked START.
2. When it is your turn, say the number on the pile, toss the cube, and count the dots.
3. Add that number to the number on your pile of stones.
4. Put a marker on the stone that has the correct sum on it.
5. Continue playing until all of the stones are covered.

Player 1
START
10

Player 2
START
20

22 15 11
25 23 26
14 24
13 21
16
12

Name _____

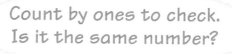
Count by ones to check.
Is it the same number?

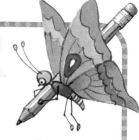

Circle groups of ten.
Count the **tens** and **ones**.
Write the numbers.

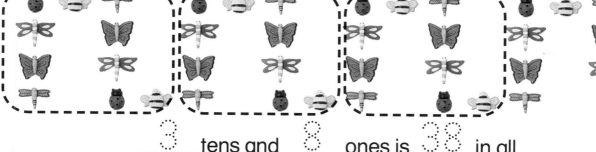

___3___ tens and ___8___ ones is ___38___ in all.

Word Bank

tens

ones

Check ✓

Circle groups of ten. Count the tens and ones.
Write the numbers.

1

_____ tens and _____ ones is _____ in all.

2

_____ tens and _____ ones is _____ in all.

Think About It   Reasoning

Can you count to 50 faster if you count by tens or by ones?
Explain.

Circle groups of ten. Count the tens and ones.
Write the numbers.

3

_____ tens and _____ ones is _____ in all.

4

_____ tens and _____ ones is _____ in all.

Problem Solving   Number Sense

Solve. Draw your answer.

5 There are 7 tens and 2 ones.
We find 1 more one.
How many are there now?

_____ tens and _____ ones is _____ in all.

6 There are 8 tens and 6 ones.
We find 1 more ten.
How many are there now?

_____ tens and _____ ones is _____ in all.

Home Connection Your child counted tens and ones.
Home Activity With your child, count at least 25 objects in your
home or outside—first by ones and then by tens.

Name ________________________

Using Tens and Ones

Learn!

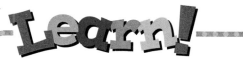

Show 47.

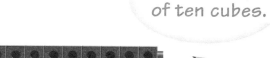

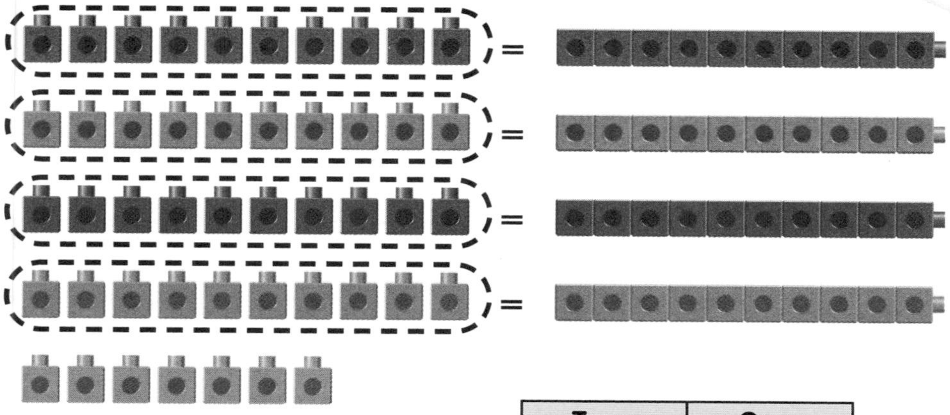

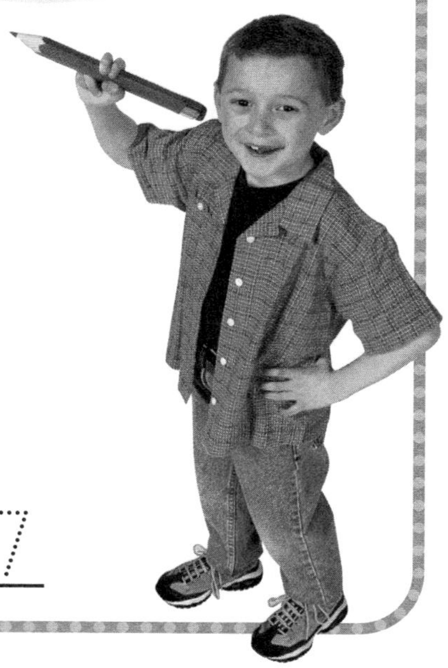

Circle groups of ten cubes.

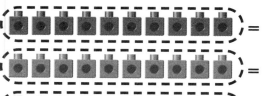

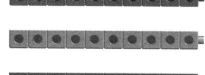

4 tens 7 ones =

Tens	Ones
4	7

= 47

Check

Show the number with cubes on Workmat 4.
Write the number of tens and ones.

1. Show 72. _____ tens _____ ones =

Tens	Ones

= _____

2. Show 35. _____ tens _____ ones =

Tens	Ones

= _____

3. Show 64. _____ tens _____ ones =

Tens	Ones

= _____

Think About It Number Sense

Which is greater, 8 ones or 2 tens? Explain.

Draw lines to match the numbers with the models.
Use cubes and Workmat 4 if you need to.

4

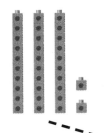 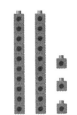  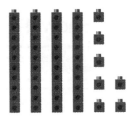

Tens	Ones
1	7

Tens	Ones
3	2

Tens	Ones
4	7

Tens	Ones
2	3

5

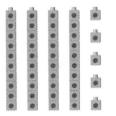   

Tens	Ones
1	6

Tens	Ones
5	4

Tens	Ones
4	5

Tens	Ones
3	6

Problem Solving   Visual Thinking

6 How many pairs of gloves are needed to show
at least 65 fingers? Draw a picture to solve
the problem. Explain your answer.

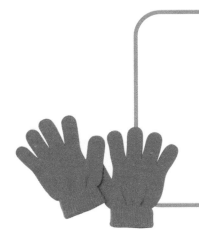

© Pearson Education, Inc.

Home Connection Your child learned to represent and write
tens and ones. **Home Activity** Have your child count and write a
two-digit number using collections of small objects, such as coins.

Number Words

The number 35 has 2 **digits**.

Number 35

3 and 5 are digits in 35 .

Number word

thirty-five

Ones	Teens	Tens
1 one	11 eleven	10 ten
2 two	12 twelve	20 twenty
3 three	13 thirteen	30 thirty
4 four	14 fourteen	40 forty
5 five	15 fifteen	50 fifty
6 six	16 sixteen	60 sixty
7 seven	17 seventeen	70 seventy
8 eight	18 eighteen	80 eighty
9 nine	19 nineteen	90 ninety

Word Bank

digit
number word

Check ✓

Write the number.

1 ninety-four 94   sixteen _____   forty _____

2 thirty-one _____   twenty-three _____   eighty-nine _____

Write the number word.

3 70 _____   32 _____

4 65 _____   11 _____

Think About It   Number Sense

Name the ones digits in seventy-nine and eighty-two.

Name the tens digits in thirty and fifty-six.

Write the number.

(5) nine _____   thirty-three _____   eighty-two _____

(6) seventy _____   seventeen _____   fifty-eight _____

(7) forty-five _____   ninety-one _____   twenty-six _____

Write the number word.

(8) 12 _____

(9) 90 _____

(10) 84 _____

(11) 49 _____

(12) 2 tens _____

(13) 1 ten 6 ones _____

(14) 15 ones _____

(15) 6 tens _____

(16) 9 tens 3 ones _____

(17) 5 tens 7 ones _____

Problem Solving Number Sense

What is the number?

(18) It is greater than thirty-five and less than forty-five. If you add the two digits, the sum is five.

Write the number word.

_____

(19) It is less than 70 and greater than 65. If you add the two digits, the sum is 14.

Write the number.

_____

Home Connection Your child learned number words.
Home Activity Name a number between 10 and 99 and ask your child to write it as a number word.

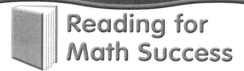

Reading for Math Success

Understand Graphic Sources: Lists

1 Making a list is a good way to think things through.

A mysterious suitcase fell off the train and popped open. "Hmm," said the detective. "No name. How can we find the owner?"

2 Help the detective list the contents.

Five _____

Seven _____

Four _____

_____ + _____ + _____ = _____ items

3 Look at the passengers. Which ones look like they might have lost something? Help the detective list them.

_____

_____

_____

4 To which one does this mysterious

suitcase belong? _____

5 Why do you think so?

_____

Think About It   Number Sense

You can make a list for just about anything.
Make a list of your three favorite names for girls
and your three favorite names for boys.

Here are two lists of names. They show 10 popular names for girls and 10 popular names for boys.

6 Beside each name, write down the number of people you know who have that name.
If you don't know anyone with that name, write 0.
If **your** name is on the list, don't forget to count yourself!

1. Emily   6. Hailey

2. Hannah   7. Ashley

3. Kaitlyn   8. Brianna

4. Madison   9. Samantha

5. Sarah   10. Jasmine

1. Jacob   6. Andrew

2. Michael   7. Joseph

3. Nicholas   8. Christopher

4. Matthew   9. Anthony

5. Joshua   10. Dylan

7 Add up the total number of girls.
Then add up the total number of boys.

Girls _____   Boys _____

Home Connection Your child looked at lists as a way of organizing information. **Home Activity** Show your child lists you use in everyday life, for example, a grocery list or an address book.

1 Make 100 as many ways as you can by using groups of ten.

What two groups of ten make 100?

Read and Understand

You need to find groups of ten that make 100.

Plan and Solve

Make an **organized list** to keep track of the groups. Use cubes and Workmat 1 if you need to.

Complete the first row. The first row says that 0 tens and 10 tens make 100.

Write the missing numbers in the chart.

Look Back and Check

Do your answers make sense? Does each row have a total of 10 tens (or 100)?

Tens	Tens	Total
0	10	100
1	9	100
2	8	100
		100
		100
		100
		100
		100
		100
		100
		100

Word Bank

organized list

Think About It   Reasoning

How does making an organized list help you?

Practice

Use groups of ten to make the number.
Use cubes and Workmat 1 if you need to.

2 Make 60.

Tens	Tens	Total
0	6	60
		60
		60
		60
		60
		60
		60

4 Make 90.

Tens	Tens	Total
0	9	90
		90
		90
		90
		90
5	4	
		90
7	2	
		90

3 Make 50.

Tens	Tens	Total
		50
		50
		50
		50
		50
		50

I see number patterns!

Home Connection Your child made organized lists with groups of ten to make given multiples of ten. **Home Activity** Ask your child to make an organized list identifying the different ways to make 70 using groups of ten.

90 ninety

© Pearson Education, Inc.

Comparing Numbers

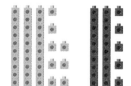  **Algebra**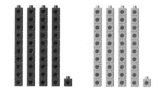

We can compare numbers by using >, <, and =.

Compare the tens.	If the tens are the same, compare the ones.	Tens and ones can be the same.

3 tens is **greater than** 2 tens.
38 is greater than 25.
38 **>** 25

4 ones is **less than** 6 ones.
24 is less than 26.
24 **<** 26

41 is **equal to** 41.
41 **=** 41

Word Bank

greater than (>)
less than (<)
equal to (=)

Check ✓

Write the numbers. Circle >, <, or =.

1

53 (>) 46

2

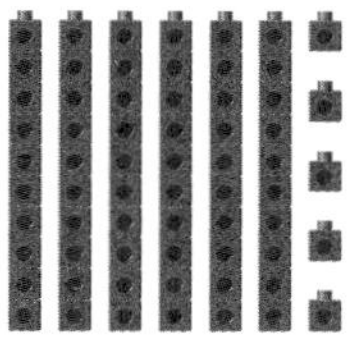

____ = ____

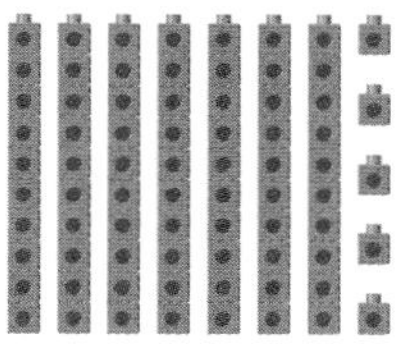

3

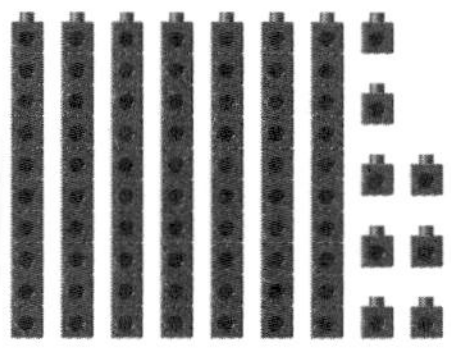

____ > ____

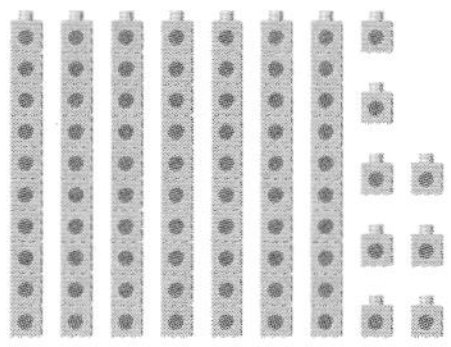

4

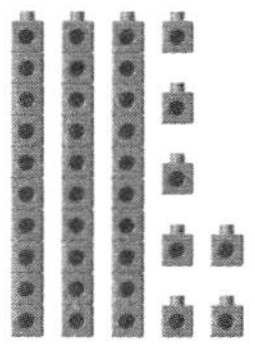

____ < ____

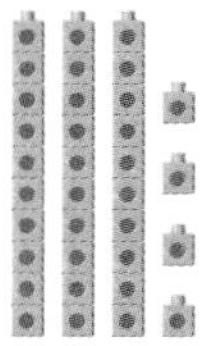

Think About It   Number Sense

Which number is greater, 46 or 64? How do you know?

Write >, <, or =.

Compare the tens first!

5 21 (>) 14   28 ◯ 82   73 ◯ 68

6 90 ◯ 86   57 ◯ 61   43 ◯ 43

7 39 ◯ 95   84 ◯ 84   65 ◯ 56

8 6 ◯ 36   99 ◯ 100   49 ◯ 35

Write a number that makes the statement true.

9 ____ < 41   77 = ____   100 > ____

10 ____ = 16   ____ > 80   ____ > 25

Problem Solving   Reasoning

What number am I?

11 My tens digit is 2 more
than my ones digit.
I am less than 100.
I am greater than 89.

____

12 My ones digit is
double my tens digit.
I am less than 42.
I am greater than 30.

____

Name _____

Circle groups of ten. Count the tens and ones.
Write the numbers.

1

_____ tens and _____ ones is _____ in all.

Write the number of tens and ones.

2

_____ tens _____ ones =

Tens	Ones

3 Use groups of ten to make 80.

Tens	Tens	Total
0	8	80
	7	80
2		80
3	5	
		80
6		
		80
8		

Write the number.

4 eleven _____

seventy-nine _____

Write the number word.

5 68 _____

13 _____

80 _____

Write >, <, or =.

6 40 ◯ 20   **7** 31 ◯ 48

100 ◯ 90   61 ◯ 16

69 ◯ 70   24 ◯ 24

Mark the related **addition** fact.

 1
$$5 + 3 = 8$$

    $5 + 2 = 7$ $3 + 5 = 8$ $8 - 5 = 3$ $2 + 3 = 5$

     Ⓐ   Ⓑ   Ⓒ   Ⓓ

Mark the fact that does not belong in the fact family.

 2 $12 - 5 = 7$ $5 + 7 = 12$ $12 - 7 = 5$ $5 + 2 = 7$

     Ⓐ   Ⓑ   Ⓒ   Ⓓ

Subtract.

3 $13 - 4 = \square$ **4** $\square = 11 - 3$

   10   8   9   17   14   13   10   8

   Ⓐ   Ⓑ   Ⓒ   Ⓓ   Ⓐ   Ⓑ   Ⓒ   Ⓓ

Add.

5 $9 + 8 = \square$ **6** $\square = 5 + 8$

   17   16   15   1   12   17   3   13

   Ⓐ   Ⓑ   Ⓒ   Ⓓ   Ⓐ   Ⓑ   Ⓒ   Ⓓ

Writing in Math

7 Write the missing number. $9 + \square = 15$
      Then write a number story that tells about this number sentence.

_____

_____

_____

_____

Name_____

 **Algebra**

You can use tens to tell **about** how many.
Find the **closest ten.**

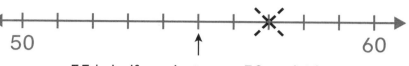

50   60

55 is halfway between 50 and 60.

57 is about __60__.

57 is closer to 60 than to 50.

Check ✓

Find the number on the number line.
Write the closest ten.

Word Bank

about

closest ten

1

20   30

26 is about _____.

2

40   50

43 is about _____.

Think About It   Number Sense

Is 45 closer to 40 or to 50?

Find the number on the number line.
Write the closest ten.

3
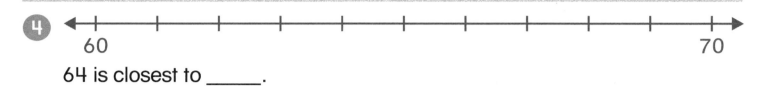

80   90

88 is closest to _____.

4

60   70

64 is closest to _____.

5

30   40

39 is closest to _____.

Write the closest ten.

6    _____

7    _____

8    _____

9 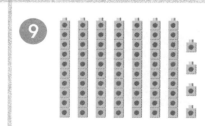   _____

Problem Solving   Reasonableness

About 40 Children Visit Pandas at Zoo!

10 Which could be the exact number of children?

68   55   39   22

_____ children

© Pearson Education, Inc.

Home Connection Your child found the closest ten to tell about how many. **Home Activity** Ask your child to find the closest ten for 34 and to explain his or her thinking.

Name_____

 **Learn!**

What is the number?

1	2	3	4	5	6	7	8	9	10
11	12	13	14	15	16	17	18	19	20
21	22	23	24	25	26	27	28	29	30
31	32	33	34	35	36	37	38	39	40
41	42	43	44	45	46	47	48	49	50
51	52	53	54	55	56	57	58	59	60
61	62	63	64	65	66	67	68	69	70
71	72	73	74	75	76	77	78	79	80
81	82	83	84	85	86	87	88	89	90
91	92	93	94	95	96	97	98	99	100

Use the hundred chart to help you.

One **before** 56 is __55__.

One **after** 53 is __54__.

__46__ is **between** 45 and 47.

Word Bank

before

after

between

Check ✓

Write the missing numbers.
Answer the questions.

1

16		
	27	28
37		39

One after 16 is __17__.

One before 28 is _____.

The number between 37 and 39 is _____.

2

		74
82		84
92		

One before 74 is _____.

One after 92 is _____.

The number between 82 and 84 is _____.

Think About It   Number Sense

Use the words **before**, **after**, and **between** to describe 47.

Write the missing numbers.

3
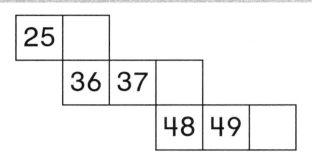

	42		44
	52		
		63	

4
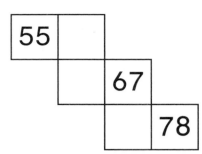

55		
	67	
		78

5

25			
	36	37	
		48	49	

6

70		72	
		82	83
	92		

7

_____, 17, _____, _____, 20

8

85, _____, _____, 88, _____

9

_____, 29, _____, _____, 32

10

_____, 70, _____, 72, _____

Write the number.

11 What number is one after 49? _____

12 What number is between 59 and 61? _____

13 What number is one before 85? _____

14 What number is one after 90? _____

> Use the hundred chart if you need to.

Problem Solving Writing in Math

15 Use the words **one greater than** and **one less than** to describe the number between 51 and 53.

Home Connection Your child identified which numbers come before, after, and between given numbers. **Home Activity** Ask your child to select a number—1 to 99—and to describe it by using *before, after,* and *between.*

Name ______________________________

Skip Counting on the Hundred Chart

Learn! Algebra

Skip counting makes **patterns** on the hundred chart.
What pattern do you see?

1	2	(3)	4	5	(6)	7	8	(9)	10
11	(12)	13	14	(15)	16	17	(18)	19	20
(21)	22	23	(24)	25	26	(27)	28	29	(30)
31	32	(33)	34	35	(36)	37	38	(39)	40
41	(42)	43	44	(45)	46	47	(48)	49	50
(51)	52	53	(54)	55	56	(57)	58	59	(60)
61	62	(63)	64	65	(66)	67	68	(69)	70
71	(72)	73	74	(75)	76	77	(78)	79	80
(81)	82	83	(84)	85	86	(87)	88	89	(90)
91	92	(93)	94	95	(96)	97	98	(99)	100

I circled the skip counts by 3s.

Word Bank

skip counting
pattern

Check

1. Finish coloring skip counts by 2s.
2. Circle skip counts by 4s.

1	2	3	(4)	5	6	7	8	9	10
11	12	13	14	15	16	17	18	19	20
21	22	23	24	25	26	27	28	29	30
31	32	33	34	35	36	37	38	39	40
41	42	43	44	45	46	47	48	49	50
51	52	53	54	55	56	57	58	59	60
61	62	63	64	65	66	67	68	69	70
71	72	73	74	75	76	77	78	79	80
81	82	83	84	85	86	87	88	89	90
91	92	93	94	95	96	97	98	99	100

Think About It Reasoning

Look at the chart. What patterns do you see?

3 Finish coloring skip counts by 5s.

4 Circle skip counts by 10s.

5 What patterns do you see with skip counts by 5s and 10s?

_____

_____

_____

1	2	3	4	5	6	7	8	9	10
11	12	13	14	15	16	17	18	19	20
21	22	23	24	25	26	27	28	29	30
31	32	33	34	35	36	37	38	39	40
41	42	43	44	45	46	47	48	49	50
51	52	53	54	55	56	57	58	59	60
61	62	63	64	65	66	67	68	69	70
71	72	73	74	75	76	77	78	79	80
81	82	83	84	85	86	87	88	89	90
91	92	93	94	95	96	97	98	99	100

Problem Solving Number Sense

6 Count by 2s. 2, 4, 6, 8, ____, ____, ____, ____

7 Count by 3s. 12, 15, 18, 21, ____, ____, ____, ____

8 Count by 5s. 30, 35, 40, 45, ____, ____, ____, ____

9 Count by 10s. 10, 20, 30, 40, ____, ____, ____, ____

10 Count backward by 2s. 20, 18, 16, 14, ____, ____, ____, ____

11 Count backward by 3s. 60, 57, 54, 51, ____, ____, ____, ____

12 Count backward by 5s. 50, 45, 40, 35, ____, ____, ____, ____

13 Count backward by 10s. 100, 90, 80, 70, ____, ____, ____, ____

Home Connection Your child learned that skip counting makes number patterns. **Home Activity** Ask your child to skip count by 2s and 4s, forward and backward, using the hundred chart.

Name ________________________

Even and Odd Numbers

Learn! Algebra

If all parts of a number match, the number is **even**.

(6)

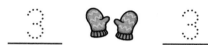

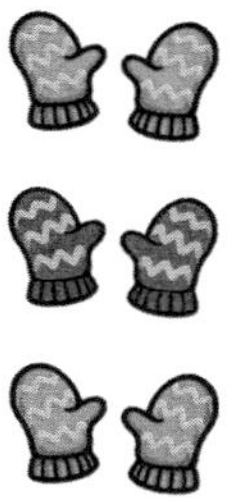

3 3

6 is an even number.

If one part of a number has no match, the number is **odd**.

(7)

3 4

7 is an odd number.

Word Bank

even
odd

Check

Write each part of the number.
Is the number odd or even?
Draw objects to show the number if you need to.

1. (15) 7 8

15 is an odd number.

2. (14) ____ ____

14 is an __________ number.

3. (17) ____ ____

17 is an __________ number.

4. (18) ____ ____

18 is an __________ number.

Think About It Number Sense

If you add two odd numbers, will the sum be odd or even?
Explain.

5 Circle the even numbers.

6 The ones digit in an even number can be

_2_____.

7 The ones digit in an odd number can be

_____.

1	②	3	④	5	6	7	8	9	10
11	12	13	14	15	16	17	18	19	20
21	22	23	24	25	26	27	28	29	30
31	32	33	34	35	36	37	38	39	40
41	42	43	44	45	46	47	48	49	50
51	52	53	54	55	56	57	58	59	60

Circle the numbers that are odd.

8 27   28   29   30

Circle the numbers that are even.

9 33   52   66   41

Write even or odd.

10 16 _____   34 _____   49 _____

11 71 _____   82 _____   57 _____

12 28 _____   100 _____   95 _____

Problem Solving   Algebra

13 The same shapes weigh the same amount. How much does each solid figure weigh?

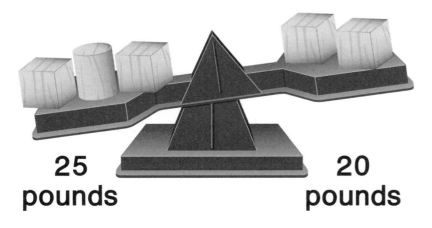

25 pounds   **20 pounds**

☐ weighs _____ pounds.

⬭ weighs _____ pounds.

Home Connection Your child learned about odd and even numbers.
Home Activity Say a number from 1 to 100 and ask your child to tell you whether it is odd or even. Then ask, "How do you know?"

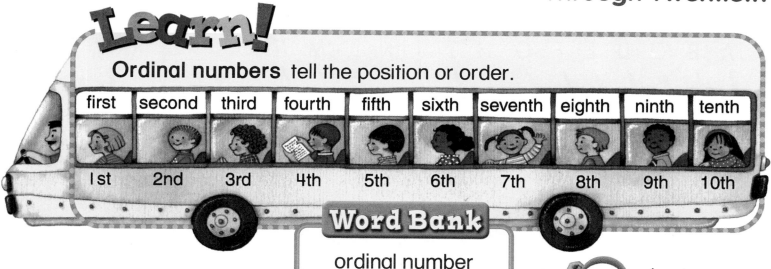

Learn!

Ordinal numbers tell the position or order.

first	second	third	fourth	fifth	sixth	seventh	eighth	ninth	tenth
1st	2nd	3rd	4th	5th	6th	7th	8th	9th	10th

Word Bank

ordinal number

Check ✓

1. Write the ordinal number next to the link in the chain.

2. Write the ordinal number words for the links between 6th and 11th.

    seventh _____

    _____

    _____

    _____

Think About It   Reasoning

Nine children are in line in front of you. What position in line are you?

If you switch places with the child in front of you, what position will you be in?

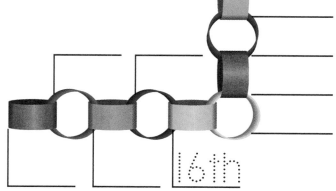

1st

6th

11th

16th

Use the pencils to solve. Write the letter or number.

A B C D E F G H I J K L M N O P Q R S T

/ / / / / / / / / / / / / / / / / / / /

1st   10th   20th

3 The sixth pencil is __F__.

4 The 3rd pencil is _____.

5 The second pencil is _____.

6 The tenth pencil is _____.

7 The 17th pencil is _____.

8 The 15th pencil is _____.

9 How many pencils are before the 12th pencil? _____

10 How many pencils are after the 15th pencil? _____

11 How many pencils are before the 20th pencil? _____

12 How many pencils are after the 11th pencil? _____

Mark your answers on the bottle caps.

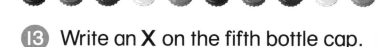

13 Write an **X** on the fifth bottle cap.

14 Circle the tenth bottle cap.

15 Write a ✓ on the 14th bottle cap.

16 Put a box around the 18th bottle cap.

Problem Solving   Reasonableness

Solve the riddle.

17 The secret letter comes after the second letter.
It comes before the 6th letter.
This letter is not the letter C.
The secret letter is not a vowel.

What is the secret letter? _____

Home Connection Your child learned ordinal numbers, 1st through 20th.
Home Activity Ask your child to put 20 small objects in a line. Then ask your child to identify the 1st, 5th, 10th, 15th, and 20th objects.

Learn!

What is the secret number?

Cross out numbers on the chart that do not fit each clue.

Clues:

It is greater than 22.
It is less than 26.
It is an even number.

20	21	22	23	24	25	26	27	28	29
30	31	32	33	34	35	36	37	38	39

The secret number is __24__.

Check ✓

Use clues to find the secret number.
Cross out the numbers on the chart
that do not fit the clues.

1 It is less than 40.
It is more than 31.
It has 3 in the ones place.

30	31	32	33	34	35	36	37	38	39
40	41	42	43	44	45	46	47	48	49

The secret number is _____.

2 It is greater than 67.
It is less than 70.
It is an odd number.

60	61	62	63	64	65	66	67	68	69
70	71	72	73	74	75	76	77	78	79

The secret number is _____.

Think About It   Reasoning

How does using clues help you find the answer?

Use clues to find the secret number.

3 It is less than 53.
It has 5 in the tens place.
It is an odd number.

40	41	42	43	44	45	46	47	48	49
50	51	52	53	54	55	56	57	58	59
60	61	62	63	64	65	66	67	68	69

The secret number is _____.

4 It is greater than 69.
It has 7 ones.

50	51	52	53	54	55	56	57	58	59
60	61	62	63	64	65	66	67	68	69
70	71	72	73	74	75	76	77	78	79

The secret number is _____.

5 It has 8 tens.
It is greater than 86.
It is an even number.

70	71	72	73	74	75	76	77	78	79
80	81	82	83	84	85	86	87	88	89
90	91	92	93	94	95	96	97	98	99

The secret number is _____.

Writing in Math

6 Choose a secret number from the chart. Write 3 clues. Ask a friend to find your secret number.

70	71	72	73	74	75	76	77	78	79
80	81	82	83	84	85	86	87	88	89
90	91	92	93	94	95	96	97	98	99

Clues: _____

_____

_____

Home Connection Your child used clues to help find a secret number.
Home Activity Give your child 6 number choices and 3 clues. Ask your child to select the secret number from the 6 choices.

 **Diagnostic Checkpoint**

Find the number on the number line.
Write the closest ten.

1

```
←|———|———|———|———|———|———|———|———|———|———|→
  30                                        40
```

37 is closest to _____.

Use clues to find the secret number.

2 It is less than 60.
It is more than 57.
It is an even number.

50	51	52	53	54	55	56	57	58	59
60	61	62	63	64	65	66	67	68	69

The secret number is _____.

3 Circle 55. Beginning with 55, circle skip counts by 5s.

4 Write an **X** on the even numbers that are circled.

5 Color the odd numbers that are circled.

51	52	53	54	55	56	57	58	59	60
61	62	63	64	65	66	67	68	69	70
71	72	73	74	75	76	77	78	79	80
81	82	83	84	85	86	87	88	89	90
91	92	93	94	95	96	97	98	99	100

Write the missing numbers.

6

21			24
	32		
	42		

7

	56		58
		77	

8 Write the letter for each block.

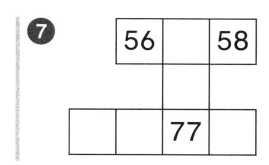

A B C D E F G H I J K L M N O P Q R S T

1st   20th

ninth block _____   18th block _____   fifth block _____

Name _____

Mark the statement that is true.

1   15 > 51   47 < 37   19 = 18   68 > 63

      Ⓐ   Ⓑ   Ⓒ   Ⓓ

Mark the missing number.

2 $\square + 5 = 10$ **3** $7 + \square = 10$

  4   15   5   10   17   3   2   1

 Ⓐ   Ⓑ   Ⓒ   Ⓓ   Ⓐ   Ⓑ   Ⓒ   Ⓓ

Add.

4 $7 + 7 = \square$ **5** $9 + 9 = \square$

  14   15   16   17   16   17   18   0

 Ⓐ   Ⓑ   Ⓒ   Ⓓ   Ⓐ   Ⓑ   Ⓒ   Ⓓ

Subtract.

6 $12 - 6 = \square$ **7** $16 - 8 = \square$

  18   6   5   7   9   24   7   8

 Ⓐ   Ⓑ   Ⓒ   Ⓓ   Ⓐ   Ⓑ   Ⓒ   Ⓓ

Writing in Math

8 Add to find the sum. $2 + 6 + 8 = \square$

Then explain how you solved the problem.

_____

_____

_____

_____

Dime, Nickel, and Penny

 **Learn!**

What is the total amount shown by the six **coins**?

| dime = 10¢ | | nickel = 5¢ | | penny = 1¢ |

10¢   20¢   25¢   30¢   31¢   32¢ total

First count by 10s.   Then count by 5s.   Then count by 1s.

 The total amount is 32 cents.
The cent sign is ¢ .

Check ✓

Count on to find the total amount.
Use coins if you need to.

1

10¢   20¢   ____   ____

Total Amount

2

____ ____ ____ ____ ____

Total Amount

Think About It   Number Sense

How many nickels do you need to equal the value of 2 dimes?
Explain.

Count on to find the total amount.

3

Total Amount

10¢ _____ _____ _____ _____

4

Total Amount

_____ _____ _____ _____ _____ _____

5

Total Amount

_____ _____ _____ _____ _____

6

Total Amount

_____ _____ _____ _____ _____ _____

Problem Solving **Writing in Math**

7 You have 6 coins that have a total value of 36¢.
Draw and label the coins.

> You can draw circles for coins. Write P, N, or D in each circle.

 Home Connection Your child skip counted by 10s, 5s, and then 1s, as necessary, to find the total value of each set of coins. **Home Activity** Select about 5 coins: pennies, nickels, and dimes. Have your child count on to find the total amount, beginning with the coin or coins of greatest value.

I earned these coins doing chores.

I **quarter** = 25¢

I **half-dollar** = 50¢

How much did Mia earn? You may use a hundred chart to count on.

50¢   75¢

Total 75¢

Word Bank

quarter
half-dollar

Check ✓

Count on to find the total amount.
You may use Workmat 6 if you need to.

1

50¢   75¢   ____   ____

Total Amount

2

____   ____   ____   ____   ____

Total Amount

Think About It   Reasoning

Is a larger coin always worth more than a smaller coin?
Explain with examples.

Count on to find the total amount.
You may use Workmat 6 if you need to.

Total Amount

_____ _____ _____ _____ _____

Total Amount

_____ _____ _____ _____ _____ _____

Total Amount

_____ _____ _____ _____ _____ _____

Problem Solving Number Sense

6 Draw more coins so that each bank has half of 50¢.

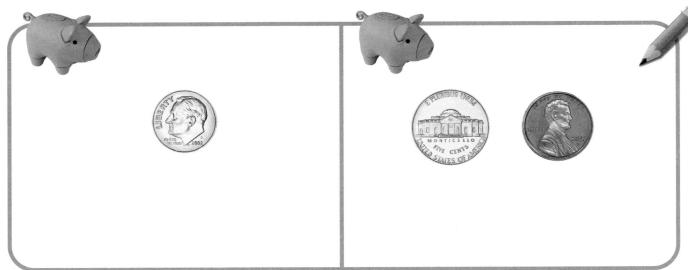

Home Connection Your child found the values of sets of coins that included quarters and half-dollars. **Home Activity** Have your child use different combinations of coins to show you 75¢.

Learn!

To count sets of coins, begin with
the coin of **greatest value**.

Then count
on to the coin of
least value.

 =

50¢   75¢   85¢   86¢

The total amount is 86¢.

Word Bank

greatest value
least value

Check ✓

Draw coins from the greatest to the least value.
Count on to find the total amount.

1

(H)

50¢ ___ ___ ___ ___

Total Amount

2

___ ___ ___ ___ ___

Total Amount

Think About It   Reasoning

Nikko counted coins in this order: 2 dimes, 1 nickel, 1 quarter.
What should he do differently? Why?

Draw coins from the greatest to the least value.
Count on to find the total amount.

3

_____ _____ _____ _____ _____

The total amount is _____.

4

_____ _____ _____ _____ _____

The total amount is _____.

5

_____ _____ _____ _____ _____

The total amount is _____.

Problem Solving Estimation

6 Jack has these coins.
About how many cents
does he have?

Hint: Find the
closest ten.

about _____

Home Connection Your child ordered and counted coins from greatest to
least value. **Home Activity** Give your child 5 or 6 coins selected randomly.
Have him or her put them in order and count the total amount.

Name_____

 **Algebra**

Does the number of coins tell you which set has more money?

Write the total amount of money in each set. Then write >, <, or =.

Number of coins __2__   Number of coins __3__

Compare the total amounts in the two sets.

$60¢$ $20¢$

Check ✓

Write the total amounts and compare them.
Write >, <, or =.

1

$31¢$ ◯ $20¢$

2

____ ◯ ____

Think About It   Reasoning

Can you use only nickels to show 40¢? Explain.

Write the total amounts and compare them.
Write >, <, or =.

3

_____ ◯ _____

4

_____ ◯ _____

5

_____ ◯ _____

Problem Solving   Reasoning

Read the clues to find out
which is Jessie's change purse.

6 Jessie has more than 20¢.
Jessie has less than 50¢.

Circle Jessie's purse.

2 quarters
1 penny

1 quarter
1 dime
1 nickel
1 penny

1 dime
1 nickel
2 pennies

 Home Connection Your child compared the total amounts of sets of coins.
Home Activity Show your child two different sets of coins, each set with a
total amount less than one dollar. Ask your child to find the set with the
greater amount.

Name_____

A **table** shows different ways to make the same amount. **Tally marks record** the number of coins.

What coins can I use to buy the seeds?

Ways to Show 60¢			
Half-Dollar	Quarter	Dime	Total Amount
I		I	60¢
	II	I	60¢
		ⅢI	60¢

Word Bank

table
tally mark
record

Check ✓

Use coins to show the same amount in different ways. Record with tally marks.

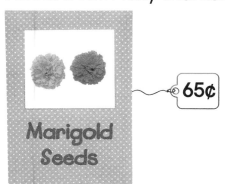

Marigold Seeds 65¢

Which row shows the least number of coins used? _____

Ways to Show 65¢			
	Half-Dollar	Dime	Nickel	Total Amount
①	I	I	I	65¢
②				
③				
④				
⑤				
⑥				

Think About It Reasoning

How does a table help you show different ways to make 65¢?

Use coins to show the same amount in different ways.
Record with tally marks.

70¢

Pumpkin Seeds

Which row shows the least number of coins used?

_____

Ways to Show 70¢			
Half-Dollar	Dime	Nickel	Total Amount
7			
8			
9			
10			
11			

86¢

Daisy Seeds

Which row shows the least number of coins used?

_____

Ways to Show 86¢			
Quarter	Dime	Penny	Total Amount
12			
13			
14			
15			

Problem Solving   Reasoning

16 Make 37¢ with fewer than 5 coins. Draw the coins you use.

Home Connection Your child found and recorded different ways to show the same amount of money. **Home Activity** Ask your child to show different ways to make 55¢ using quarters, dimes, and nickels.

To make **change**, count on from the **price** to the amount given.

Begin with pennies. Then use nickels.

Price:	You give:	You get:
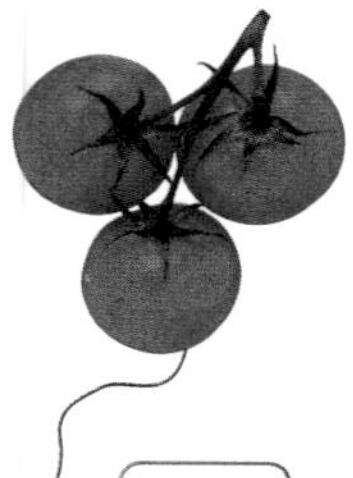 🍅 43¢	50¢	43¢  44¢ 45¢ 50¢ Your change is 7¢.

Check ✓

Word Bank

change
price

Count on from the price.
Write the amount of change given.

Price:	You give:	You get:	Change:
1  🥬 18¢	20¢	18¢  ____ ____	
2  🫑 32¢	40¢	32¢  ____ ____ ____ ____	

Think About It   Reasoning

If you paid for the celery with a quarter, how much change
would you get? Explain. Use coins if you need to.

Count on from the price.
Draw the coins you would get for change.
Write the amount of change you get.

Price:	You give:	You get:		Change:
3 6¢	10¢	6¢ ⓟ ⓟ ⓟ ⓟ 7¢ 8¢ 9¢ 10¢		
4 41¢	50¢	41¢		
5 88¢	90¢	88¢		
6 95¢	100¢	95¢		

Problem Solving **Algebra**

Write the amounts.

7 Chet paid 15¢ for the ball and the car. He got 2¢ in change.
How much did both toys cost?

$$15¢ - 2¢ = \underline{\hspace{1.5cm}}$$

How much did the ball cost?

$$\underline{\hspace{1.5cm}} = 9¢ + \underline{\hspace{1.5cm}}$$

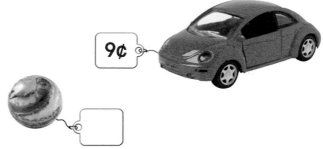

9¢

Home Connection Your child made change by counting on from the cost of the item up to the amount given. **Home Activity** Use coins and household items to help your child pretend to find change of 10¢ or less.

120   one hundred twenty

© Pearson Education, Inc.

Name _____

Learn!

To write 1 dollar, begin with the **dollar sign**. You can put a **decimal point** to separate the dollar from the cents.

dollar bill   **dollar coin**

one dollar = 100¢

Word Bank

dollar bill
dollar coin
dollar sign ($)
decimal point (.)

Check ✓

Use coins to show $1.00. Draw the coins.
Write the number of coins.

1 Use only half-dollars.

_____ half-dollars = $1.00

2 Use only quarters.

_____ quarters = $1.00

3 Use only dimes.

_____ dimes = $1.00

Think About It   Reasoning

Would it take more nickels or more dimes to make $1.00?
How do you know?

Chapter 3 ★ Lesson 18

Write each total amount.
Circle sets of coins that equal $1.00.

4

Total Amount

5

Total Amount

6

Total Amount

7

Total Amount

Problem Solving Algebra

8 What two coins will make the statement true?

    = $1.00

 Home Connection Your child identified coins with a total value of one dollar. **Home Activity** Have your child use coins to show you other ways to make $1.00.

© Pearson Education, Inc.

Dorling Kindersley

Today most people around the world use bills and coins as money.

Look at the pile of money at the bottom of this page. There are **ten thousand** $100 bills. That is one million dollars!

1 Which is worth more, ten $10 bills or one $100 bill?

_____

2 Which is worth more, twenty $5 bills or one $100 bill?

_____

Fun Fact!

Ten thousand $100 bills weigh about 320 ounces or 20 pounds. That's as much as three newborn babies might weigh!

Here are the first United States coins:

1793 copper cent

1794 silver dollar

1795 gold $10 "eagle"

3 Circle the group of coins that has the greater value.

4 Max has a collection of 12 coins from other countries. You can see 5 of the coins below. How many coins are inside the envelope?

_____ coins are inside the envelope.

Germany

Greece

United Kingdom

France

Japan

In 1976, a Bicentennial Quarter was issued in celebration of the 200th birthday of the United States.

5 **Writing in Math**

Draw your own coin. Give it a name and tell how much it is worth.

Dear Family,

Today my class started Chapter 8, **Time, Data, and Graphs.** I will learn how to tell time to five minutes. And I will make different kinds of graphs to organize and display information that I collect. Here are some of the math words I will be learning and some things we can do to help me with my math.

Love,

_____

Math Activity to Do at Home

Go on a "clock hunt." Ask your child to write down the locations of clocks in your home. Then, as you go around the house, ask your child to tell you the time on each clock. Repeat the activity several times at different times of the day.

Books to Read Together

Reading math stories reinforces concepts. Look for these titles in your local library:

What Time Is It?
By Sheila Keenan
(Scholastic, 2000)

Lemonade for Sale
By Stuart J. Murphy
(HarperCollins, 1998)

Take It to the NET
More Activities
www.scottforesman.com

My New Math Words

midnight 12 o'clock at night; the middle of the night.

noon 12 o'clock in the daytime; the middle of the day.

line plot A collection of data with an **X** placed above each number on a number line for each piece of data collected is called a line plot.

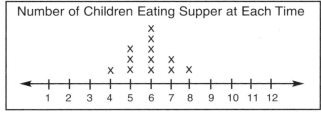

Number of Children Eating Supper at Each Time

Tick Tock Around the Clock

What You Need

2 dot cubes

4 game markers
   for each player ⚪ ⚫

How to Play

1. Take turns tossing the cubes.
2. Add the dots. If the sum is 3, 6, 9, or 12, place a marker on that hour on your clock.
3. The first player to cover 12, 3, 6, and 9 is the winner. **Hurry up! The clock is ticking!**

Player 1

Player 2

Name _____

 **Learn!** —

The **hour hand** and **minute hand**
work together to show you the time.

minute
hand

hour
hand

8:00   8:10   8:30   8:55

There are
60 minutes in an **hour**
and 30 minutes
in a **half hour**.

Word Bank

hour hand
minute hand
hour
half hour

Check ✓

Write the time.

1

2

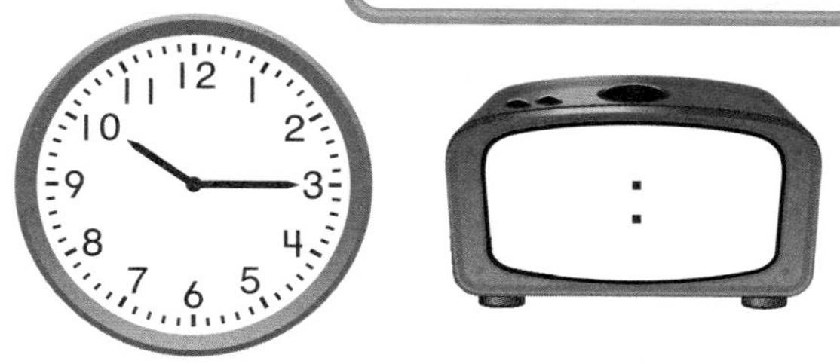

3

4

Think About It   Reasoning

Why do we write **2:05** and not **2:5**
for the time shown on the clock?

Practice

Draw the clock hands for each time.

5

6

7

8

9

10

11

12

Problem Solving Reasoning

13 The time is 7:55. Is the hour hand closer to the 7 or the 8? Why?

14 The time is 7:05. Is the hour hand closer to the 7 or the 8? Why?

15 The time is 3:10. Is the hour hand closer to the 3 or the 4? Why?

Home Connection Your child identified times to five minutes.
Home Activity Draw several clock faces. Have your child draw the hour and minute hands to show times to 5 minutes, times such as 9:20 and 1:35.

 **Learn!**

2:00
2 o'clock

2:15
15 minutes after 2
quarter past 2

2:30
30 minutes after 2
half past 2

2:45
45 minutes **after** 2

Word Bank

quarter past
half past
after

Check ✓

Write the time or draw the minute hand to show
the time. Then circle another way to say the time.

1   | : |

quarter past 7

half past 7

2   1:45

1 o'clock

45 minutes after 1

3   | : |

30 minutes after 11

quarter past 11

Think About It   Reasoning

At half past 2, the hour hand is halfway
between the 2 and the 3. Why?

Write the time or draw the minute hand to show
the time. Then circle another way to say the time.

4

35 minutes after 3

half past 3

5

15 minutes after 9

5 minutes after 9

6   **4:30**

half past 4

quarter past 4

7   **8:10**

10 minutes after 8

8 o'clock

8

quarter past 12

45 minutes after 12

Problem Solving Reasoning

9 Jill's baseball game starts at 45 minutes
after 2. Joe's game starts at quarter
past 2. Whose game starts first?
How do you know?

Home Connection Your child identified times *after* a given hour.
Home Activity Give your child several times *after* the hour and ask him
or her to draw a clock to show the times.

© Pearson Education, Inc.

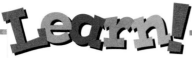

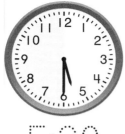

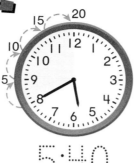

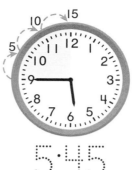

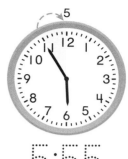

Name ______________________

Telling Time Before the Hour

Learn!

5:30

30 minutes **before** 6

5:40

20 minutes **before** 6

5:45

15 minutes before 6
quarter to 6

5:55

5 minutes **before** 6

Times after the half hour are often read as times before the next hour.

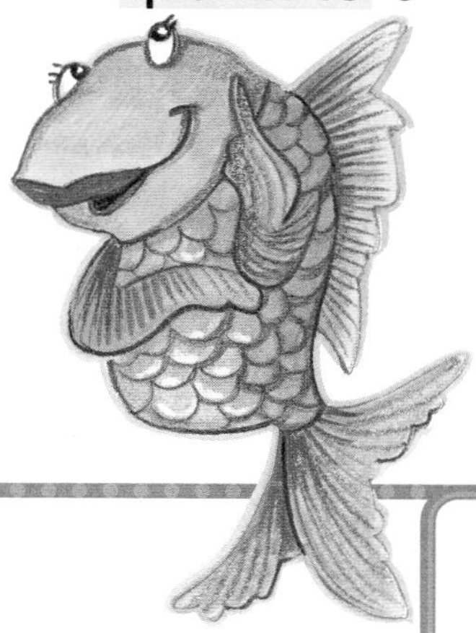

Word Bank
before
quarter to

Check

Write the time or draw the minute hand to show the time. Then write the time before the hour.

1

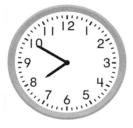

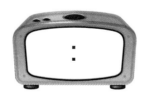

10 minutes before _____

2

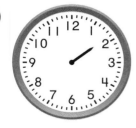

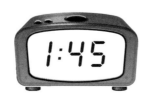

quarter to _____

Think About It Reasoning

Name a time that is the same number of minutes before one hour as it is after one hour.

Write the time or draw the minute hand to show the time. Then write the time before the hour.

25 minutes before _____

20 minutes before _____

quarter to _____

5 minutes before _____

Problem Solving Writing in Math

Take your time!

 Write 3 ways to say the time shown.

_____

_____

_____

 **Home Connection** Your child identified times between the half hour and the hour. **Home Activity** Write a time between the half hour and the hour, such as 7:45. Have your child tell you the time as "_____ minutes before _____."

Name _____

About how long does it take to paint a house?

about 3 _____ minutes ~~(days)~~

I know a house cannot be painted in 3 minutes. It takes about 3 days.

Check ✓

How long will each activity take? Circle the estimated time.

1 Combing hair

about 2 _____ ~~(minutes)~~ hours

2 Baking a cake

about 1 _____ hour day

3 Tying shoes

about 3 _____ minutes days

4 Watching a movie

about 2 _____ hours days

Think About It   Reasoning

Does writing the alphabet take minutes, hours, or days?
How do you know?

Circle the amount of time each activity would take.

5 Drawing a picture

(about 5 minutes)

about 5 hours

about 5 days

6 Playing at the beach

about 4 minutes

about 4 hours

about 4 days

7 Doing a puzzle

about 3 minutes

about 3 hours

about 3 days

8 Brushing your teeth

about 2 minutes

about 2 hours

about 2 days

9 Going on a trip

about 7 minutes

about 7 hours

about 7 days

10 Opening a gift

about 1 minute

about 1 hour

about 1 day

Problem Solving Number Sense

11 Tim spends 60 minutes doing homework.
Janna spends 1 hour giving her dog a bath.
Circle the true statement.

Doing homework takes more time than bathing a dog takes.

Doing homework and bathing a dog take the same amount of time.

Doing homework takes less time than bathing a dog takes.

Home Connection Your child estimated whether a given activity takes minutes, hours, or days to complete. **Home Activity** Talk about activities at home that take minutes, hours, or days to complete.

Learn!

They started at 1 o'clock.
They finished at 3 o'clock.
How long did it take to see the zoo?

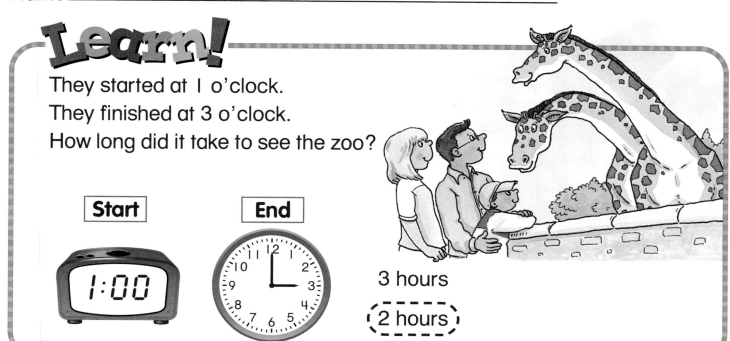

Start
1:00

End

3 hours

(2 hours)

Check ✔

Write the times. Circle how long each activity lasted.
Use a clock if you need to.

Start   **End**

1 Go swimming.

(2 hours)

1 hour

9:00   11:00

2 Play hopscotch.

30 minutes

2 hours

_____   _____

Think About It   Reasoning

About how long does it take you to get ready
for school in the morning?

Draw the clock hands and write the end time for each activity.
Use a clock if you need to.

| **Starts** | **Lasts** | **Ends** |

3 **Clean your room.**

1 hour

7:00

4 **Watch a school play.**

1 hour and
30 minutes

5:00

5 **Read a short book.**

15 minutes

8:00

Problem Solving   Number Sense

Solve. Use a clock if you need to.

6 Angel leaves her house at 6:45 in the morning.
She travels to school by bus for 45 minutes.
What time does she get to school?   _____

7 Michael's favorite movie starts at 4:00.
The movie is 1 hour and 10 minutes long.
What time will the movie end?   _____

Home Connection Your child determined how much time had passed
between the start and end of a given activity. **Home Activity** Note the
starting and ending times of an activity, such as eating dinner or doing
homework. Have your child determine how long the activity lasted.

> There are 24 hours in a day.

From **midnight** until noon is **A.M.**

10:00 A.M.

From **noon** until midnight is **P.M.**

10:00 P.M.

Word Bank

midnight
A.M.
noon
P.M.

Check ✓

Circle A.M. or P.M. for each event shown.

1 Eating breakfast

8:00 (A.M.) or P.M.

2 Doing homework

5:00 A.M. or P.M.

3 Waking up

7:00 A.M. or P.M.

4 Walking the dog

3:30 A.M. or P.M.

Think About It   Reasoning

Why are there only 12 numbers on a clock when there are 24 hours in a day?

Draw lines to match the events to the times.

5   8:00 A.M.   2:00 P.M.   8:00 P.M.

6   9:00 A.M.   12:00 P.M.   9:00 P.M.

7   10:00 A.M.   6:00 P.M.   10:00 P.M.

Problem Solving   Number Sense

Solve. Use a clock if you need to.

8 Jack and Tom started playing basketball at 11:00 A.M. They quit at 1:00 P.M. How long did they play?

_____

9 The movie started at 10:30 A.M. It lasted 2 hours and 30 minutes. At what time did the movie end?

_____

Learn!

A calendar helps us keep track of days, weeks, months, and years!

Word Bank

calendar

Check ✓

Write the month, year, and dates for this month.

1

Month _____				Year _____		
Sunday	Monday	Tuesday	Wednesday	Thursday	Friday	Saturday

Use the calendar to answer the questions.

2 What is the last day of this month? _____

3 What day is the 23rd of the month? _____

Think About It   Reasoning

Do all months have the same number of days?
How do you know?

One Year						

January

S	M	T	W	T	F	S
				1	2	3
4	5	6	7	8	9	10
11	12	13	14	15	16	17
18	19	20	21	22	23	24
25	26	27	28	29	30	31

February

S	M	T	W	T	F	S
1	2	3	4	5	6	7
8	9	10	11	12	13	14
15	16	17	18	19	20	21
22	23	24	25	26	27	28

March

S	M	T	W	T	F	S
1	2	3	4	5	6	7
8	9	10	11	12	13	14
15	16	17	18	19	20	21
22	23	24	25	26	27	28
29	30	31				

April

S	M	T	W	T	F	S
			1	2	3	4
5	6	7	8	9	10	11
12	13	14	15	16	17	18
19	20	21	22	23	24	25
26	27	28	29	30		

May

S	M	T	W	T	F	S
					1	2
3	4	5	6	7	8	9
10	11	12	13	14	15	16
17	18	19	20	21	22	23
24/31	25	26	27	28	29	30

June

S	M	T	W	T	F	S
	1	2	3	4	5	6
7	8	9	10	11	12	13
14	15	16	17	18	19	20
21	22	23	24	25	26	27
28	29	30				

July

S	M	T	W	T	F	S
			1	2	3	4
5	6	7	8	9	10	11
12	13	14	15	16	17	18
19	20	21	22	23	24	25
26	27	28	29	30	31	

August

S	M	T	W	T	F	S
						1
2	3	4	5	6	7	8
9	10	11	12	13	14	15
16	17	18	19	20	21	22
23/30	24/31	25	26	27	28	29

September

S	M	T	W	T	F	S
		1	2	3	4	5
6	7	8	9	10	11	12
13	14	15	16	17	18	19
20	21	22	23	24	25	26
27	28	29	30			

October

S	M	T	W	T	F	S
				1	2	3
4	5	6	7	8	9	10
11	12	13	14	15	16	17
18	19	20	21	22	23	24
25	26	27	28	29	30	31

November

S	M	T	W	T	F	S
1	2	3	4	5	6	7
8	9	10	11	12	13	14
15	16	17	18	19	20	21
22	23	24	25	26	27	28
29	30					

December

S	M	T	W	T	F	S
		1	2	3	4	5
6	7	8	9	10	11	12
13	14	15	16	17	18	19
20	21	22	23	24	25	26
27	28	29	30	31		

Use the calendar to answer the questions.

4 How many months have 30 days? _____

5 What month is the sixth month of the year? _____

6 What month comes just before November? _____

7 What day is October 6th on this calendar? _____

8 Which month has neither 30 nor 31 days? _____

Problem Solving   Reasoning

Solve.

9 Ann and Rachel are both 7 years old. Ann's birthday is in August.
Rachel's birthday is in May. It is April now. Who is older?
How do you know?

_____

_____

Name _____

Learn! Algebra

Equivalent Times	
one quarter hour	15 minutes
one half hour	30 minutes
one hour	60 minutes

Equivalent Times	
1 day	24 hours
1 week	7 days
1 year	12 months

"Equivalent" means "same."

How many hours are in 1 day?

Word Bank

equivalent

Check ✓

Use the tables to solve each problem.

1 My bus ride home is 30 minutes long. Is my ride one quarter hour long or one half hour long?

_____

2 Aunt Sandy lived in Canada for 12 months. Did she live there for 1 day, 1 week, or 1 year?

_____

3 Sam and Ken went camping for 3 days. Is that more than a week or less than a week?

_____

4 I played volleyball for one and a half hours today. How many minutes did I play?

_____

Think About It   Reasoning

How many minutes are in 2 hours?
Explain.

Morning Schedule

8:30– 9:30	Reading	
9:30–10:30	Math	10 + 2 = 12
10:30–10:45	Recess	
10:45–11:30	Art	
11:30–12:15	Lunch	

Use the schedule to answer these questions.

5 How many hours long is Reading? _____

How many minutes is this? _____

6 Which other class is as long as Reading? _____

7 Which two activities are each 45 minutes long? _____

_____

8 Which activity is 15 minutes long? _____

Problem Solving Visual Thinking

9 Write the time for each clock. Find the pattern.
What will the last clock show?
Draw the hands and write the time.

_____ _____ _____ _____

Home Connection Your children answered questions involving equivalent times. **Home Activity** Name the times listed in the first column of each table on Student Book Page 305. Have your child name an equivalent time.

Name _____

Write the time. Then circle another way to say the time.

half past 10

20 minutes
before 11

___ : ___

quarter past 4

10 minutes
before 5

___ : ___

Circle the amount of time each activity would take.

3

about 30 minutes

about 30 hours

about 30 days

4

about 2 minutes

about 2 hours

about 2 days

Write the times. Then circle how long the activity lasted.

5 Pick vegetables.

Start	End

3 hours

4 hours

_____   _____

Use the calendar to answer the questions.

6 How many days are in the month? _____

7 What day is the 18th of the month? _____

8 How many days are in 1 week? _____

November						
S	M	T	W	T	F	S
			1	2	3	4
5	6	7	8	9	10	11
12	13	14	15	16	17	18
19	20	21	22	23	24	25
26	27	28	29	30		

Name _____

Add or subtract.

1
9
+ 3

Ⓐ 6
Ⓑ 9
Ⓒ 21
Ⓓ 12

2
79
− 59

Ⓐ 20
Ⓑ 19
Ⓒ 29
Ⓓ 59

Which is the closest ten?

3

70 ———————————— 80

77 is closest to ___.

70   75   80   10
Ⓐ   Ⓑ   Ⓒ   Ⓓ

Which shape is congruent to this shape?

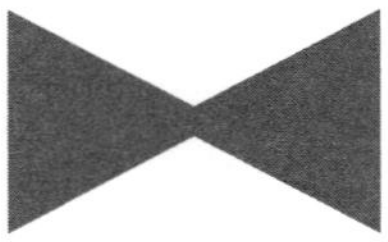

4

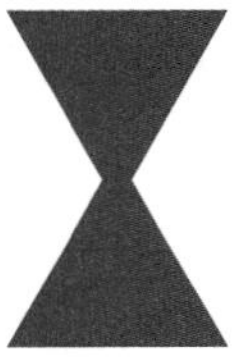

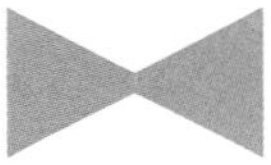

Ⓐ   Ⓑ   Ⓒ   Ⓓ

---

5 Mark the pair of numbers that has the sum of 50.

20 and 15   32 and 18   14 and 70   50 and 50
Ⓐ   Ⓑ   Ⓒ   Ⓓ

Writing in Math

6 Explain which is the better way to add.

79
+ 19

paper and pencil

mental math

_____

_____

Name _____

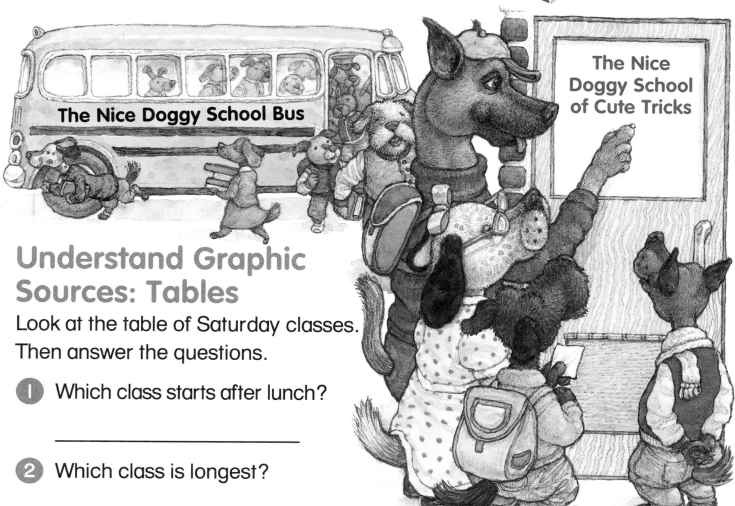

The Nice Doggy School Bus

The Nice Doggy School of Cute Tricks

Understand Graphic Sources: Tables

Look at the table of Saturday classes. Then answer the questions.

1 Which class starts after lunch?

_____

2 Which class is longest?

_____

3 Which class is shortest?

_____

4 Which class is earliest?

_____

5 Which class starts at the same time as Sitting Up?

_____

Class	Starts	Ends
Rolling Over	10:00	12:00
Shaking Paws	8:00	10:00
Sitting Up	10:00	11:00
Fetching Sticks	1:00	3:00
Jumping Through Hoops	9:00	12:00

Think About It   Reasoning

What is the greatest number of classes a dog could take in one day? Explain your thinking.

6 Read the information about dogs and look at the pictures.

There are more than 300 kinds or breeds of dogs.
The breeds can be placed in 7 groups.
Here are some examples.

Breed: St. Bernard
Group: Working dogs
Height: 26–30 inches
Weight: 140–200 pounds

Breed: Chihuahua
Group: Toy dogs
Height: 5 inches
Weight: 1–6 pounds

Breed: Beagle
Group: Hounds
Height: 13–15 inches
Weight: 18–30 pounds

Breed: Scottish Terrier
Group: Terriers
Height: 9–10 inches
Weight: 18–22 pounds

Breed: Golden Retriever
Group: Sporting dogs
Height: 22–24 inches
Weight: 55–75 pounds

Breed: Collie
Group: Herding dogs
Height: 22–26 inches
Weight: 50–75 pounds

Breed: Dalmatian
Group: Nonsporting dogs
Height: 19–23 inches
Weight: 40–50 pounds

7 Pick your 3 favorite breeds. Write their information in the table.
Then answer questions about your favorites.

Breed	Group	Height	Weight

8 Which of your picks is the tallest? _____

9 Which of your picks weighs the least? _____

Home Connection Your child organized information in a table.
Home Activity With your child, look for a table used in everyday life—
for example, a train schedule, a table of television programs, or a schedule
of sporting events, showing home and away games.

Learn!

Read and Understand

What kinds of plants did the children plant in the class garden?
How many of each kind of plant?

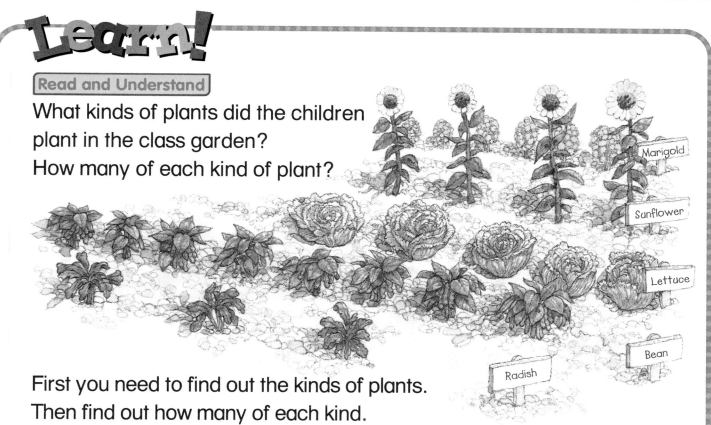

First you need to find out the kinds of plants.
Then find out how many of each kind.

Plan and Solve

You can make a table. Make tally marks to show how many of each kind.

What kinds of plants are in the garden?

There are ___8___ bean plants, ___3___ radish plants, _____ lettuce plants, _____ marigold plants, and _____ sunflower plants.

Look Back and Check

How did making a table help you answer the questions?

Classroom 2A's Garden	
Kind	**Number**
Bean	⦙⦙⦙⦙ ⦙⦙⦙
Radish	⦙⦙⦙
Lettuce	⊬⊬
Marigold	⊬⊬⎮
Sunflower	⎮⎮⎮⎮

Think About It   Number Sense

Are there more bean plants and radish plants or bean plants and sunflower plants?

The children in Class 2B drew crayons to show their favorite colors.
Complete the table. Use tally marks.

1

Favorite Colors						
Color	Red					
Number						

2 How many children are in Class 2B? _____ children

3 How many children named red as their favorite color? _____ children

4 Do more children like green or yellow? _____

How many more? _____ more children

5 What color is the favorite of most children? _____

6 What color did two children name as their favorite? _____

Visual Thinking

Use the table to solve the problem.

7 How many children in all are in Grades 2 and 3?

_____ children

Grade	Number of Children
2	ⅢⅢ ⅢⅢ ⅢⅢ ⅢⅢ ⅢⅢ
3	ⅢⅢ ⅢⅢ ⅢⅢ ⅢⅢ III

Home Connection Your child used tally marks to record data in a chart and used the chart to answer questions. **Home Activity** Ask your child questions that can be answered using the above tables, such as: "How many more children are in Grade 2 than are in Grade 3?"

Taking a **survey** is one way to collect information, or **data**.

What is your favorite flower?

Favorite Flowers		
Tulip	Daisy	Rose
ⅢⅠ	Ⅲ	Ⅲ

Make tally marks to record.

Check ✓

Write a question. Take a survey.
Complete the chart.

Word Bank

survey
data

What is your favorite _____?		
_____	_____	_____

1. What did most people choose as their favorite? _____

2. What did the least number of people choose as their favorite? _____

3. How many people did you survey? _____

Think About It   Reasoning

Would you get the same data if you asked your parents the survey question instead of your classmates? Explain.

Use the survey to answer the questions.

Favorite Playground Toys	
Toy	**Number of Children**
Bars	~~HHT~~ ~~HHT~~ ~~HHT~~
Slide	~~HHT~~ ~~HHT~~ ~~HHT~~ |||
Swings	~~HHT~~ ~~HHT~~ ||||

4 Which toy is the favorite of the
greatest number of children? _____

5 Which toy did the least number of
children choose? _____

6 How many children chose the swings? _____ children

7 How many more children chose
the slide than chose the bars? _____ children

8 How many children in all answered
the survey? _____ children

Problem Solving   Number Sense

Solve.

9 If 8 more children choose the swings,
what will be the new total for swings? _____ children

10 What will be the number of children
in all who answered the survey? _____ children

Home Connection Your child collected, organized, and used data from
a survey to solve problems. **Home Activity** Have your child survey family
members and record results using tally marks.

Learn!

You can collect and show data using a **Venn diagram**.

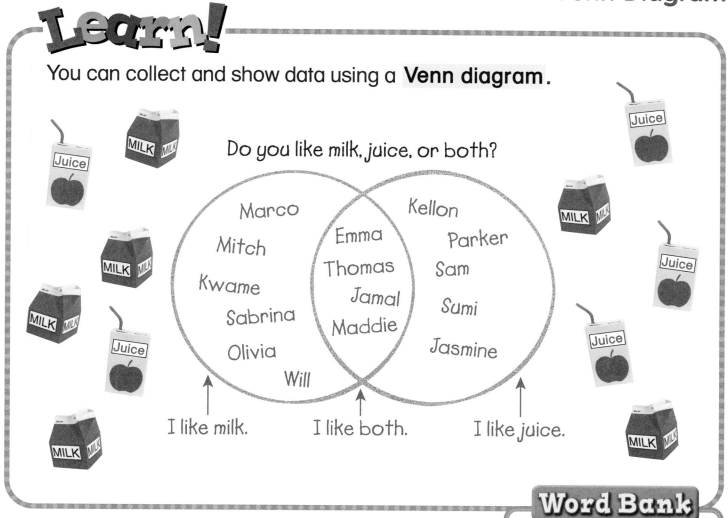

Do you like milk, juice, or both?

Marco
Mitch
Kwame
Sabrina
Olivia
Will

Emma
Thomas
Jamal
Maddie

Kellon
Parker
Sam
Sumi
Jasmine

I like milk.   I like both.   I like juice.

Word Bank

Venn diagram

Check ✓

Use the diagram to answer the questions.

1. How many children like milk? _10_ children

2. How many children like juice? _____ children

3. How many children like both milk and juice? _____ children

4. How many children like milk but **not** juice? _____ children

5. How many children like juice but **not** milk? _____ children

6. How many children were surveyed? _____ children

Think About It   Number Sense

How many more children like milk than like juice?
Explain.

7 Ask seven children the question below. Record the data.

Do you like to draw or write or both?

I like to draw. →   ← I like to write.

↑
I like to draw and write.

Use the diagram to answer the questions.

8 How many children like to draw?   _____ children

9 How many children like to draw but not write?   _____ children

10 How many children like to write?   _____ children

11 How many children like to write but not draw?   _____ children

Problem Solving Visual Thinking

12 Who likes all 3 kinds of fruit?

_____

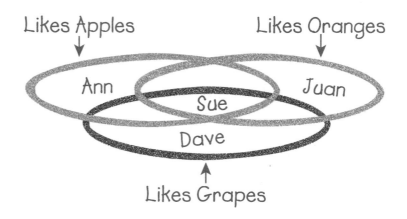

Likes Apples   Likes Oranges

Ann   Sue   Juan

Dave

Likes Grapes

Home Connection Your child collected and organized data and then used this information to solve problems. **Home Activity** Look for various kinds of diagrams and graphs in the newspaper and discuss them with your child.

Name _____

Use the table to solve the problems.

Favorite Zoo Animals	
Kind	Number
Lion	|||
Tiger	|||||
Elephant	⌣⌣⌣⌣⌣	
Giraffe	
Polar bear	||

1 Make tally marks to show that 5 children chose the giraffe as their favorite zoo animal.

2 Which animal is the favorite of the most children?

_____

3 Which animal is the favorite of the fewest children?

_____

Use the survey to answer the questions.

What is your favorite season?	
Winter	⌣⌣⌣⌣⌣	
Spring	||||
Summer	⌣⌣⌣⌣⌣ ⌣⌣⌣⌣⌣	
Fall	||

4 How many children chose winter as their favorite season?

_____ children

5 How many more children like spring than like fall?

_____ more children

Use the diagram to answer the questions.

I like dogs.　　I like cats.

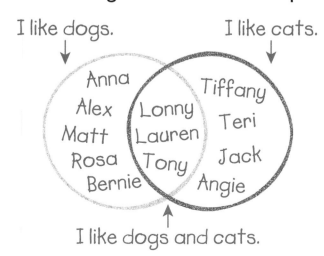

Anna
Alex
Matt
Rosa
Bernie
Lonny
Lauren
Tony
Tiffany
Teri
Jack
Angie

I like dogs and cats.

6 How many children like both dogs and cats?

_____ children

7 How many children like dogs but not cats?

_____ children

Name ____________________

Cumulative Review and Test Prep

1 What number is shown?

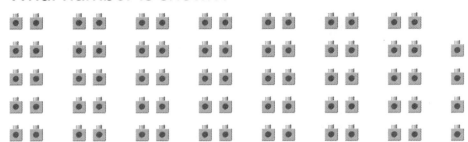

Ⓐ 64
Ⓑ 70
Ⓒ 74
Ⓓ 47

2 What amount of money do both sets show?

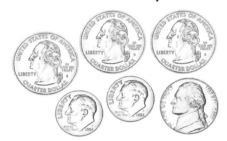

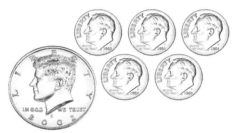

$1.00	75¢	90¢	50¢
Ⓐ	Ⓑ	Ⓒ	Ⓓ

3 What solid figure could you trace to make this plane shape?

Ⓐ

Ⓑ

Ⓒ

Ⓓ

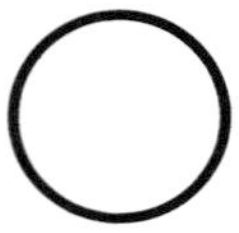

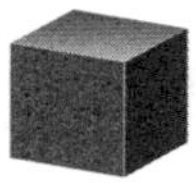

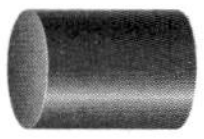

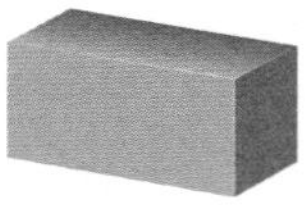

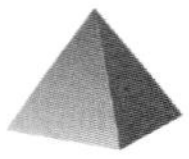

Find the difference.

4 □

$$\begin{array}{r} 52¢ \\ -\ 29¢ \\ \hline \end{array}$$

Ⓐ 12¢
Ⓑ 10¢
Ⓒ 31¢
Ⓓ 23¢

5 □

$$\begin{array}{r} 26¢ \\ -\ 17¢ \\ \hline \end{array}$$

Ⓐ 9¢
Ⓑ 19¢
Ⓒ 43¢
Ⓓ 11¢

Writing in Math

6 Write 3 ways to say the time shown.

____

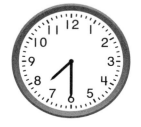

Name _____

A **pictograph** helps you compare information.

Favorite Fruits	
 Grapes	유유유유유유유
🍎 Apple	유유유유유유유유유
🍌 Banana	유유유유

Each 유 = I child.

How many children like apples best?

 9

Which fruit is the favorite of the fewest children?

banana

 **Word Bank**

pictograph

Check ✓

① Which food does your class like best?
Make a pictograph to find out. Complete the graph.

Favorite Foods	
🍔 Hamburger	
🍕 Pizza	
🌮 Taco	

Each 유 = I child.

② Which food is favored by the most children? _____

③ Which food is favored by the fewest children? _____

④ How many children chose tacos? _____ children

Think About It   Reasoning

What if 5 more children choose tacos as their favorite food?
Would the class's favorite food be the same?

Use the graph to answer the questions.

Favorite Book	
A	𝕩 𝕩 𝕩 𝕩 𝕩 𝕩
B	𝕩 𝕩 𝕩 𝕩 𝕩 𝕩 𝕩 𝕩 𝕩
C	𝕩 𝕩 𝕩

Each 𝕩 = I child.

5 Which book is favored by the most children?

_____

6 How many children like C best?

____ children

7 Which book is the favorite of 6 children?

_____

Use the graph to answer the questions.

Rice cereal	Oat cereal	Wheat cereal

Favorite Cereals

Each 🍲 = 2 children.

8 What is the favorite cereal?

_____

9 How many children like rice cereal best?

2 , 4 , _____ children

10 How many children like oat cereal best?

2 , _____ , _____ , _____ children

Problem Solving Number Sense

11 Write the number sentence that tells how many more children chose oat cereal than chose wheat cereal. Solve.

_____

_____ more children

Home Connection Your child created and analyzed pictographs.
Home Activity Have your child compare rice cereal and wheat cereal in the above pictograph. How many children like each kind of cereal? How many more children like rice cereal than like wheat cereal?

I took a survey to find out how many children ride the bus to school. Then I made a bar graph.

Do you ride a bus to school?

Grade	Number of Children
1	~~HHH~~ ~~HHH~~
2	~~HHH~~ ~~HHH~~ ~~HHH~~ I
3	~~HHH~~ ~~HHH~~ IIII
4	~~HHH~~ ~~HHH~~ ~~HHH~~ ~~HHH~~
5	~~HHH~~ ~~HHH~~ ~~HHH~~ III

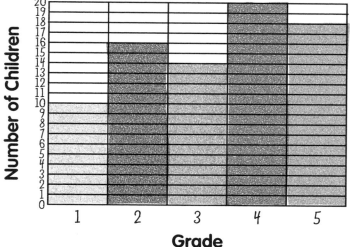

Children Who Ride a Bus

How many children in Grade 4 ride the bus to school?   20

Check ✓

Use the bar graph to answer the questions.

1 How many children ride the bus in Grade 2?

_____

2 Do more children ride the bus in Grade 3 or Grade 4?

_____

3 Which grade has the fewest bus riders? How many?

_____

4 Which grade has the most bus riders? How many?

_____

Think About It   Number Sense

How many bus riders are there in all?
Tell how you know.

5 Take a survey. Ask classmates what they most like to do outside.
Make tally marks to keep track of what each classmate says.

Favorite Outside Activities	
Ride bike	
Skateboard	
Play games	
Jump rope	

6 Make a bar graph. Color one box
for each time an activity was chosen.

Favorite Outside Activities

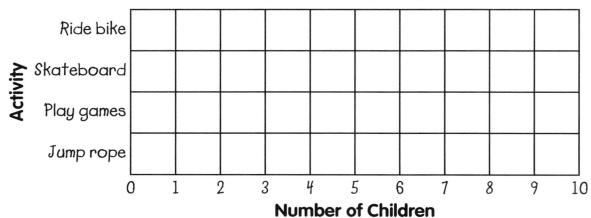

Use the graph to answer each question.

7 Which activity is favored by the most children? _____

8 Which activity is favored by the fewest children? _____

9 Do more children like to ride a bike or play games? _____

Problem Solving Writing in Math

10 Write one way that tally charts and
bar graphs are alike and one
way that they are different.

Home Connection Your child gathered and used data from tally
charts and bar graphs. **Home Activity** Ask your child a question
that can be answered using the above graph.

Name _____

How many books did you read this month?

Books	0	1	2	3	4	5	6	7	8	9	10
Tallies	I	II	II	I	⊮⊩	⊮⊩	⊮⊩I	III	IIII	I	I
Children	1	2	2	1	5	5	6	3	4	1	1

Books Read This Month

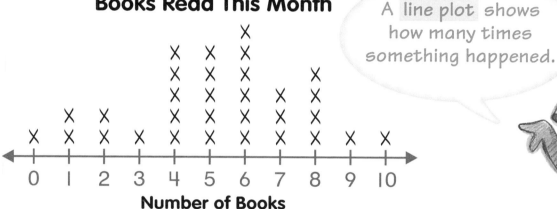

Number of Books

A **line plot** shows how many times something happened.

How many children read 4 books? ___5___ children

Check ✓

1. How many children read 8 books? _____ children

2. How many books did the most children read? _____ books

3. What was the least number of books read? _____ books

4. How many children read 1 or 2 books? _____ children

5. Did more children read 6 or 7 books? _____ books

Word Bank

line plot

Think About It Number Sense

How many children were surveyed?
Tell your strategy for figuring this out.

Use the line plot to answer the questions.

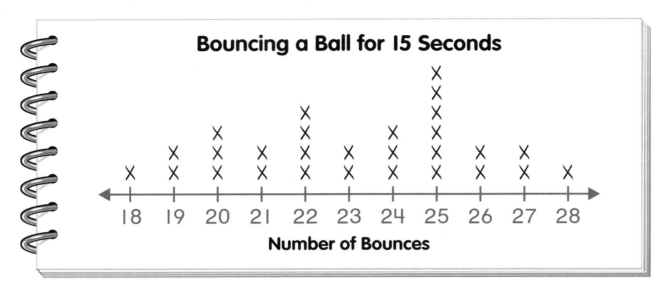

Bouncing a Ball for 15 Seconds

Number of Bounces

6 How many children bounced the ball 20 times?

_____ children

7 What is the greatest number of times a child bounced the ball?

_____ times

8 What is the least number of times a child bounced the ball?

_____ times

9 How many children bounced the ball 25 or more times?

_____ children

10 How many children bounced the ball 22 or fewer times?

_____ children

11 How many children in all bounced the ball?

_____ children

Problem Solving Reasonableness

Circle the answer that is more reasonable.

12 Ginny bounced the ball for 15 seconds.
She bounced the ball _____ times.   2   22

13 Tyrone bounced the ball for 30 seconds.
He bounced the ball _____ times.   45   450

Home Connection Your child analyzed line plots to answer questions.
Home Activity Have family members bounce a ball for 15 seconds and record the number of bounces. Add the data to the graph above. Discuss how the graph changed when you added the new data.

Name _____

Learn! Algebra

Look at the coordinate graph. Can you tell me which musical instrument is located at (C, 3)?

(C, 3) is an **ordered pair**.
It names a point on the **grid**.

A _____piano_____ is **located** at (C, 3).

Find the Musical Instruments

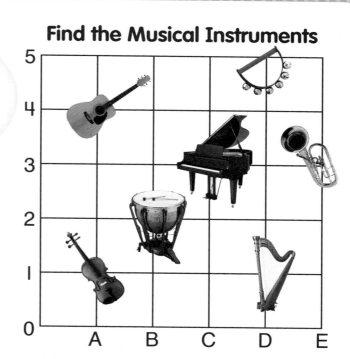

Word Bank

coordinate graph
ordered pair
grid
located

Check ✓

Circle the picture to show which toy is located at each ordered pair.

1 (E, 3)

2 (D, 1)

3 (A, 1)

4 (B, 2)

5 (D, 5)

6 (A, 4)

Think About It   Reasoning

Draw a new instrument on the grid. Name its location using an ordered pair.

Find the Farm Animals

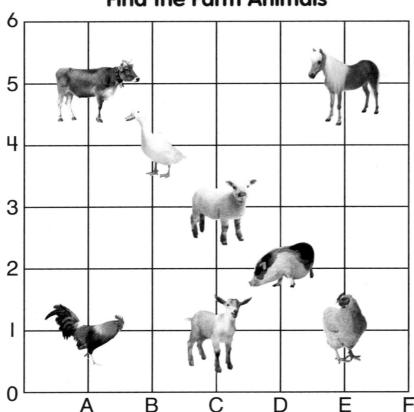

Write the ordered pair where each farm animal is located.

7 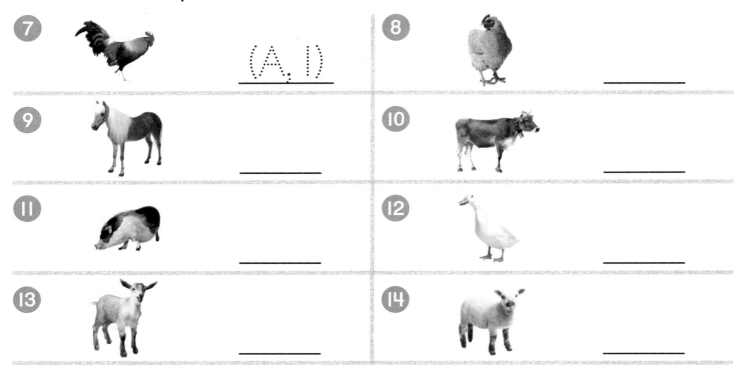 (A, 1)

8 _____

9 _____

10 _____

11 _____

12 _____

13 _____

14 _____

Problem Solving Writing in Math

15 Tell how you would find the ordered pair that tells the location of the pig.

Home Connection Your child used ordered pairs to locate points on a grid. **Home Activity** Name an ordered pair, such as (D, 5), and have your child locate it with his or her finger.

How many butterfly cards does Eva have? There are 7 cards next to "Butterfly." Each picture stands for 5 cards. Count by 5s.

Eva's Insect Cards							
Butterfly							
Grasshopper							
Beetle							

I 🦋 = 5 cards.

5, 10, 15, ____, ____, ____, ____

Eva has _35_ butterfly cards.

Check ✓

Use the graph to answer the questions.

1 How many grasshopper cards does Eva have?

_____

2 Does Eva have more grasshopper cards or butterfly cards?

_____

3 How many more butterfly cards than grasshopper cards does Eva have?

_____

4 Eva bought 5 more butterfly cards. How many butterfly cards does she have now?

_____

Think About It   Reasoning

How many more beetle cards does Eva need to buy to have 20 beetle cards in all? Tell how you know.

Coin Collections

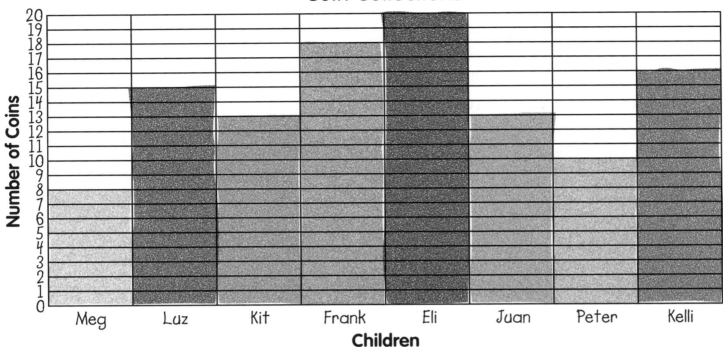

Number of Coins

Meg Luz Kit Frank Eli Juan Peter Kelli

Children

Use the graph to answer the questions.

5 Who has the most coins in his or her collection? _____

6 Who has the fewest? _____

7 Which two children have the same number of coins? _____

8 Who has 15 coins? _____

9 How many more coins does Kelli have than Peter? _____ more coins

10 How many coins do Frank and Meg have altogether? _____ coins

---

Reasonableness

Circle the answer that makes more sense.

11 How many coins are there in all in the 8 collections?

30   113

 Home Connection Your child used data from a pictograph and a bar graph to solve problems. **Home Activity** Have your child ask you a question that can be answered using one of the graphs.

Name _____

 Dorling Kindersley

Do You Know...
that a caterpillar makes a covering called a chrysalis? Then the caterpillar is called a pupa. After the pupa grows and changes, it breaks out of its chrysalis. When it breaks out, it is a butterfly!

1. This pupa is starting to break out of its chrysalis. Write the time.

   _____ o'clock

2. Look! The butterfly has pushed all the way out of the chrysalis. Write the time.

   _____ : _____

3. Now it is 20 minutes after 12. The butterfly is waiting until its wings harden before it tries to fly. Draw the minute hand to show the time.

4. Two hours later the adult butterfly flies away. Draw the clock hands. Write the time.

   _____ : _____

5 This butterfly landed on a flower at 4:00. It rested there for 5 minutes. Then it flew away. It flew away at

_____:_____.

6 There are 11 butterflies in the garden. 6 more break out of their chrysalises. How many butterflies are in the garden now?

_____ + _____ = _____ butterflies

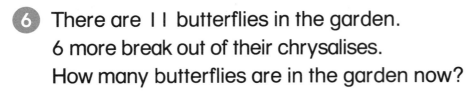

7 22 children in a class voted for their favorite butterflies. If 12 children chose painted ladies, how many children chose other kinds of butterflies?

_____ ◯ _____ = _____ children

Writing in Math

8 Write a story about time. Tell about a caterpillar changing into a butterfly.

© Pearson Education, Inc.

Home Connection Your child learned how to solve problems by applying his or her math skills. **Home Activity** Draw a clock and ask your child to draw the hands to show times such as 8:00, 8:05, or 8:20.

Name _____

Diagnostic
Checkpoint

Answer each question.

Rock Collections

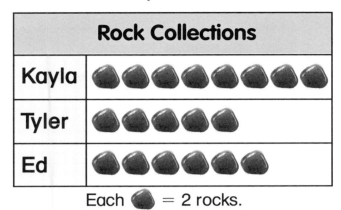

Kayla	🪨🪨🪨🪨🪨🪨🪨🪨
Tyler	🪨🪨🪨🪨🪨
Ed	🪨🪨🪨🪨🪨🪨

Each 🪨 = 2 rocks.

1 Who has the most rocks?

_____

Favorite Vegetables

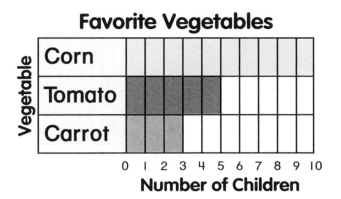

	Corn										
Vegetable	Tomato										
	Carrot										

0 1 2 3 4 5 6 7 8 9 10
Number of Children

2 How many children were asked to name their favorite vegetable?

_____ children

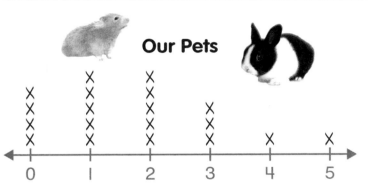

Our Pets

```
        X
    X   X
X   X   X
X   X   X   X
X   X   X   X   X       X
|   |   |   |   |   |
0   1   2   3   4   5
```

Number of Pets

3 How many children have 2 pets?

_____ children

4 How many children have 4 or 5 pets?

_____ children

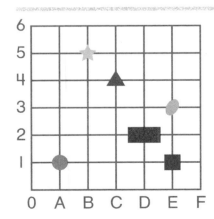

```
6
5       ★
4       ▲
3           ●
2       ▬▬
1   ●       ▪
  0 A B C D E F
```

Write the ordered pair where each shape is located.

5 ★ _____   **6** ● _____

7 ▪ _____   **8** ▬▬ _____

9 ● _____   **10** ▲ _____

I like music → ↓   ← I like sports

Ian
Jack Marcy Max
Sue   Nate
        Sharon

↑ I like music and sports

11 How many children like music and sports?

_____ children

Chapter 8 ★ Section C

three hundred thirty-one   **331**

Name_____

1 Which number sentence completes the fact family?

$$4 + 5 = 9 \qquad 5 + 4 = 9 \qquad 9 - 4 = 5$$

$$9 - 5 = 4 \qquad 8 - 4 = 4 \qquad 5 + 5 = 10 \qquad 9 - 0 = 9$$

    Ⓐ   Ⓑ   Ⓒ   Ⓓ

2 Which picture shows a line of symmetry?

   Ⓐ   Ⓑ   Ⓒ   Ⓓ

Find the sum.

3

$$\begin{array}{r} \square \\ 49 \\ + \ 5 \\ \hline \end{array}$$

  Ⓐ 44
  Ⓑ 55
  Ⓒ 53
  Ⓓ 54

4

$$\begin{array}{r} \square \\ 51 \\ + \ 6 \\ \hline \end{array}$$

  Ⓐ 56
  Ⓑ 57
  Ⓒ 45
  Ⓓ 67

Find the difference.

5

Tens	Ones
□	□
3	3
− 1	6

  Ⓐ 13
  Ⓑ 7
  Ⓒ 17
  Ⓓ 14

6

Tens	Ones
□	□
6	8
− 4	5

  Ⓐ 23
  Ⓑ 11
  Ⓒ 20
  Ⓓ 13

Writing in Math

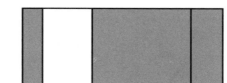

7 Does this picture show $\frac{3}{4}$? Explain.

Range and Mode

How many pets would you like to have in your classroom?

The girls in Room 110 said:
3, 1, 3, 1, 1, 2, 3, 3, 1, 3, 2

The girls' graph shows the girls' answers. The most popular answer is the **mode.**

The mode is __3__.

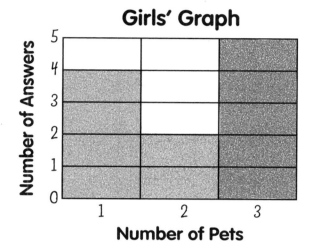

Girls' Graph

Number of Answers (vertical axis): 0, 1, 2, 3, 4, 5
Number of Pets (horizontal axis): 1, 2, 3

The **range** is the difference between the greatest answer and the least answer.

The range is 3 − 1, or __2__.

The boys in Room 110 said:
3, 7, 7, 2, 2, 3, 1, 3, 7, 7, 7, 7

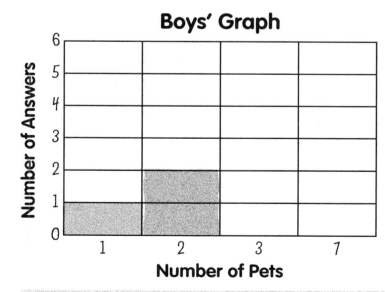

Boys' Graph

Number of Answers (vertical axis): 0, 1, 2, 3, 4, 5, 6
Number of Pets (horizontal axis): 1, 2, 3, 7

1. Complete the boys' graph.

2. What is the mode? _____

3. What is the range?

   _____ − _____, or _____

4. How could you change the mode in the girls' graph by adding two more answers?

   _____

Writing in Math

5. Put all of the girls' and boys' answers together. Make a new graph. How do the mode and the range change?

Learning with Technology

Use a Computer to Find Elapsed Time

1. Under **Rides** in the table below, make a list of rides you want to go on at the amusement park.

2. Under **Elapsed Time,** write how many minutes you think it will take to go on each ride.
   10 minutes? 15 minutes? 20 minutes?

Rides	Elapsed Time	Starting Time	Ending Time
Ferris wheel	10 minutes	6:00 P.M.	6:10 P.M.
		6:10 P.M.	

3. On a computer, go to the Time eTool.
   Set the clock to 6:00 P.M.

4. Set the elapsed time to the time you think your ride will last.

5. In your table, write down the ending time for this ride.

6. Now, set the starting time of the clock to the ending time of the first ride you went on.

7. Follow the same steps for all of the rides on your list.

Think About It   Reasoning

If you have to leave the amusement park at 7:00 P.M., will you have enough time to go on all of your rides?

Home Connection Your child made a table of amusement park rides and used a computer to show the starting time and ending time for each ride.
Home Activity Ask your child to explain how he or she used a computer to find the starting time and the ending time for one of the rides listed in his or her table.

Name_____

Read Together

Plan How to Find the Answer

You can use problem-solving strategies to help you find answers on tests.

One strategy is reading a table. Another strategy is writing a number sentence.

Test-Taking Strategies

Understand the Question

Get Information for the Answer

Plan How to Find the Answer

Make Smart Choices

Use Writing in Math

1 How many more children chose running than chose swimming?

Ⓐ 3 more children

Ⓑ 4 more children

Ⓒ 5 more children

Ⓓ 7 more children

Read the table.

Compare the two numbers:

_____ – _____ = _____

Fill in the answer bubble.

4 more chldren chose running than chose swimming.

Our Favorite Sports	
Sport	**Number of Children**
Swimming	|||
Running	卌 ||
Basketball	卌

Your Turn

Choose a strategy to solve the problem. Then fill in the answer bubble.

2 How many children voted for their favorite sport?

Ⓐ 10 children Ⓒ 15 children

Ⓑ 12 children Ⓓ 16 children

3 How many fewer children chose basketball than chose running?

Ⓐ 1 fewer child Ⓒ 3 fewer children

Ⓑ 2 fewer children Ⓓ 5 fewer children

Home Connection Your child prepared for standardized tests by using problem-solving strategies to answer math questions.
Home Activity Ask your child to describe the strategy he or she used to solve Exercise 2.

Name _____

 # Be a Weather Watcher

We all like to know when it is going to rain or snow, and whether it is going to be hot or cold. Can you use a thermometer to find out what the temperature is?

Measuring Temperature

1 For five days, measure the temperature once in the morning and once in the afternoon.

2 Write the morning temperature and the afternoon temperature for each day in the table below.

3 Find the difference between the morning temperature and the afternoon temperature each day.

Temperature	Day 1	Day 2	Day 3	Day 4	Day 5
Morning					
Afternoon					
Difference					

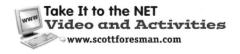
Take It to the NET
Video and Activities
www.scottforesman.com

Home Connection Your child measured air temperature twice a day and found the difference between the two readings.
Home Activity Watch a weather report on TV or look in the newspaper with your child to find the high and low temperatures for the day. Ask your child to find the difference between the two.

Chapter Test

Write the time. Circle another way to say the time.

1

half past 1

quarter to 2

Circle the amount of time each activity would take.

2

about 1 minute

about 1 hour

about 1 day

3

about 1 minute

about 1 hour

about 1 day

Draw the clock hands and write the end time.

4 Go to the amusement park.

Starts	Lasts	Ends

3 hours

12:00 _____   _____

Answer the questions.

5 How many minutes are in one half hour? _____

6 How many days are in one week? _____

Use the survey to answer the questions.

What Should We Do?	
Go to movie	卌 l
Go to park	lll
Go swimming	卌 卌 ll

7 Which activity do most children want to do?

_____

8 Do more children want to go to a movie or to a park?

_____

Use the graph to answer the questions.

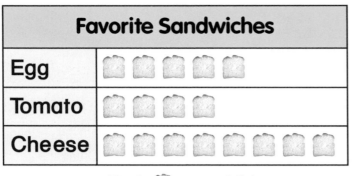

Favorite Sandwiches	
Egg	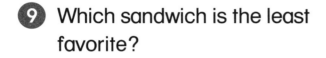
Tomato	
Cheese	

Each 🍞 = I child.

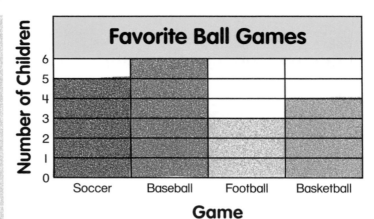

9 Which sandwich is the least favorite?

_____

10 How many children were asked to name their favorite ball game?

_____ children

Answer the questions.

Fruit Snack Time

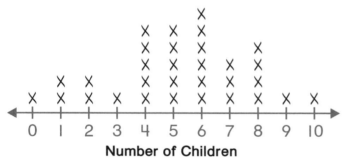

Number of Children

11 How many children ate fruit 4 times? _____ children

12 What is the most times children ate fruit? _____ times

Write the ordered pair.

Zoo Animals

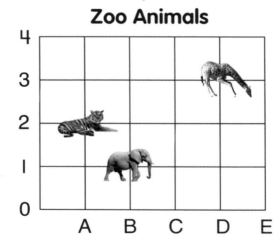

13 🐅 _____

14 🐘 _____

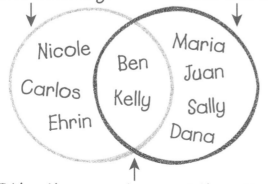

I like the country.   I like the city.

Nicole   Ben   Maria
              Juan
Carlos   Kelly   Sally
Ehrin   Dana

I like the country and the city.

15 How many children like only the country?

_____ children

16 How many children like the city and the country?

_____ children

338   three hundred thirty-eight

2 76 is closest to ____.

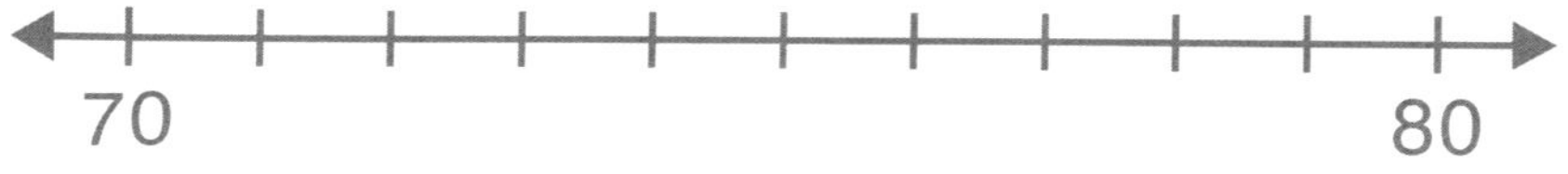

- Ⓐ 60
- Ⓑ 70
- Ⓒ 80
- Ⓓ 90

(number line from 70 to 80)

Mark the number that makes the statement true.

3 5 + ____ = 14,
so 14 − 5 = ____.

- Ⓐ 5
- Ⓑ 7
- Ⓒ 9
- Ⓓ 11

4 6 + ____ = 11,
so 11 − 6 = ____.

- Ⓐ 4
- Ⓑ 5
- Ⓒ 6
- Ⓓ 7

5 In how many months did it rain 2 or fewer days?

Rainy Days

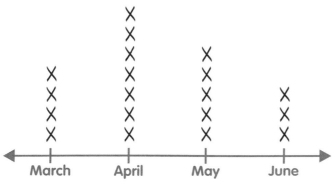

0	1	2	3
Ⓐ	Ⓑ	Ⓒ	Ⓓ

6 How many days did it snow during these four months?

Snowy Days

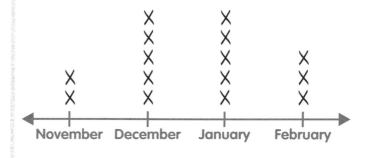

4	5	10	15
Ⓐ	Ⓑ	Ⓒ	Ⓓ

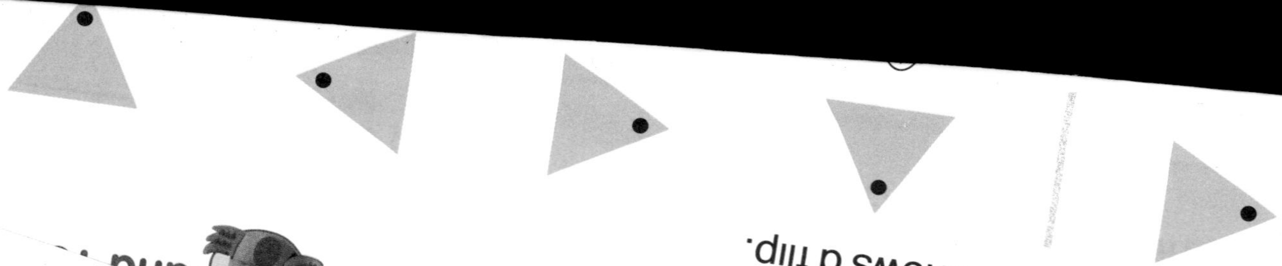

10 95 and _____

40 and _____ is 100.

Count on from the price.
Draw the coins you would get for change.
Write the amount of change.

Price:	You give:	You get:	Change:
11 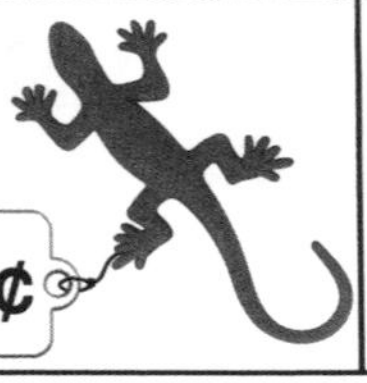 ![lizard] 42¢	50¢	42¢	

Writing in Math

12 José used about $\frac{3}{4}$ of the milk in a big bowl of cereal. Is there enough milk for another big bowl of cereal? Explain.

_____

_____

Read Together

How Many Miles to Allentown?

Allentown

A New Adaptation of a Classic Mother Goose Rhyme
Illustrated by Hector Borlasca

This Math Storybook belongs to

_____

9A

Home-School Connection

Dear Family,

Today my class started Chapter 9, **Measurement and Probability**. I will learn about ways to measure length, weight, and how much something holds. I will also learn how to predict how likely or unlikely it is that certain things will happen. Here are some of the math words I will be learning and some things we can do to help me with my math.

Love,

_____

Math Activity to Do at Home

Go on a measuring tool hunt with your child. Look for rulers, tape measures, yardsticks, measuring cups and spoons, and scales. You also may want to have your child look at the measurements listed on various food products.

Books to Read Together

Reading math stories reinforces concepts. Look for these titles in your local library:

Measuring Penny
By Loreen Leedy
(Holt, 2000)

If You Hopped Like a Frog
By David M. Schwartz
(Scholastic, 1999)

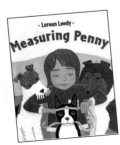

Take It to the NET
More Activities
www.scottforesman.com

My New Math Words

inch A unit of measure used to measure the lengths of small objects.

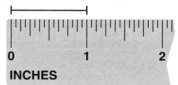

foot A unit of length equal to 12 inches.

yard A unit of length equal to 36 inches, or 3 feet.

cup A unit of volume for liquids.

pint A unit of volume for liquids, equal to 2 cups.

quart A unit of volume for liquids, equal to 4 cups or 2 pints.

Can You Get Home by Suppertime?

What You Need

I dot cube
I small game marker ⬤

How to Play

1. Place your marker on START.
2. Toss the cube. In this game,

   | 1 = 1 ten |
   | 2 = 2 tens |

3. You need 1 to move 10 miles to the next marker.
4. You need 2 to move 20 miles to the next marker.
5. If you get 3, 4, 5, or 6, you have to toss again!
6. How many tosses do you think it will take you to get to each marker? Write your predictions and record your tosses on the chart.

Recording Chart		
Mile Marker	Number of Tosses to Get There *(Predictions)*	Number of Tosses to Get There *(Tally Marks)*
20 miles		
40 miles		
60 miles		
70 miles Allentown!		
90 miles		
110 miles		
130 miles		
140 miles Suppertime!		
	TOTAL:	TOTAL:

START

20 miles

40 miles

60 miles

70 Miles

Allentown!

90 miles

110 miles

130 miles

140 Miles

Home by Suppertime!

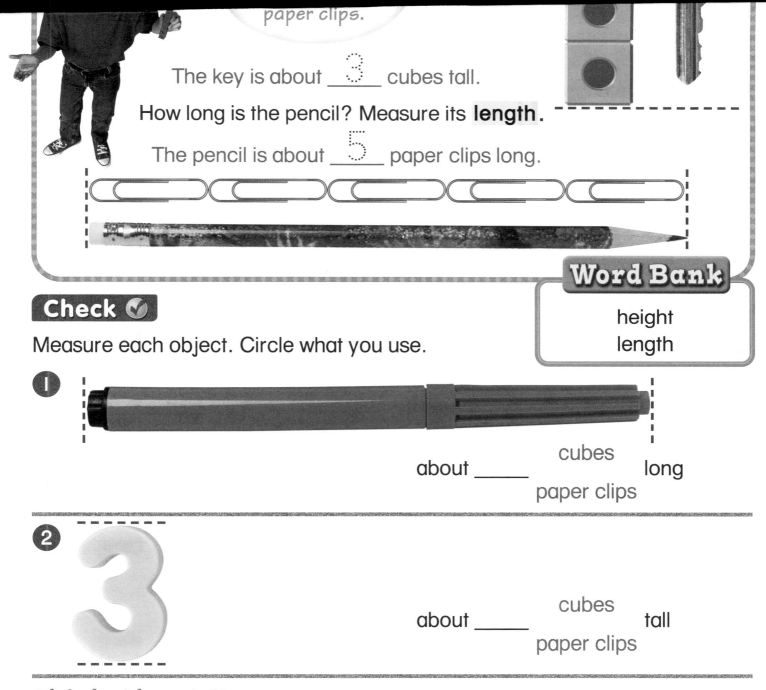

The key is about __3__ cubes tall.

How long is the pencil? Measure its **length**.

The pencil is about __5__ paper clips long.

Check ✓

Measure each object. Circle what you use.

Word Bank

height
length

1

about _____ cubes / paper clips long

2

about _____ cubes / paper clips tall

Think About It   Reasoning

Why do you get different answers when you measure
the same object using cubes and paper clips?

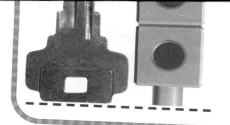

Learn!

How tall is the key? Measure its **height.**

You can measure
using cubes or

6

about _____ cubes
paper clips tall

Problem Solving Visual Thinking

Circle the pencil that is the longest.

7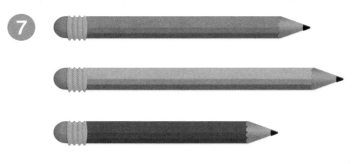

8

Home Connection Your child measured the length and height of objects using cubes or paper clips. **Home Activity** Have your child measure objects at home using blocks, pennies, or paper clips.

© Pearson Education, Inc.

Name ______________________________

Understanding Length and Height

Learn!

How tall is the key? Measure its **height**.

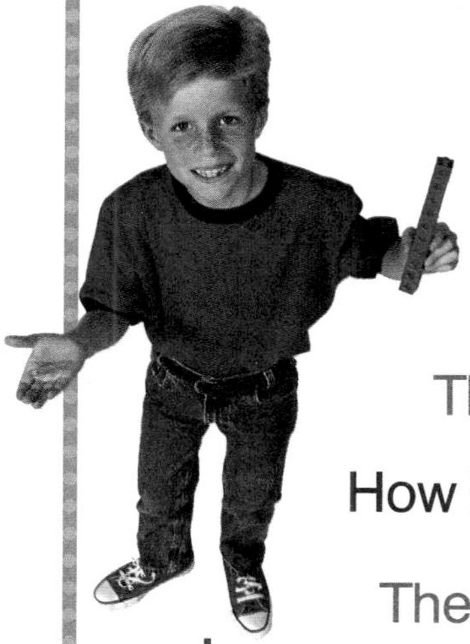

You can measure using cubes or paper clips.

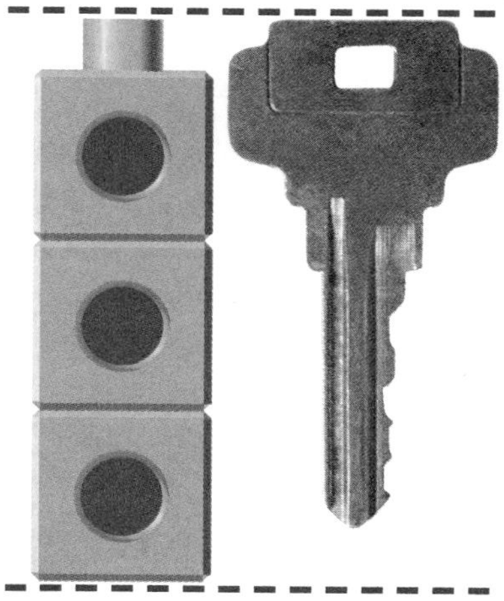

The key is about __3__ cubes tall.

How long is the pencil? Measure its **length**.

The pencil is about __5__ paper clips long.

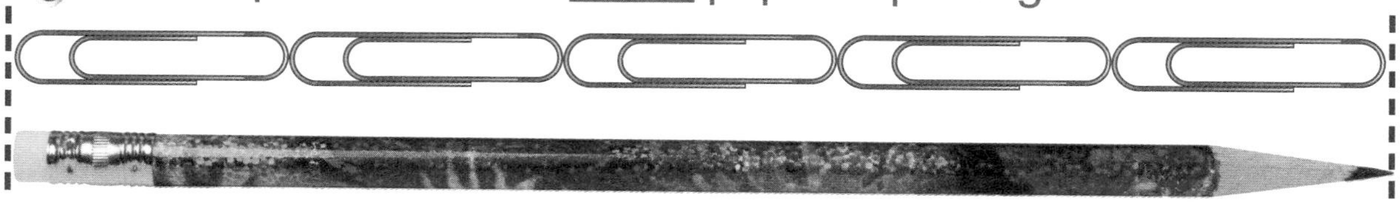

Word Bank

height
length

Check

Measure each object. Circle what you use.

1

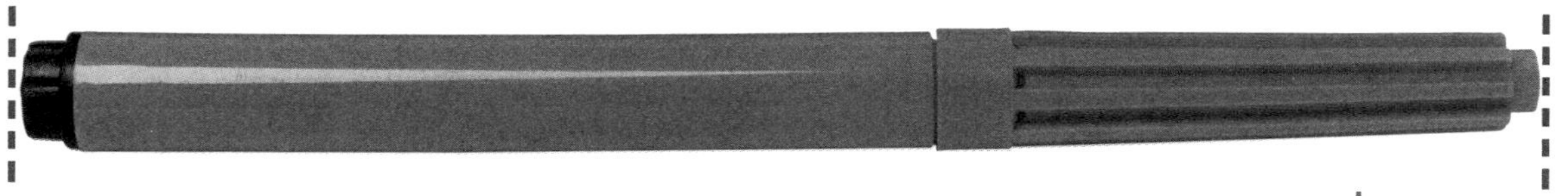

about _____ cubes / paper clips long

2

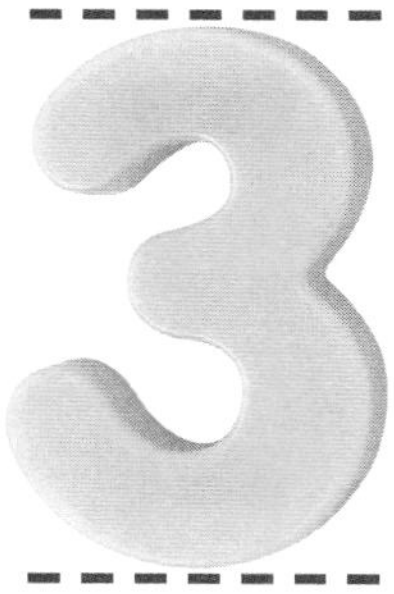

about _____ cubes / paper clips tall

Think About It Reasoning

Why do you get different answers when you measure the same object using cubes and paper clips?

Measure each classroom object using cubes or paper clips.
Circle the word or words that make sense.

3

about _____ cubes
paper clips long

4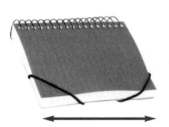

about _____ cubes
paper clips tall

5

about _____ cubes
paper clips long

6

about _____ cubes
paper clips tall

Problem Solving   Visual Thinking

Circle the pencil that is the longest.

7 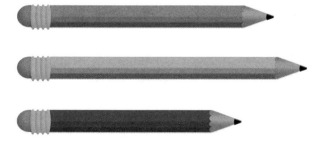   **8**

Home Connection Your child measured the length and height of objects using cubes or paper clips. **Home Activity** Have your child measure objects at home using blocks, pennies, or paper clips.

© Pearson Education, Inc.

Name_____

The paper clip is about 1 **inch** long.
Look at the **ruler**.
How long is the notebook?
There are 12 inches in one **foot**.

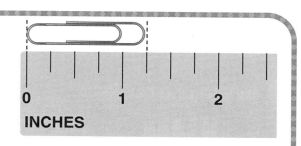

The notebook is about __12__ inches long.

The notebook is about __1__ **foot** long.

Check ✓

Estimate the length or height of each object.
Then use a ruler to measure.

Word Bank

inch (in.)
ruler
foot (ft)

	Estimate.	Measure.
① height of a table 	about _____ feet	about _____ feet
② length of a forearm 	about _____ inches	about _____ inches
③ length of a shoe 	about _____ inches	about _____ inches

Think About It   Number Sense

If there are 12 inches in 1 foot, how many inches
are in 2 feet? How do you know?

Estimate the length or height of each object.
Then use a ruler to measure.

	Estimate.	Measure.
4 length of a bookshelf 	about _____ feet	about _____ feet
5 length of an eraser 	about _____ inches	about _____ inches
6 height of a chair 	about _____ feet	about _____ feet

Problem Solving Reasonableness

Circle the better estimate for the length or height of each object.

7

The height of a door is
about 7 inches.
about 7 feet.

8

The length of a spoon is
about 6 inches.
about 6 feet.

9

The height of a tree is
about 20 inches.
about 20 feet.

Home Connection Your child estimated and measured the lengths and heights of objects in inches using a ruler. **Home Activity** Help your child measure household objects using a ruler.

Learn!

What is the **width** of the door?
There are 3 feet in 1 **yard**.
There are 36 inches in 1 yard.

The door is about _____ yard wide.

We measure feet with a ruler.
We measure yards with a **yardstick**.

Word Bank

width
yard (yd)
yardstick

Check ✓

Estimate the width, height, or length of each object.
Then use a ruler or yardstick to measure.

		Estimate.	Measure.
1	width of a chalkboard	about _____ yards	about _____ yards
2	height of a table	about _____ feet	about _____ feet
3	length of a crayon	about _____ inches	about _____ inches

Think About It   Reasoning

Would you measure the length of the playground
using yards or inches? Explain.

Estimate the width, height, or length of each object.
Then use a ruler or yardstick to measure.

	Estimate.	Measure.
4  width of a desktop	about _____ feet	about _____ feet
5  length of a rug	about _____ yards	about _____ yards
6 height of a wastebasket	about _____ inches	about _____ inches

Problem Solving Reasonableness

Circle inches, feet, or yards.

7

The flower is about 12 inches tall.
yards

8

The dog is about 3 feet long.
yards

9

The adult is about 5 inches tall.
feet

Home Connection Your child estimated and measured objects in inches, feet, and yards. **Home Activity** Choose several household objects. Ask your child if it would be easier to measure them in inches, feet, or yards.

How wide is the large paper clip? Look at the **centimeter ruler**.

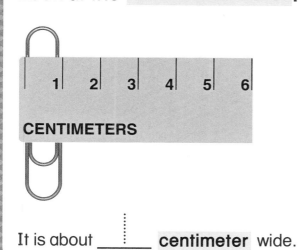

CENTIMETERS

It is about _____ **centimeter** wide.

How tall is the easel? Look at the **meterstick**.

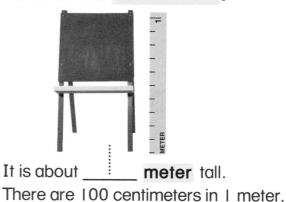

It is about _____ **meter** tall.
There are 100 centimeters in 1 meter.

Word Bank

centimeter (cm)
centimeter ruler
meter (m)
meterstick

Check ✓

Estimate the length or height of each object.
Then use a ruler to measure.

	Estimate.	Measure.
1 a classroom shelf	about _____ meters	about _____ meters
2  connecting cubes	about _____ centimeters	about _____ centimeters

Think About It   Reasoning

Find an object that is about 5 centimeters long.
Find an object that is about 1 meter tall.

Estimate the length or height of each object.
Then use a ruler to measure it.

	Estimate.	Measure.
3 length of a book	about _____ cm	about _____ cm
4 height of a room	about _____ m	about _____ m
5 width of a lunchbox	about _____ cm	about _____ cm

Problem Solving Writing in Math

6 Andie says that her dollhouse is about 8 meters tall. Do you think this is a good estimate? Why or why not?

_____

_____

_____

 Home Connection Your child measured objects using centimeters and meters. **Home Activity** Have your child measure several household objects using a centimeter ruler. Ask your child, "Which is a smaller unit of measurement, a centimeter or a meter?"

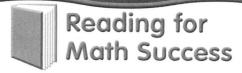

Reading for Math Success

Visualize

1 Look at these groups of stars. A group of stars is called a **constellation.** Long, long ago, people looked up into the night sky and imagined pictures in the stars. Some of these star-pictures were of animals. Match each constellation to the animal it looks like.

2 Today scientists try to visualize how big the universe is.

How many stars do you think there are?

Ⓐ About 1 hundred   Ⓒ About 1 million

Ⓑ About 3 thousand   Ⓓ More than 1 million

Think About It   Number Sense

Write these numbers.

1 hundred _____   1 million _____

3 thousand _____

3 The sun is a star. It is the star nearest to Earth. How far away do you think the sun is?

Ⓐ About 12 miles

Ⓒ About 15 thousand miles

Ⓑ About 6 hundred miles

Ⓓ About 93 million miles

4 First, make 154 **X**'s.

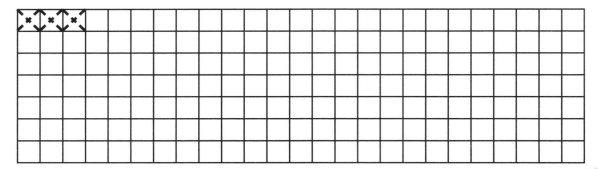

Now think about this: If you took off in a rocket, it would take you **154 days** to reach the sun. That's more than **5 months.** (No one can really go to the sun, because it's too hot.)

5 Pretend you are standing next to a skyscraper with a dog beside you. If you were the planet **Earth,** the dog would be the size of the **moon.** And the skyscraper would be the size of the **sun.** The sun is big!

Home Connection Your child visualized distance and size, and talked about the relative magnitude or "size" of numbers. **Home Activity** Talk with your child about what each of you visualizes doing tomorrow. Write down your plans. Then check back to see if things went according to plans.

© Pearson Education, Inc.

Read and Understand

The distance around a shape is called its **perimeter**. The space inside a shape is called its **area**. What is the perimeter of this rectangle? What is its area?

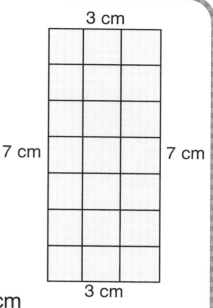

3 cm

7 cm   7 cm

3 cm

Plan and Solve

You can measure the length of each side and then add all the lengths together.

__3__ cm + __7__ cm + __3__ cm + __7__ cm = __20__ cm

The perimeter of this rectangle is __20__ centimeters.

Now, to find the area of this rectangle, you can count the **square units** inside it.

The area of this rectangle is __21__ square units.

Look Back and Check

Do your answers make sense?
Is there more than one way to add the lengths of the sides?

Word Bank

perimeter
area
square unit

Check ✓

1 Find the **perimeter** and the **area** of each shape.

perimeter:_____ cm

area:_____ square units

Find the **perimeter** and the **area** of each shape.

2

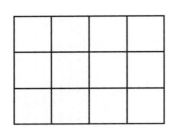

perimeter:___14___ cm

area:___12___ square units

3

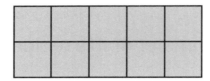

perimeter:_____ cm

area:_____ square units

4

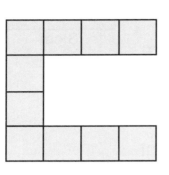

perimeter:_____ cm

area:_____ square units

5

perimeter:_____ cm

area:_____ square units

Writing in Math

6 How can you find the number of square units inside of this trapezoid?

_____

_____

_____

_____

Home Connection Your child found the perimeters and the areas of various shapes. **Home Activity** Ask your child to tell how many square units are NOT inside the trapezoid in Exercise 6. *(2: 1 whole square unit and two half square units, which combine to make another whole)*

Which holds more, the cup or the bowl?

Capacity is the amount a container can hold.

I think the bowl will hold more rice than the cup.

Word Bank

capacity

Check ✓

Find objects like the ones shown. Does each object hold more or less than a paper cup?
Write **more than** or **less than.**
Then measure to find out.

		Estimate.	Measure.
❶	🥄	less than	less than
❷	🪣		
❸	🫙		

Think About It   Number Sense

If 2 cups of rice fill 1 bowl,
how many cups of rice will fill 3 bowls?

Practice

Circle the object that holds the most.

4

5   

6      

Circle the object that holds the least.

7    

8      

9

Problem Solving   Writing in Math

10 Tell why it makes more sense to drink water from a glass rather than from a teaspoon.

_____

_____

_____

_____

Home Connection Your child estimated, measured, and ordered objects by capacity. **Home Activity** Show your child several containers and have him or her tell you which container holds the most.

Name _____

 **Algebra**

We use these units to measure capacity.

2 **cups** = I **pint**

4 **cups** = 2 **pints** = I **quart**

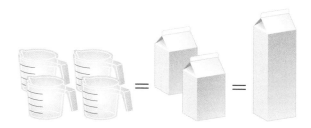

How many pints
are the same as 4 cups?

4 cups = __2__ pints

Word Bank

cup (c)
pint (pt)
quart (qt)

 Check ✔

Write how many cups, pints, or quarts
hold the same amount.

1

I quart = _____ cups

2

I pint = _____ cups

3

_____ quart = 2 pints

4

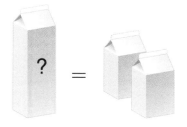

_____ pints = 4 cups

Think About It   Number Sense

How many pints are the same as 2 quarts?

Circle the number of containers that hold the same amount.

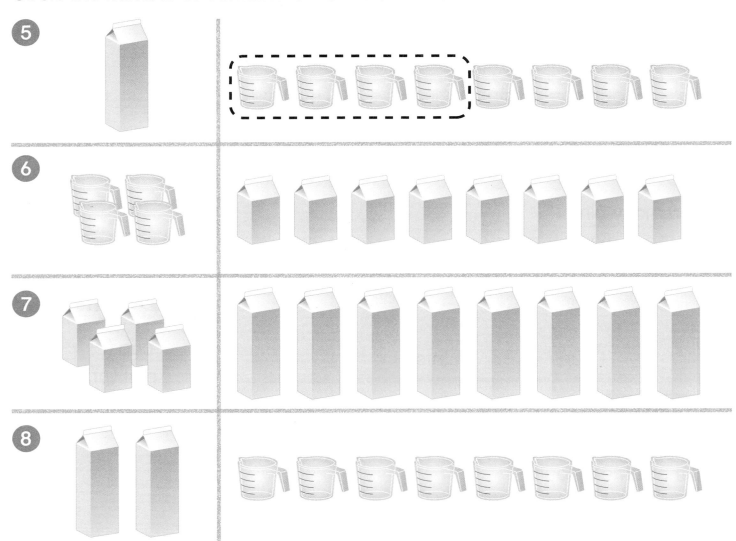

5

6

7

8

Problem Solving   Visual Thinking

Use the pictures to answer the questions.
Write **more than** or **less than**.

9 Does a gallon hold more than or less than 5 quarts?

_____

10 Does a gallon hold more than or less than 1 pint?

_____

 Home Connection Your child compared the capacities of cups, pints, and quarts. **Home Activity** Have your child identify cup, pint, and quart containers at home. Have him or her tell which containers hold the most and which hold the least.

Name _____

Does the glass hold more than or less than 1 **liter**?

This holds less than 1 liter.

This holds about 1 liter.

This holds more than 1 liter.

The glass holds ___less than___ 1 liter.

Word Bank

liter (L)

Check ✓

Does each object hold **more than** or **less than** 1 liter?
Complete each sentence.

1

The pool holds _____ 1 liter.

2

The mug holds _____ 1 liter.

3

The fish bowl holds _____ 1 liter.

Think About It   Reasoning

Name some things that hold more than a liter.

Name some things that hold less than a liter.

About how many liters does the object hold?
Circle the better estimate.

4

(about 3 liters)

about 30 liters

5

about 10 liters

about 1 liter

6

about 5 liters

about 50 liters

7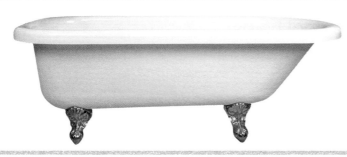

about 90 liters

about 9 liters

Problem Solving   Number Sense

Solve.

8 In Mexico, gasoline is sold in liters.
If 1 liter of gasoline costs 6 pesos,
how much does 4 liters cost?

____ pesos

Home Connection Your child compared the capacities of objects to a liter and then estimated how many liters an object holds.
Home Activity Help your child find objects that hold about a liter, less than a liter, and more than a liter.

Name _____

**Learn!**

How many cubes does it take to fill this box? Make the shape to find out.

It takes ___8___ cubes to fill the box.

The **volume** of the box is 8 **cubic units**.

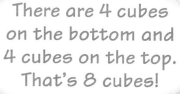
There are 4 cubes on the bottom and 4 cubes on the top. That's 8 cubes!

Word Bank

volume

cubic units

Check ✓

Use cubes to show how many it takes to fill each box. Write how many cubes you use.

1

_____ cubes

2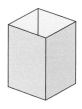

_____ cubes

3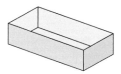

_____ cubes

Think About It   Reasoning

What can you say about the volumes of Boxes A and B? How do you know?

A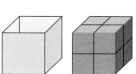

B

Circle the number of cubes that will fit in each box.

4 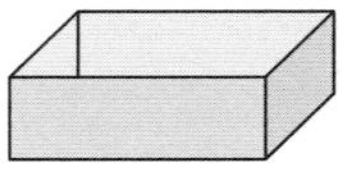 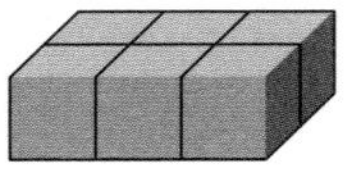 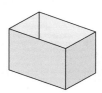 5 cubes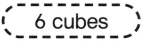

5 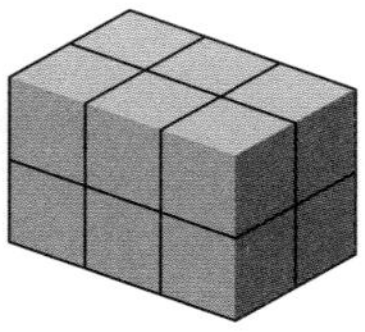 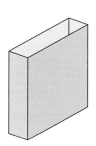  12 cubes 15 cubes

6 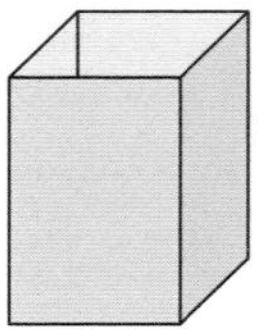 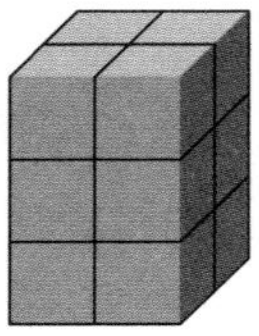   12 cubes 20 cubes

7 12 cubes 16 cubes

Problem Solving   Visual Thinking

8 If 16 cubes fit in Box A, how many cubes do you think will fit in Box B?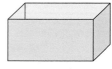

_____ cubes

            A 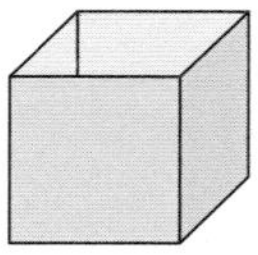   B

How do you know?

_____

_____

Home Connection Your child explored the concept of volume by determining how many cubes fill a box. **Home Activity** Have your child tell you how he or she figured out how many cubes were in each box in Exercises 5–7.

Name _____

 Diagnostic Checkpoint

Circle the better estimate.

1

about 100 inches

about 100 yards

2

about 15 centimeters

about 15 meters

3

about 1 liter

about 10 liters

Circle the object that holds more.

4

5

Measure using cubes or an inch ruler.

6

about _____ cubes long

7

about _____ inches tall

Find the perimeter.

8

_____ inches

Circle the number of cubes that will fit in the box.

9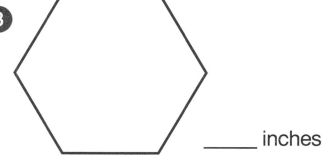

10 cubes   16 cubes

Name_____

Mark the time.

1

   Ⓐ 2:35

   Ⓑ 7:05

   Ⓒ 7:10

   Ⓓ 2:10

2

   Ⓐ 4:10

   Ⓑ 4:50

   Ⓒ 5:10

   Ⓓ 5:50

Add on to find the other part of 100. Mark the answer.

3   50 and _____ is 100.

50	60	40	30
Ⓐ	Ⓑ	Ⓒ	Ⓓ

4   35 and _____ is 100.

55	75	65	15
Ⓐ	Ⓑ	Ⓒ	Ⓓ

Mark the shape that is congruent to the first shape.

5

Ⓐ	Ⓑ	Ⓒ	Ⓓ

6

Ⓐ	Ⓑ	Ⓒ	Ⓓ

Mark the addition problem that shows an estimate.

7   22 + 59

20 + 60	20 + 50	30 + 50	30 + 60
Ⓐ	Ⓑ	Ⓒ	Ⓓ

Writing in Math

8 Find the difference. Tell why you need to regroup.

_____

_____

$$\begin{array}{r} 61 \\ -\ 28 \\ \hline \end{array}$$

Which **weighs** more? Which weighs less?

We can check using a balance scale.

I think that 20 cubes weigh more than the pencil.

The cubes weigh __more than__ the pencil.

The pencil weighs __less than__ the cubes.

Word Bank

weight

Check ✓

Find objects like the ones shown. Estimate if the object weighs more than or less than 20 cubes. Then weigh the object using a balance.

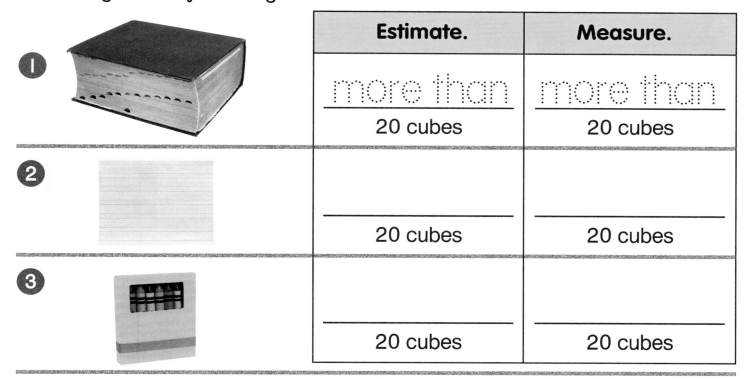

	Estimate.	Measure.
1	more than 20 cubes	more than 20 cubes
2	_____ 20 cubes	_____ 20 cubes
3	_____ 20 cubes	_____ 20 cubes

Think About It   Reasoning

Find an object that you think weighs about the same as 20 cubes. How can you tell how much the object weighs?

Circle the object that weighs more.

Circle the object that weighs less.

Problem Solving Reasoning

9 Name 3 objects that you think weigh less than a watermelon.

_____ _____ _____

Home Connection Your child estimated and measured the weight of objects, and identified which of two objects weighs more or less.
Home Activity Take 5 objects from the kitchen shelf. Have your child line up the objects from heaviest to lightest.

This is 1 **pound** of butter.
There are 16 **ounces** in 1 pound.

About how much does each object or group of objects weigh?

less than 1 pound   about 1 pound   more than 1 pound

Word Bank

pound (lb)
ounce (oz)

Check ✓

Does each object weigh more than
or less than 1 pound?
Circle **more** or **less**.

 1      (more)
     less

2      more
     less

3      more
     less

4      more
     less

5      more
     less

6      more
     less

Think About It   Number Sense

How many ounces are in 2 pounds?

About how much does each object weigh?
Circle the better estimate.

 7

(about 1 ounce)

about 1 pound

8

about 8 ounces

about 8 pounds

9

about 3 ounces

about 3 pounds

10

about 5 ounces

about 5 pounds

11

about 3 ounces

about 3 pounds

12

about 15 ounces

about 15 pounds

13

Pasta

about 2 ounces

about 2 pounds

14

about 8 ounces

about 8 pounds

Problem Solving Algebra

Solve.

15 1 pound is 16 ounces.
How many ounces are in
a half pound?

_____

1 pound = 16 ounces

$\frac{1}{2}$ pound = ? ounces

 Home Connection Your child estimated and compared the weights of objects using ounces and pounds. **Home Activity** Have your child find items in your home that are measured in ounces and/or pounds.

Name _____

This large jar of peanut butter measures about 1 **kilogram**.
There are 1,000 **grams** in 1 kilogram.
A marker cap measures about 1 gram.

About how much does each object or group of objects measure?

| less than 1 kilogram | about 1 kilogram | more than 1 kilogram |

Word Bank

kilogram (kg)
gram (g)

Check ✓

Does each object measure more than or less than
1 gram or 1 kilogram? Write **more than** or **less than**.

1

_____ 1 gram

2

_____ 1 kilogram

3

_____ 1 gram

4

_____ 1 kilogram

Think About It   Reasoning

Would you use grams or kilograms to find out how
much 2 paper clips measure? Explain.

About how much does each object measure?
Circle the better estimate.

5
(about 30 grams)
about 30 kilograms

6
about 500 grams
about 500 kilograms

7
about 5 grams
about 5 kilograms

8
about 4 grams
about 4 kilograms

9
about 2 grams
about 2 kilograms

10
about 65 grams
about 65 kilograms

Problem Solving   Number Sense

Solve.

$$1{,}000 \text{ g} = 1 \text{ kg}$$

11 If 1 large paper clip measures about 1 gram, how many paper clips measure about 1 kilogram?

about _____ paper clips

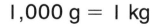

Temperature: Fahrenheit and Celsius

Learn!

What is the **temperature**? You can measure temperature in **degrees** Fahrenheit or in degrees Celsius.

It is _68_ °F.

degrees **Fahrenheit (°F)**

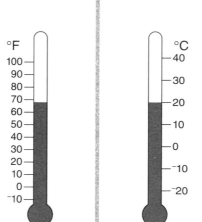

It is _20_ °C.

degrees **Celsius (°C)**

Word Bank

temperature
Fahrenheit (°F)
Celsius (°C)
degrees

Check ✓

Write each temperature.
Circle the hottest temperature in each row.

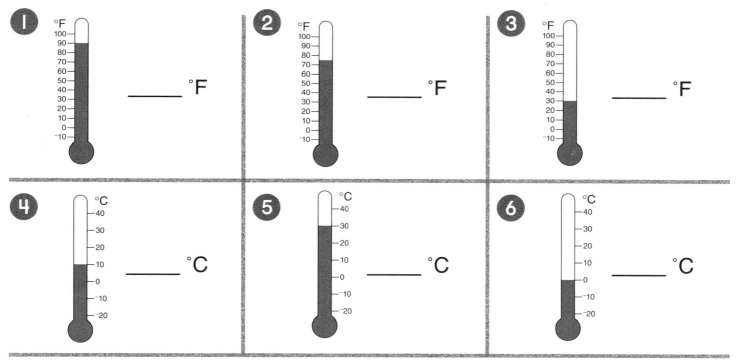

1 _____ °F

2 _____ °F

3 _____ °F

4 _____ °C

5 _____ °C

6 _____ °C

Think About It Reasoning

It is 82°F. Would you go swimming or sledding outdoors? Why?

Practice

Color to show the temperature.
Circle hot or cold to tell about the temperature.

7 95°F

hot

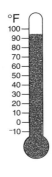

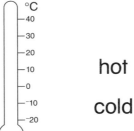

cold

8 2°C

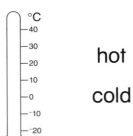

hot

cold

9 40°C

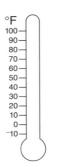

hot

cold

10 13°F

hot

cold

11 28°F

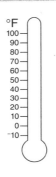

hot

cold

12 36°C

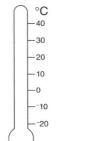

hot

cold

Problem Solving **Writing in Math**

13 Tell about the things you would do if it were 65°F outside.

____

____

____

Home Connection Your child read temperatures and learned how to show temperatures on a thermometer. **Home Activity** Help your child read the temperature on a home thermometer or find the temperature of your state in the newspaper.

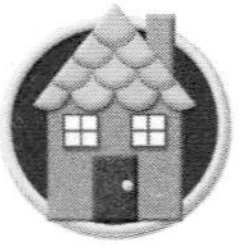

Name _____

Circle the object that weighs more.

1

2

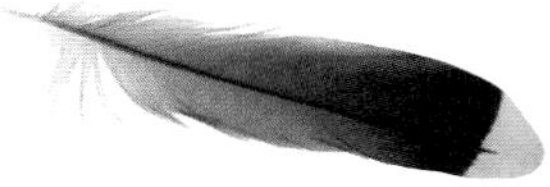

Circle the better estimate.

3

about 2 ounces

about 2 pounds

4

about 2 ounces

about 2 pounds

5

about 9 grams

about 9 kilograms

6

about 1 gram

about 1 kilogram

Color to show the temperature.
Circle **hot** or **cold** to tell about the temperature.

7 3°F

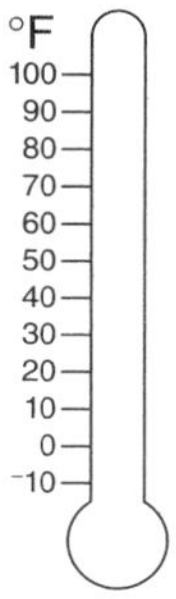

°F
100
90
80
70
60
50
40
30
20
10
0
-10

hot

cold

8 34°C

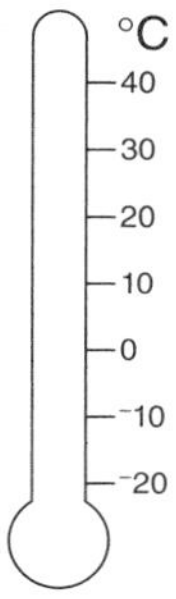

°C
40
30
20
10
0
-10
-20

hot

cold

Name _____

Mark the fraction that tells how much is shaded.

1

Ⓐ $\frac{1}{4}$

Ⓑ $\frac{1}{3}$

Ⓒ $\frac{1}{2}$

Ⓓ $\frac{1}{5}$

2

Ⓐ $\frac{1}{2}$

Ⓑ $\frac{1}{3}$

Ⓒ $\frac{1}{4}$

Ⓓ $\frac{1}{6}$

Mark the time.

3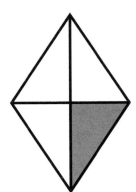

Ⓐ 2 minutes

Ⓑ 2 hours

Ⓒ 2 days

Ⓓ 2 weeks

Raking leaves

4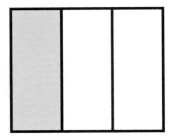

Ⓐ 15 hours

Ⓑ 15 days

Ⓒ 15 minutes

Ⓓ 15 weeks

Walking around the block

Mark the total amount.

5

Ⓐ 75¢

Ⓑ 85¢

Ⓒ 95¢

Ⓓ $1.00

Writing in Math

6 Write 3 sentences about the calendar. Tell the name of the month. Tell how many days are in the month. Name the date with a star.

_____

_____

_____

_____

© Pearson Education, Inc.

Name _____

Let's **predict** what might happen! Write the color.

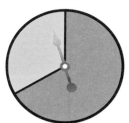

It is **more likely** that the spinner will land on

_____green_____.

It is **less likely** that you will pick

_____purple_____.

It is **equally likely** that you will pick

_____blue or red_____.

Word Bank

predict
more likely
less likely
equally likely

Check ✓

Put some cubes in a bag.
Then make a prediction. Pull out one cube, record the results, and put the cube back. Do this 10 times.

1 Use 10 red cubes and 2 blue cubes.
Are you more likely to pick red or blue cubes?

_____

2 Use 4 blue cubes and 8 red cubes.
Are you less likely to pick red or blue cubes?

_____

Think About It   Reasoning

You have 12 cubes. It is equally likely that you will pick a red cube or a blue cube. How many cubes do you have of each color? Explain.

If you were to spin once, which color is the spinner
most likely to land on?

3
red
(dashed box) yellow

4
red
yellow

5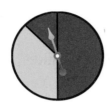
red
yellow
blue

6
red
yellow
blue

If you were to spin once, which color is the spinner
least likely to land on?

7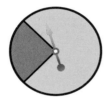
green
yellow

8
green
yellow

9
green
purple
red

10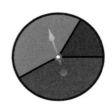
green
purple
red

Problem Solving   Reasoning

Write **more likely, less likely,** or **equally likely**
to answer the question.

11 How likely is it that the spinner will land on red?

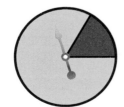      

_____   _____   _____

Home Connection Your child predicted the outcome of
activities using the terms *more likely, less likely,* and *equally likely.*
Home Activity Draw several spinners with equal and unequal
sections colored. Have your child tell you which color the spinner
is more likely to land on.

Learn!

Put 10 purple cubes and 10 orange cubes in a bag. If you pick 10 cubes, predict the outcome.

Compare your predictions with your results.

It is **certain** that you will pick purple or orange cubes.

It is **probable** that you will pick an orange cube.

It is **impossible** that you will pick a red cube.

Number of: purple cubes _____ orange cubes _____

Check ✔

Put 20 green cubes and 5 yellow cubes in a bag.
If you pull out 10 cubes, predict the outcome.
Circle the missing word to complete the sentence.

Word Bank

certain
probable
impossible

❶ It is _____ that you will pick a yellow cube.

probable

impossible

❷ It is _____ that you will pick a red cube.

impossible

probable

Pick 10 cubes and record the results.

❸

Number of: green cubes _____ yellow cubes _____

Think About It   Reasoning

There are 5 blue cubes and 20 red cubes in a bag.
Is it more probable to pick a blue cube or a red cube?
Why?

Use the tally chart to help you answer the questions.
Circle the missing word to complete the sentence.

Marbles	
Purple	卌 卌 卌 ‖
Red	卌 ‖‖

4 There are more _____ marbles in the jar.

purple

red

5 You can pick one marble. It is _____ that you will pick a purple marble.

probable

certain

6 It is _____ that you will pick a yellow marble.

probable

impossible

7 It is _____ that you will pick a purple or a red marble.

probable

certain

Problem Solving   Reasoning

8 There are red, yellow, and green marbles in each jar.
Color the marbles to match the description below each jar.

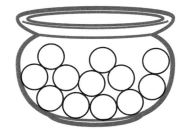   

It is most probable
to pick a green marble.

It is least probable
to pick a green marble.

Home Connection Your child predicted, recorded, and analyzed results of probability experiments. **Home Activity** Have your child put 12 coins in a bag, predict the results from picking 10 coins, and record the results.

Name _____

If you spin once, which color is the spinner most likely to land on?

1    blue

red

2    blue

red

green

Which color is the spinner least likely to land on?

3    blue

purple

yellow

4 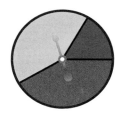   blue

red

yellow

Use the tally chart to help you answer.
Circle the missing word to complete the sentence.

Cubes	
Yellow	|||||
Red	||||| |||||	

5 If you pick one cube, it is _____ that
you will choose a red or a yellow cube.

impossible

certain

6 It is _____ that you will pick a red cube.

certain

probable

Write a number sentence for each part of the problem.

7 There are 76 beads in the bag.
38 of the beads are orange and the
rest are green. How many beads
are green?

_____ beads

Jamie pulled out 30 of the green beads.
How many green beads were left?

_____ beads

How much is left? Mark the best estimate.

1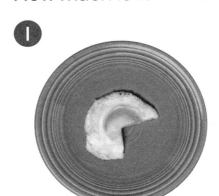

   Ⓐ about $\frac{1}{4}$

   Ⓑ about $\frac{1}{2}$

   Ⓒ about $\frac{3}{4}$

   Ⓓ about $\frac{7}{8}$

2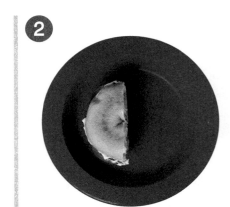

   Ⓐ about $\frac{1}{3}$

   Ⓑ about $\frac{1}{2}$

   Ⓒ about $\frac{1}{4}$

   Ⓓ about $\frac{2}{3}$

Use the diagram to answer the questions. Mark your answer.

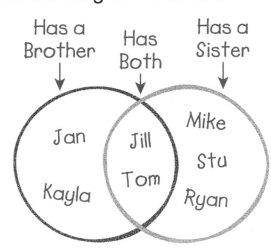

Has a Brother   Has Both   Has a Sister

Jan   Jill   Mike

Kayla   Tom   Stu   Ryan

3 How many children have only a brother?

    2   3   4   5

    Ⓐ   Ⓑ   Ⓒ   Ⓓ

4 How many children have a brother?

    2   4   5   7

    Ⓐ   Ⓑ   Ⓒ   Ⓓ

Mark the object that weighs more than a pound.

5

    Ⓐ   Ⓑ   Ⓒ   Ⓓ

Writing in Math

6 Tell the best way to solve 30 + 25.
Then add to find the sum.

_____

_____

_____

Choosing a Measuring Tool

Circle the measuring tool you would use.

1 How long is the clown's shoe?

2 How cold is it outside?

3 Which dog is heavier?

4 How much water does the dish hold?

Writing in Math

 5 Name all the units you might use.

 Home Connection Your child chose the right tool to measure an object.
Home Activity Ask your child to explain two of his or her answers above.

Use a Computer to Find Perimeter

You can use a computer to find the perimeters of different shapes.

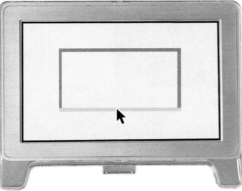

1 Go to the Geometry Drawing eTool on a computer.

2 Draw a rectangle in the Geoboard workspace.

3 Find the length of each side of your rectangle. Record these lengths on a separate sheet of paper.

4 Use the tool to find the perimeter. Write the perimeter on your paper.

5 Repeat Exercises 1–4 for a **pentagon** and a **hexagon**.

Think About It   Reasoning

How did your computer find the perimeter of each shape? Use the lengths on your sheet of paper to help you explain your thinking.

Home Connection Your child used a computer to find the perimeters of different shapes.
Home Activity Ask your child to draw a shape with 4 or 5 sides, measure each side to the nearest inch, and then find the perimeter of the shape to the nearest inch.

Name _____

Read Together

Make Smart Choices

Removing wrong answer choices can help you find the correct answer choice.

Test-Taking Strategies

Understand the Question

Get Information for the Answer

Plan How to Find the Answer

Make Smart Choices

Use Writing in Math

① Matt has 78¢. He spends 15¢ for a pencil. How much money does he have left?

Ⓐ 78¢ + 15¢ = 93¢

Ⓑ 78¢ − 15¢ = 63¢

Ⓒ 78¢ + 5¢ = 83¢

Ⓓ 78¢ − 25¢ = 53¢

Do I need to add or subtract?

Do you need to add or subtract to solve this problem? Since Matt spent money, you need to subtract. Which two answer choices are **not** subtraction sentences?

Now look at the two subtraction sentences. Which one answers the question?

Fill in the answer bubble.

Your Turn

Solve another problem about Matt.
Fill in the answer bubble.

② After Matt bought the pencil, he earned 35¢.
How much money does he have now?

Ⓐ 63¢ − 45¢ = 18¢   Ⓒ 63¢ + 35¢ = 98¢

Ⓑ 63¢ − 35¢ = 28¢   Ⓓ 53¢ + 35¢ = 88¢

Home Connection Your child prepared for standardized tests by eliminating wrong answer choices to help find the correct answer choice. **Home Activity** Ask your child to explain why three of the answer choices are wrong in Exercise 2.

Name _____

When Is a Foot Not a Foot?

How many inches long do you think your foot is?
Is your foot 1 foot long? Work with a partner to
find out.

Measuring Up

1 Take off your shoes. Stand on a large piece
of paper. Have your partner trace your foot.
Then trace your partner's foot.

2 Use a ruler. Find the length of your foot and
then your partner's foot to the nearest inch.
Write your names and the measurements
in the table.

Name	Foot Length (in inches)

3 Make a tally chart like the one below to show the lengths of the feet
for the children in your class.

Length	Number of Children
_____ inches	
_____ inches	
_____ inches	

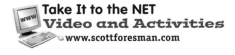

Home Connection Your child measured the length of his or her foot
and made a chart showing the lengths of classmates' feet.
Home Activity With your child, trace the foot of a member of your
family and measure its length to the nearest inch.

© Pearson Education, Inc.

Name _____

Measure with cubes. Then measure with a centimeter ruler.

1

about _____ cubes   about _____ centimeters

Find the perimeter and the area of this shape.

2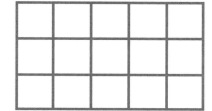

perimeter: _____ cm

area: _____ square units

Circle the object that holds less.

3     **4**

Does it hold more than or less than 1 liter? Circle **more** or **less**.

5   more

less

6   more

less

Circle the object that weighs less.

7     **8**

Circle the best estimate.

9    about 5 inches

about 5 feet

about 5 yards

10    about 3 grams

about 3 kilograms

11 Write the temperature.

_____ °F

12 Circle the number of cubes that will fit in the box.

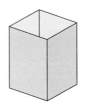

18 cubes

12 cubes

Write a number sentence for each part of the problem.

13 On Monday, the temperature was 62°F.
On Tuesday it was 25°F warmer.
What was the temperature?   _____ degrees F

On Wednesday, the temperature was
30°F cooler than on Tuesday.
What was the temperature?   _____ degrees F

If you were to spin once, which color is the spinner
most likely to land on?

14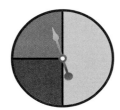

red

yellow

green

15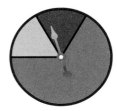

red

yellow

green

Use the tally chart to help you answer.
Circle the missing word to complete the sentence.

Cubes	
Red	⊦⊦⊦ ‖
Blue	‖

16 If you pick one cube, it is _____ that
you will choose a red cube.

probable

certain

17 It is _____ that you will pick a green cube.

certain

impossible

"Let's See," Said Betty Bee

Written by John Carlisle

Illustrated by K. Michael Crawford

Mail

Mail

This Math Storybook belongs to

_____

"Let's see," said Betty Bee.

Betty was planning a Big Family Picnic.
And she didn't want to forget anyone.

"Aunt Rose has **122** bees in her family.
Aunt Tulip has **144** bees in her family.
Aunt Bluebell has **231** bees in her family.
That's **497** bees, plus my **3** aunts," Betty said to herself.
"And then there are those **500** cousins!"

"That's **1,000** bees! There will be **1,000** bees
at our picnic!"

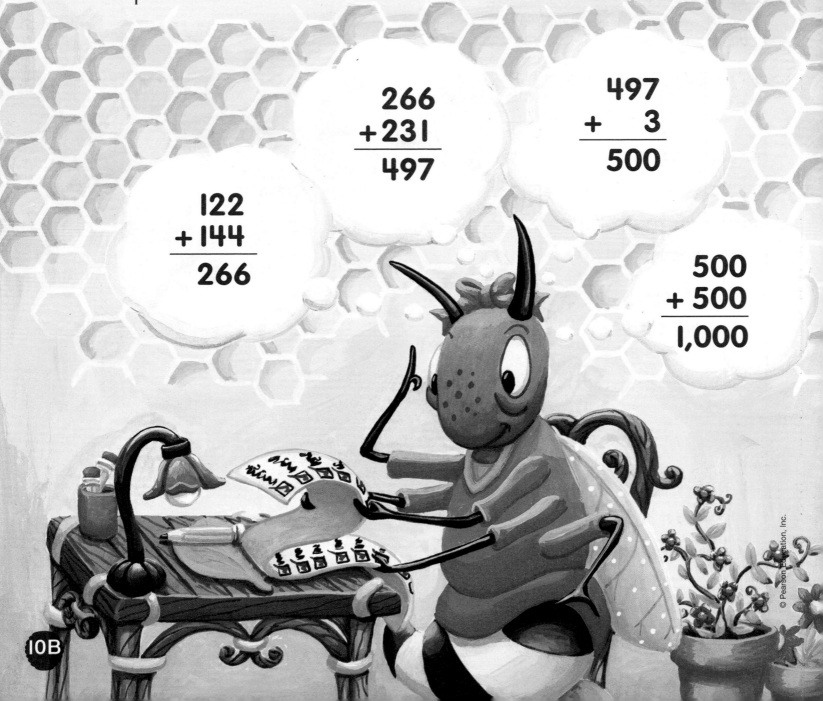

So Betty Bee sent out **1,000** invitations.

And she got back **1,000** letters saying Yes.

Everyone was coming!

Betty had a LOT of work to do.

"Let's see," said Betty Bee.

"If I seat **100** bees at each table,
I'll need **10** tables."

"Now, what should we eat? Hmmm.
I think I will plan for **500** pollen treats
and **500** nectar treats."

"Yes, this sounds like a good plan
to me," said Betty Bee.

"**10** tables. **1,000** seats. **1,000** treats. Perfect!"

1,000 + 1 = 1,001

The Big Day arrived at last.

Betty's whole family came.

Everyone sat down at a table.
Everyone, that is, except Betty.

Everyone had something to eat.
Everyone, that is, except Betty.

"Let's see," said Betty Bee,
scratching her head.

Wait a minute!

There were **1,001** bees at the Big Family Picnic.

Betty had forgotten to count herself!

But Betty didn't care.

Even though she felt a little silly
for making such a simple mistake,
she decided just to have a great time
with her family. Good idea, right?

Dear Family,

Today my class started Chapter 10, **Numbers to 1,000.** I will learn how to build, read, write, compare, and order numbers to 1,000. I will also learn more about the value of each digit in a 3-digit number. Here are some of the math words I will be learning and some things we can do to help me with my math.

Love,

_____

Math Activity to Do at Home

Collect 1,000 of something! (Pennies work particularly well, but paper clips, craft sticks, reinforcement labels, and stickers work well too.) Organize your collection by tens and hundreds and talk about it as 1,000 ones, as 100 tens, and as 10 hundreds. Have fun!

Books to Read Together

Reading math stories reinforces concepts. Look for these titles in your local library:

Millions of Cats
By Wanda Ga'g
(Penguin Putnam,
1996)

Math Curse
By Jon Scieszka and
Lane Smith (Penguin
Putnam, 1995)

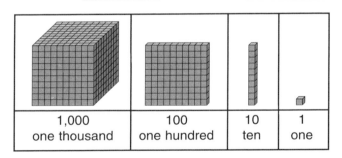

My New Math Words

Our place-value number system is based on groups of ten. It takes 10 ones to make 1 ten. It takes 10 tens to make 1 hundred. And it takes 10 **hundreds** to make 1 **thousand.**

1,000 one thousand	100 one hundred	10 ten	1 one

Here is a number written in **standard form:**

456

Here is the same number written in **expanded form:**

400 + 50 + 6

Take It to the NET
More Activities
www.scottforesman.com

Don't Get Stung!

What You Need

1 game marker
for each player

How to Play

1. Place your markers on START.
2. Take turns moving from hive to hive.
   Whenever you land on a new hive,
   your partner says, "I challenge you!"
3. Then your partner tells you what you have to do:

   · Name the numbers that are **1 more** and **1 less.**
   OR
   · Name the numbers that are **2 more** and **2 less.**
   OR
   · Name the numbers that are **10 more** and **10 less.**

4. If your partner thinks you have answered incorrectly,
   you have to work together to find the answers.
5. Keep playing until both of you make it
   to FINISH without getting stung!

Name _____

Building 1,000

How many tens make 100?

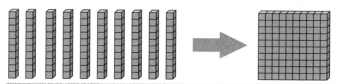   10 tens make 1 hundred.

How many **hundreds** make 1,000? 10 hundreds make 1 **thousand**.

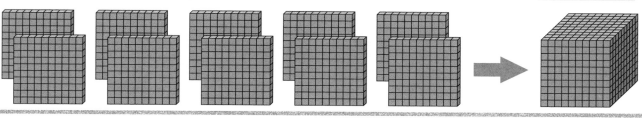

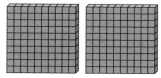

100 less is __100__.   __200__   100 more is __300__.

Word Bank

hundreds
thousand

Check ✓

Use crayons.

1 Circle 200 with a red crayon.

2 Circle 500 with a green crayon.

3 Circle 700 with a blue crayon.

4 Circle 1,000 with an orange crayon.

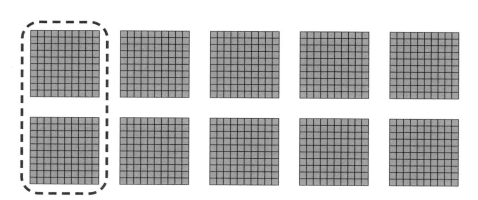

Think About It   Number Sense

Count by 100s to 1,000. How do you know how many ones you are counting?

Chapter 10 ★ Lesson 1   three hundred ninety-one   **391**

Write how many. Use models if you need to.

5

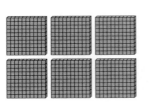

100 less is __200__.

_300_

100 more is __400__.

6

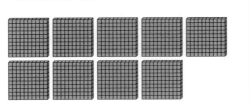

100 less is _____.

_____

100 more is _____.

7

100 less is _____.

_____

100 more is _____.

8

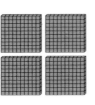

100 less is _____.

_____

100 more is _____.

Problem Solving **Algebra**

Solve.

9 How many pounds would you need to put on the right side to balance the scale?

_____ pounds

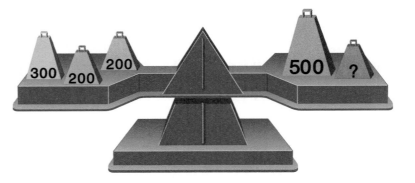

Home Connection Your child counted by 100s to 1,000.
Home Activity Have your child count aloud by 100s to 1,000.

What number do the models show?

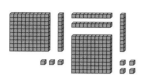

1. Count the hundreds.
2. Count the tens.
3. Count the ones.

Hundreds	Tens	Ones
2	4	7

247

This is a **three-digit number** because it has three **digits**.

Word Bank

three-digit number
digit

Check ✓

Write the numbers.
Use models and Workmat 5 if you need to.

1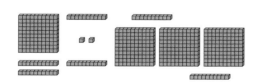

Hundreds	Tens	Ones
4	6	2

_____

2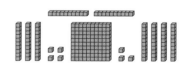

Hundreds	Tens	Ones

_____

3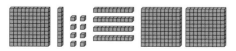

Hundreds	Tens	Ones

_____

4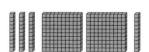

Hundreds	Tens	Ones

_____

Think About It Number Sense

What does the zero mean in each number:
30, 506, 680?

Write the numbers.

Use models and Workmat 5 if you need to.

 5

Hundreds	Tens	Ones

_____

 6

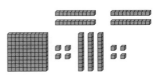

Hundreds	Tens	Ones

_____

 7

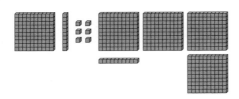

Hundreds	Tens	Ones

_____

 8

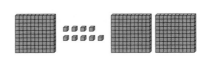

Hundreds	Tens	Ones

_____

 9

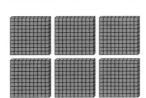

Hundreds	Tens	Ones

_____

 10

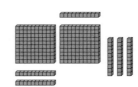

Hundreds	Tens	Ones

_____

Problem Solving Reasoning

Use the clues to find the number.

11 What is the number?
- The hundreds digit is 4.
- The ones digit is 8.
- The tens digit is 5.

_____

12 What is the number?
- The tens digit is 6.
- The ones digit is 3.
- The hundreds digit is 9.

_____

Home Connection Your child counted hundreds, tens, and ones to make three-digit numbers. **Home Activity** Have your child make the greatest and least possible numbers with the digits 7, 3, and 9. *(973 and 379)*

394 three hundred ninety-four

Learn!

What are some ways to write numbers?

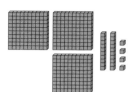

I write the hundreds first, then the tens, and then the ones.

300 + 20 + 4
expanded form

324
standard form

three hundred twenty-four
number word

Word Bank

expanded form
standard form
number word

Check ✓

Read the number. Write the number in expanded form. Then write it in standard form.

1 two hundred fifty-three

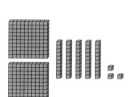

200 + 50 + 3   253

2 six hundred twelve

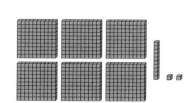

_____ + _____ + _____   _____

Think About It   Number Sense

How do you know when to write a zero in these numbers?

one hundred ninety-two   one hundred ninety   one hundred nine

Circle the models to match the expanded form.
Write the number in standard form.

3

$400 + 50 + 6$
four hundred fifty-six

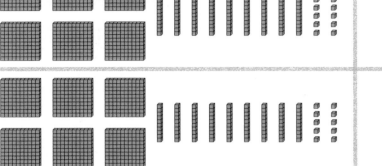

$\underline{456}$

4

$300 + 80 + 2$
three hundred eighty-two

_____

5

$100 + 8$
one hundred eight

_____

Circle the models to match the standard form.
Write the number in expanded form.

6

678

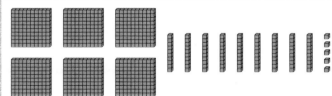

_____ + _____ + _____
six hundred seventy-eight

7

340

_____ + _____ + _____
three hundred forty

Problem Solving   Mental Math

Write the total.

8 The school bought 6 cartons of
crayons and 18 boxes of crayons.
How many boxes of crayons
did the school buy in all?

_____ boxes

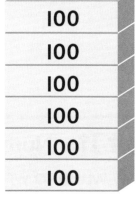

| 100 |
| 100 |
| 100 |
| 100 |
| 100 |
| 100 |

1 carton = 100 boxes

 Home Connection Your child wrote numbers in expanded form and
standard form. **Home Activity** Ask your child to explain what those
terms mean.

 **Algebra**

You can use models, drawings, or **mental math**
to add or subtract hundreds and tens.

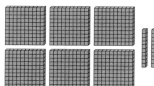

Think
$40 + 30 = 70$

$$645 + 30 = 675$$
$$645 + 300 = 945$$

6 hundreds plus 3 hundreds is
9 hundreds.

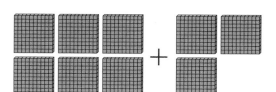

Think
$300 - 200 = 100$

$$368 - 200 = 168$$
$$368 - 20 = 348$$

6 tens minus 2 tens is 4 tens.

Word Bank

mental math

Check ✓

Use models, drawings, or mental math
to solve the problems.

$$471 - 10 = \underline{\qquad}$$
$$471 - 100 = \underline{\qquad}$$

 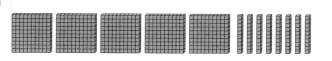

$$580 - 50 = \underline{\qquad}$$
$$580 - 500 = \underline{\qquad}$$

Think About It   Number Sense

How does a number change when you add 30? 300?

Practice

Use models, drawings, or mental math to solve the problems.

3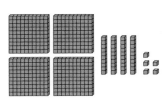

$$445 - 20 = \underline{\hspace{2cm}}$$
$$445 - 200 = \underline{\hspace{2cm}}$$

4

$$286 + 10 = \underline{\hspace{2cm}}$$
$$286 + 100 = \underline{\hspace{2cm}}$$

5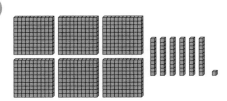

$$661 + 30 = \underline{\hspace{2cm}}$$
$$661 + 300 = \underline{\hspace{2cm}}$$

6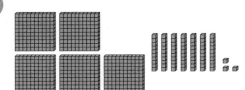

$$573 - 40 = \underline{\hspace{2cm}}$$
$$573 - 400 = \underline{\hspace{2cm}}$$

Problem Solving   Writing in Math

Solve.

7 Blake School has 263 students.
Parker School has 20 more students than Blake School.
How many students does Parker School have?   \underline{\hspace{2cm}} students

 8 Write a story problem like the one in Exercise 7.
Ask a classmate to solve it.

Home Connection Your child used mental math, drawings, or models to add and subtract multiples of 10 and 100.
Home Activity Ask your child to explain how he or she solved Exercise 6.

 **Algebra**

To **compare** numbers, start with the digit that has the greatest place value.

324 ◯ 168

Compare the hundreds first.

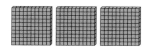

300 is **greater than** 100,

so 324 168

239 ◯ 253

If the hundreds are **equal**, compare the tens.

30 is **less than** 50,

so 239 253

If the tens are equal, compare the ones. 497 492

Word Bank

compare
equals (=)
greater than (>)
less than (<)

Check ✓

Compare. Write >, <, or =.
Use models if you need to.

1 475 ◯ 189   260 ◯ 260   732 ◯ 756

2 603 ◯ 544   162 ◯ 182   877 ◯ 877

3 139 ◯ 391   475 ◯ 375   903 ◯ 903

4 262 ◯ 232   950 ◯ 950   950 ◯ 1,000

Think About It   Number Sense

How would you compare 235 and 78?

Compare. Write >, <, or =.
Use models if you need to.

⑤ 148 ◯ 172   502 ◯ 502   246 ◯ 231

⑥ 800 ◯ 399   653 ◯ 660   413 ◯ 305

⑦ 728 ◯ 728   450 ◯ 440   926 ◯ 854

⑧ 1,000 ◯ 999   286 ◯ 189   408 ◯ 413

Problem Solving   Visual Thinking

⑨ Draw lines to show which pony each child raised.

Kirk said:

My pony weighs less than Jenny's pony.

Natalie said:

My pony weighs more than Kirk's pony.

Jenny said:

My pony weighs less than 240 pounds.

Home Connection Your child compared three-digit numbers.
Home Activity Ask your child whether 106 is less than or is greater than 601 and to explain how he or she knows.

Name_____

 Algebra

There are many ways to make 1,000.

I have 750 points.
I need 1,000 points to win.
How many more points
do I need?

Count on to make 1,000.
First, count on by 100s. Then count on by 10s.

750 850 950   950 960 970 980 990 1,000

    100   200   10   20   30   40   50

$750 + \underline{250} = 1,000$ $\underline{250}$ points

Check ✓

Count on to solve each problem.

1 Paul has 550 points.
He needs 1,000 points to win.
How many more points does
he need?

$550 + \underline{} = 1,000$

_____ points

2 Grace has 600 points.
She needs 1,000 points to win.
How many more points does
she need?

$600 + \underline{} = 1,000$

_____ points

Think About It   Reasoning

How many 50s are in 100?
How many 500s are in 1,000?

Count on to solve each problem.

3 Michelle has 950 points.
How many more points does
she need to get to 1,000?

$$950 + \underline{\hspace{1cm}} = 1,000$$

_____ points

---

4 Pat has 450 points.
If he needs 1,000 points to win,
how many more points does
he need?

$$450 + \underline{\hspace{1cm}} = 1,000$$

_____ points

---

5 Brian has 300 points.
How many more points does
he need to get to 1,000?

$$300 + \underline{\hspace{1cm}} = 1,000$$

_____ points

---

6 Elena has 250 points.
She needs 1,000 points to win.
How many more points does
she need?

$$250 + \underline{\hspace{1cm}} = 1,000$$

_____ points

---

7 Mutaz has 900 points.
How many more points does
she need to get to 1,000?

$$900 + \underline{\hspace{1cm}} = 1,000$$

_____ points

Problem Solving   Number Sense

Skip count by 50s.

8   50,   100,   150,   200,   _____,

300,   350,   _____,   450,   _____,

550,   _____,   650,   700,   _____,

_____,   _____,   900,   _____,   1,000

© Pearson Education, Inc.

Home Connection Your child found two numbers that together make 1,000.
Home Activity Ask your child to solve and explain: 850 + _____ = 1,000. *(150)*

Name _____

Write how many. Use models if you need to.

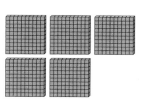

100 less is _____. _____ 100 more is _____.

Circle the models to match the standard form.
Write the number in expanded form.

2 516 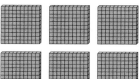 _____ + _____ + _____

Use models, drawings, or mental math to solve the problem.

3 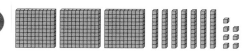 377 − 20 = _____

377 − 200 = _____

Compare. Write >, <, or =. Use models if you need to.

4 217 ◯ 217   165 ◯ 191   493 ◯ 394

Write the number. Use models and Workmat 5 if you need to.

5

Hundreds	Tens	Ones

_____

Count on to solve.

6 Doug has 200 points.
He needs 1,000 points to win.
How many more points does
he need?

200 + _____ = 1,000

_____ points

Mark the fraction that names the shaded part.

1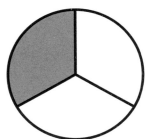

Ⓐ $\frac{1}{5}$

Ⓑ $\frac{1}{4}$

Ⓒ $\frac{1}{3}$

Ⓓ $\frac{1}{2}$

2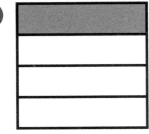

Ⓐ $\frac{1}{2}$

Ⓑ $\frac{1}{3}$

Ⓒ $\frac{1}{4}$

Ⓓ $\frac{1}{6}$

Mark the number sentence that will help solve the problem.

3 Sylvia bought a brush for 35¢ and a comb for 20¢.
How much did she spend in all?

35¢ + 20¢ = __   35¢ − 20¢ = __   25¢ + 20¢ = __   35¢ + 35¢ = __

    Ⓐ   Ⓑ   Ⓒ   Ⓓ

Mark the time shown on the clocks.

4

Ⓐ 20 minutes before 11

Ⓑ 20 minutes after 11

Ⓒ 40 minutes after 11

Ⓓ 40 minutes before 11

Mark the answer.

5 How many cups are in 2 pints?

  2   4   6   8

 Ⓐ   Ⓑ   Ⓒ   Ⓓ

Writing in Math

6 There are 3 digits in a number.
What is the digit with the
greatest value?

_____

_____

_____

Name_____

The **data chart** tells how many children play each sport in the Woodland School District.

Sports Children Play	
Sport	**Number of Children**
Soccer	710
Football	435
Basketball	286
Track	509
Baseball	628

Check ✓

Use data from the chart to answer the questions.

1 How many children play football?   ꜰ̲4̲3̲5̲ children

2 How many children are on the
track team?   _____ children

3 Which sport do 600 + 20 + 8
children play?   _____

4 Seven hundred ten children
play which sport?   _____

5 Do more children play basketball
or football?   _____

Word Bank

data
chart

Think About It   Reasoning

Why would you record data in a chart?

Use data from the chart to answer the questions.

Baseball Infield

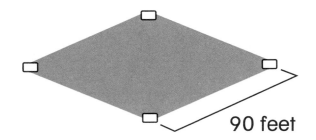

90 feet

Lengths of Playing Spaces	
Sport	Length of Field/Court
Football	360 feet
Soccer	390 feet
Baseball	90 feet
Basketball	94 feet

6 Which field is longer,
a football field or a soccer field?

_____

7 A basketball court is how many
feet long, in tens and ones?

_____ tens _____ ones

8 Which game space is
300 + 60 feet long?

_____

Reasonableness

Circle the number or word that makes more sense.

9 Together two football fields are
about $\begin{smallmatrix} 80 \\ 800 \end{smallmatrix}$ feet long.

10 Together a soccer field
and a baseball infield are
about $\begin{smallmatrix} 100 \\ 500 \end{smallmatrix}$ feet long.

11 Two baseball infields are $\begin{smallmatrix} \text{shorter} \\ \text{longer} \end{smallmatrix}$
than one soccer field.

12 Together, a football field and a
baseball infield are $\begin{smallmatrix} \text{shorter} \\ \text{longer} \end{smallmatrix}$ than
a soccer field and a basketball
court.

Home Connection Your child used data from a chart to answer questions.
Home Activity Have your child ask you a question that can be answered
using data from one of the charts on Pages 405–406.

Name _____

 **Algebra**

What are the missing numbers?

_131_, 132, 133, _134_, 135, 136, _137_, 138

131 is **before** 132.   134 is **after** 133.   137 is **between** 136 and 138.

Check ✓

Write the missing numbers.

 1

201	202	203	204	205	206	207	208	209	210
211	212		214	215		217	218	219	220
221	222	223		225	226	227		229	230
231		233	234		236	237	238	239	240
241	242	243		245	246		248		250
	252		254	255		257	258	259	
261		263	264		266	267		269	270
271	272	273		275	276		278		280
281	282	283	284			287	288	289	
	292		294	295	296	297		299	300

Word Bank

before
after
between

Think About It   Number Sense

What numbers would be in the row that comes after 300?

What numbers would be in the row that comes before 201?

Write the number that comes after.

② 123, 124   539, _____   168, _____

③ 699, _____   407, _____   999, _____

Write the number that comes before.

④ _____, 156   _____, 482   _____, 299

⑤ _____, 260   _____, 803   _____, 400

Write the number that comes between.

⑥ 153, _____, 155   118, _____, 120   810, _____, 812

⑦ 799, _____, 801   628, _____, 630   209, _____, 211

Write the number.

⑧ What number is one before 357? _____

⑨ What number is one after 682? _____

⑩ What number is between 499 and 501? _____

Problem Solving Reasoning

Find the pattern. Write the next three numbers.

What's the pattern?

⑪ 250, 252, 254, _____, _____, _____

⑫ 760, 750, 740, _____, _____, _____

⑬ 115, 110, 105, _____, _____, _____

⑭ 899, 896, 893, _____, _____, _____

Home Connection Your child identified the positions of numbers as before, after, or between other numbers. **Home Activity** Ask your child what number is between 150 and 152. *(151)*

Name_____

Learn! Algebra

Put the numbers in **order** from **least** to **greatest**.

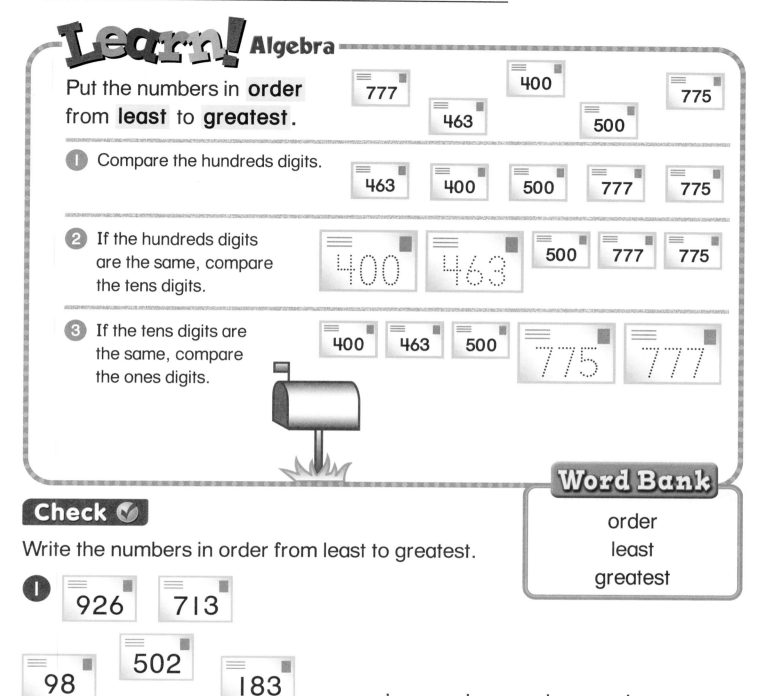

777   400   775
463   500

1 Compare the hundreds digits.

463   400   500   777   775

2 If the hundreds digits are the same, compare the tens digits.

400   463   500   777   775

3 If the tens digits are the same, compare the ones digits.

400   463   500   775   777

Word Bank
order
least
greatest

Check ✓

Write the numbers in order from least to greatest.

1 926   713   98   502   183

_____, _____, _____, _____, _____

2 608   36   247   615   822

_____, _____, _____, _____, _____

Think About It   Reasoning

When you order numbers, how can the number of digits be a clue?

Write the numbers in order from least to greatest.

3 (756, 812, 321, 765, 365) ____, ____, ____, ____, ____

4 (171, 143, 170, 209, 109) ____, ____, ____, ____, ____

5 (538, 382, 627, 566, 340) ____, ____, ____, ____, ____

Write the numbers in order from greatest to least.

6 (904, 940, 611, 573, 601) ____, ____, ____, ____, ____

7 (264, 320, 227, 302, 229) ____, ____, ____, ____, ____

8 (461, 783, 720, 451, 490) ____, ____, ____, ____, ____

Problem Solving Writing in Math

Use the space on the right to solve the problems.

9 In the numbers 411 to 430, are there more even or odd numbers? How do you know?

_____

_____

10 In the numbers 411 to 431, are there more even or odd numbers? How do you know?

_____

_____

Home Connection Your child ordered two- and three-digit numbers.
Home Activity Have your child write the following numbers in order from least to greatest: 401, 395, 410, 399, 411. *(395, 399, 401, 410, 411)*

Predict and Verify

1 Read this knock-knock joke:

> **Knock knock.**
> Who's there?
> **Tennis.**
> Tennis who?
> **Tennis five plus five!**

2 Now read this knock-knock joke:

> **Knock knock.**
> Who's there?
> **Banana.**
> Banana who?
> **Knock knock.**
> Who's there?
> **Banana.**
> Banana who?
> **Knock knock.**
> Who's there?
> **Orange.**
> Orange who?
> **Orange you glad I didn't say banana?**

3 How is the second knock-knock joke different?

——————————————————————————

——————————————————————————

Think About It   Reasoning

Predict which number will come next in this pattern: 10, 8, 6, 4, _____
How do you know?

4 Look at the rows of dots below.
What pattern do you see?

_____

_____

_____

5 Now use the dots to play a game with a partner.

Each partner takes a turn crossing out either **one dot** or **two dots**
on a single line. One partner can use the letter **X**.
The other partner can use a checkmark (**✔**).

The winner is the one who does NOT have to cross off the last dot!

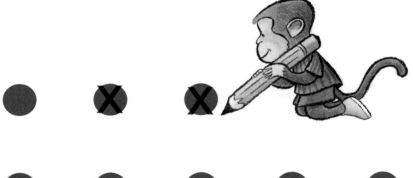

© Pearson Education, Inc.

Home Connection Your child is learning to look for patterns in both reading and math. **Home Activity** Help your child look for patterns around the house in wallpaper, tiles, carpeting, and so on.

 **Algebra**

What number **pattern** will help you find the number that comes next in this skip-counting sequence?

247   257   267   277   287   297   307   ____

Read and Understand

Find the number pattern that will help you think of the next skip-counting number.

> The tens digits increase by 1. Each number increases by 1 ten.

Plan and Solve

Look for the digits that change.
Do they **increase** or **decrease**?

What is the next number? __317__

Look Back and Check

How does knowing a number pattern help you find the next skip-counting number?

Word Bank

pattern
increase
decrease

Check ✓

Write the missing numbers. Describe the pattern.

❶ 600, 620, 640, 660, 680, _____, _____, _____

_____

❷ 200, 225, 250, 275, _____, _____, _____

_____

Think About It   Reasoning

Show a pattern in which the numbers decrease by 10.

Write the missing numbers. Describe the pattern.

3 200, 190, 180, 170, _____, _____, _____

_____

4 600, 550, 500, 450, _____, _____, _____

_____

Write the number that is 20 less.

5   560   361   837   494

_____   _____   _____   _____

What pattern do you see? _____

Write the number that is 200 more.

6   172   607   583   381

_____   _____   _____   _____

What pattern do you see? _____

Write the number that is 200 less.

7   640   905   728   462

_____   _____   _____   _____

What pattern do you see? _____

Reasoning

Find the pattern. Write the missing numbers.

8   25,   50,   75,   100,   _____,   150,

175,   _____,   225,   250,   _____,   300,

325,   _____,   _____,   _____,   425,   _____

Home Connection Your child looked for skip-counting patterns to solve problems. **Home Activity** Have your child continue and then describe this pattern: 525, 530, 535, 540, ____, ____, ____. *(545, 550, 555)*

Rescue Vehicles

Name _____

 Dorling Kindersley

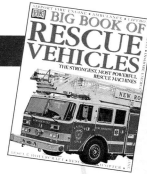
BIG BOOK OF RESCUE VEHICLES
THE STRONGEST, MOST POWERFUL RESCUE MACHINES

Do You Know...

that fire engines often respond when someone calls for an ambulance? Firefighters are trained to handle medical emergencies until an ambulance arrives.

① One fire engine carries 700 gallons of water.

How much is 100 gallons less than that?

_____ gallons

How much is 100 gallons more than that?   _____ gallons

② The aerial platform on this fire engine can be raised 100 feet.

How much is 10 feet less than that?   _____ feet

How much is 10 feet more than that?   _____ feet

③ A fire engine responded to 100 alarms in April.
It responded to 145 alarms in May.
How many times did it respond
in those two months?

_____ times

4 A fireboat pumped about
125 gallons of water in 1 second.
Record the number of hundreds,
tens, and ones in 125.

_____ hundred

_____ tens

_____ ones

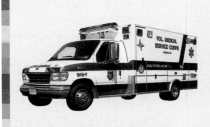
5 One fireboat is 134 feet long.
Another fireboat is 107 feet long.
Compare these two lengths.
Write >, <, or =.

134 ◯ 107

6 An all-weather lifeboat
responded to an alarm
at 10 minutes to 6.
What is another way
to write this time?

_____ : _____

7 Writing in Math

Write a number story about a fire engine.
Use four numbers between 400 and 600.
At the end of your story, list the numbers
in order from least to greatest.

Home Connection Your child learned how to solve problems by applying
his or her math skills. **Home Activity** Give your child some numbers, such as
136 or 247, and have them tell you the number of hundreds, tens, and ones.

Name _____

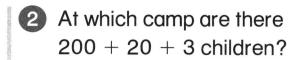
Use data from the chart to answer the two questions.

1 Are there more children at Camp A or Camp B?

_____

2 At which camp are there 200 + 20 + 3 children?

_____

Children at Camp	
Camp	**Number of Children**
A	220
B	223
C	105
D	33

Write the number that comes after.

3 438, _____   116, _____   795, _____

Write the number that comes between.

4 564, _____, 566   206, _____, 208   353, _____, 355

Write the numbers in order from greatest to least.

5 (815, 336, 306, 845, 363) _____, _____, _____, _____, _____

Write the missing numbers. Describe the pattern.

6 910, 810, 710, 610, _____, _____, _____

_____

7 135, 145, 155, 165, _____, _____, _____

_____

Mark the fraction that is green.

1

$\frac{2}{6}$ $\frac{1}{6}$ $\frac{4}{6}$ $\frac{1}{2}$
(A)   (B)   (C)   (D)

---

2 About how long would this take?

Ⓐ about 3 minutes

Ⓑ about 3 hours

Ⓒ about 3 days

Ⓓ about 3 months

---

3 Mark the number of children who like only spaghetti.

0   1   2   4
(A)   (B)   (C)   (D)

Likes Spaghetti   Likes Pizza

Pam
Ralph   Amy   Nora
Liz   Mike
Tim

Likes Both

---

4 What is the crayon's length?

about 2 inches   about 3 feet   about 3 inches   about 3 meters
(A)   (B)   (C)   (D)

Writing in Math

5 Color the spinner so that you are more likely to land on red than blue.

Chapter 10 ★ Section B

Name _____

Order on the Number Line

You can write numbers in order
if you locate them on the number line.

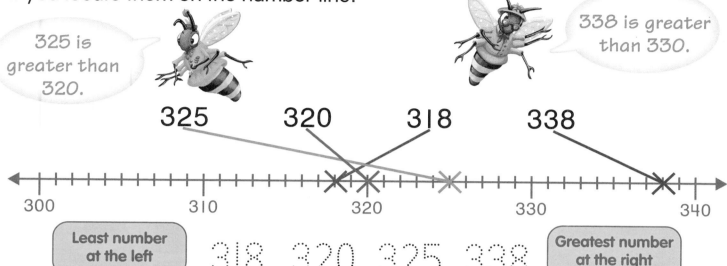

325 is greater than 320.

338 is greater than 330.

325   320   318   338

300   310   320   330   340

Least number at the left   318, 320, 325, 338   **Greatest number at the right**

Find these numbers on the number line.
Write them in order.

1 317, 302, 325, 335   _____, _____, _____, _____

2 304, 334, 324, 314   _____, _____, _____, _____

---

780   790   800   810   820

3 803, 790, 787, 807   _____, _____, _____, _____

4 791, 812, 792, 820   _____, _____, _____, _____

Writing in Math

5 How can you compare two numbers on a number line?

 Home Connection Your child located numbers on a number line and wrote them in order. **Home Activity** Ask your child to explain how he or she did Exercise 3.

Name _____

Find Patterns Using a Calculator

You can use a calculator to find patterns.

Press . Press the keys that you see below.

Write what the display shows each time you press .

1

Display: __50__ _____ _____

The pattern is count by __25s__.

2

Display: _____ _____ _____

The pattern is count by _____.

3

Display: _____ _____ _____

The pattern is count by _____.

4

Display: _____ _____ _____

The pattern is count by _____.

I like to look for patterns!

Think About It   Number Sense

In Exercise 4, what calculator key would you press to find the next number in the pattern?

 Home Connection Your child used a calculator to find patterns and to count by 25s, 50s, 100s, and 500s. **Home Activity** Ask your child to explain how he or she found the pattern in Exercise 3.

© Pearson Education, Inc.

Read Together

Use Writing in Math

Some math tests ask you to write your answer and explain your thinking. You can use words from the problem to help you do this.

Test-Taking Strategies
- Understand the Question
- Get Information for the Answer
- Plan How to Find the Answer
- Make Smart Choices
- **Use Writing in Math**

1 What number is 10 more than 370? How do you know?

380 is 10 more than 370. I know this

because 370 + 10 = 380.

The girl who solved this problem thought, "370 has 7 tens. So the answer has 8 tens. The answer is 380." Then she used words from the problem to help her write her answer.

Which words from the problem did she use? If you can find some of them, raise your hand.

Your Turn

Read and solve the problem. Then use words from the problem to help you write your answer.

I see some words I can use!

2 What number is 100 more than 589? How do you know?

_____

_____

_____

_____

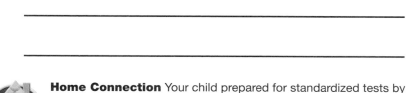

Home Connection Your child prepared for standardized tests by learning how to use words from a math problem to completely answer the question. **Home Activity** Have your child explain which words in Exercise 2 helped him or her solve the problem.

Name _____

Discover Math in Your World

 Read Together

Your Money at Work!

Why is it a good idea to put money in a bank? The bank pays you a small amount of money called **interest**.

When this happens, your money makes more money for you!

You Can Bank on It!

Miguel, Sara, and Philip are saving money for college.

1 Miguel had $375 in his savings account.
He **withdrew** $100. How much is in his account now? _____

2 Sara has $1,000 in her savings account.
Tom has $450 in his savings account.
Who has more money in the bank, Sara or Tom? _____

How much more? _____ more

3 Philip is **depositing** money in his account.
He gives the bank teller two $100 bills and
nine $10 bills. How much money is Phil depositing? _____

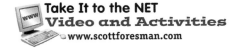 **Take It to the NET
Video and Activities**
www.scottforesman.com

 Home Connection Your child solved problems about saving money in a bank. **Home Activity** Ask your child to explain how he or she solved one of the problems on this page.

Name _____

Write how many. Use models if you need to.

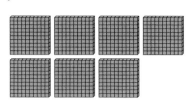

100 less is _____. _____ 100 more is _____.

Circle the models to match the expanded form.
Write the number in standard form.

$500 + 30 + 9$
five hundred thirty-nine

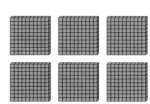 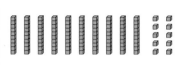 _____

Use models, drawings, or mental math to solve the problem.

$681 - 30 =$ _____

$681 - 300 =$ _____

Write the numbers in order from least to greatest.

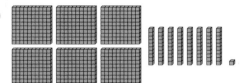 _____, _____, _____, _____, _____

Write the number. Use models and
Workmat 5 if you need to.

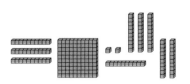

Hundreds	Tens	Ones

_____

Count on to solve.

6 Clay has 650 pennies. He needs
1,000 pennies. How many more
pennies does he need?

_____ pennies

Compare. Write >, <, or =.

7 350 ◯ 340   811 ◯ 811   672 ◯ 762

Write the number that comes before.

8 _____, 390   _____, 741   _____, 582

Write the number that comes after.

9 619, _____   400, _____   299, _____

Write the number that comes between.

10 100, _____, 102   509, _____, 511   998, _____, 1,000

Write the number that is 30 more.

11   407   813   956   260

    _____   _____   _____   _____

What pattern do you see? _____

Use data from the chart to answer the questions.

12 Write the number of fish in order
from least to greatest.

_____, _____, _____, _____

13 Are there more goldfish or more guppies?

_____

School Fish	
Fish	**Number**
Goldfish	177
Guppies	259
Neon tetras	128
Angelfish	163

Writing in Math

14 Write a story using data from the chart.
In your story, compare the number of goldfish
to the number of angelfish.

_____

_____

Name_____

Mark the related addition fact.

$$3 + 6 = 9$$

$3 + 3 = 6$	$6 + 3 = 9$	$9 - 3 = 6$	$4 + 5 = 9$
Ⓐ	Ⓑ	Ⓒ	Ⓓ

Mark the statement that is true.

②

$21 = 12$	$68 < 67$	$50 > 49$	$73 < 70$
Ⓐ	Ⓑ	Ⓒ	Ⓓ

$329 > 328$	$151 = 150$	$486 < 475$	$516 > 561$
Ⓐ	Ⓑ	Ⓒ	Ⓓ

Mark the total.

④

57¢	62¢	87¢	92¢
Ⓐ	Ⓑ	Ⓒ	Ⓓ

Mark the other part of 100.

⑤ **20 and _____ is 100.**

- Ⓐ 20
- Ⓑ 45
- Ⓒ 60
- Ⓓ 80

⑥ **65 and _____ is 100.**

- Ⓐ 25
- Ⓑ 35
- Ⓒ 40
- Ⓓ 45

⑦ **Which pair shows a flip?**

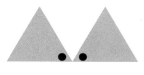   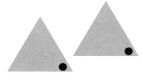 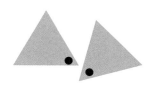

Ⓐ	Ⓑ	Ⓒ	Ⓓ

Add in any order.

8

24	45	62	21	3
15	35	17	43	27
+ 36	+ 10	+ 8	+ 29	+ 50

Subtract to find the difference.

9

52¢	68¢	79¢	81¢	37¢
− 41¢	− 39¢	− 25¢	− 53¢	− 16¢

Write the fraction for the shaded part.

10    **11**    **12**

____   ____   ____

Writing in Math

13 Circle the congruent shapes.
Tell why they are congruent.

_____

_____

14 Write the time on the digital clock.
Then write a story that tells about
what you might do at this time.

_____

_____

_____

CHAPTER 11

Addition and Subtraction of Three-Digit Numbers

Read Together

Who Has That Many Toothpicks?

Written by Mary Durkee
Illustrated by Jill Meyerhoff

This Math Storybook belongs to

____

11A

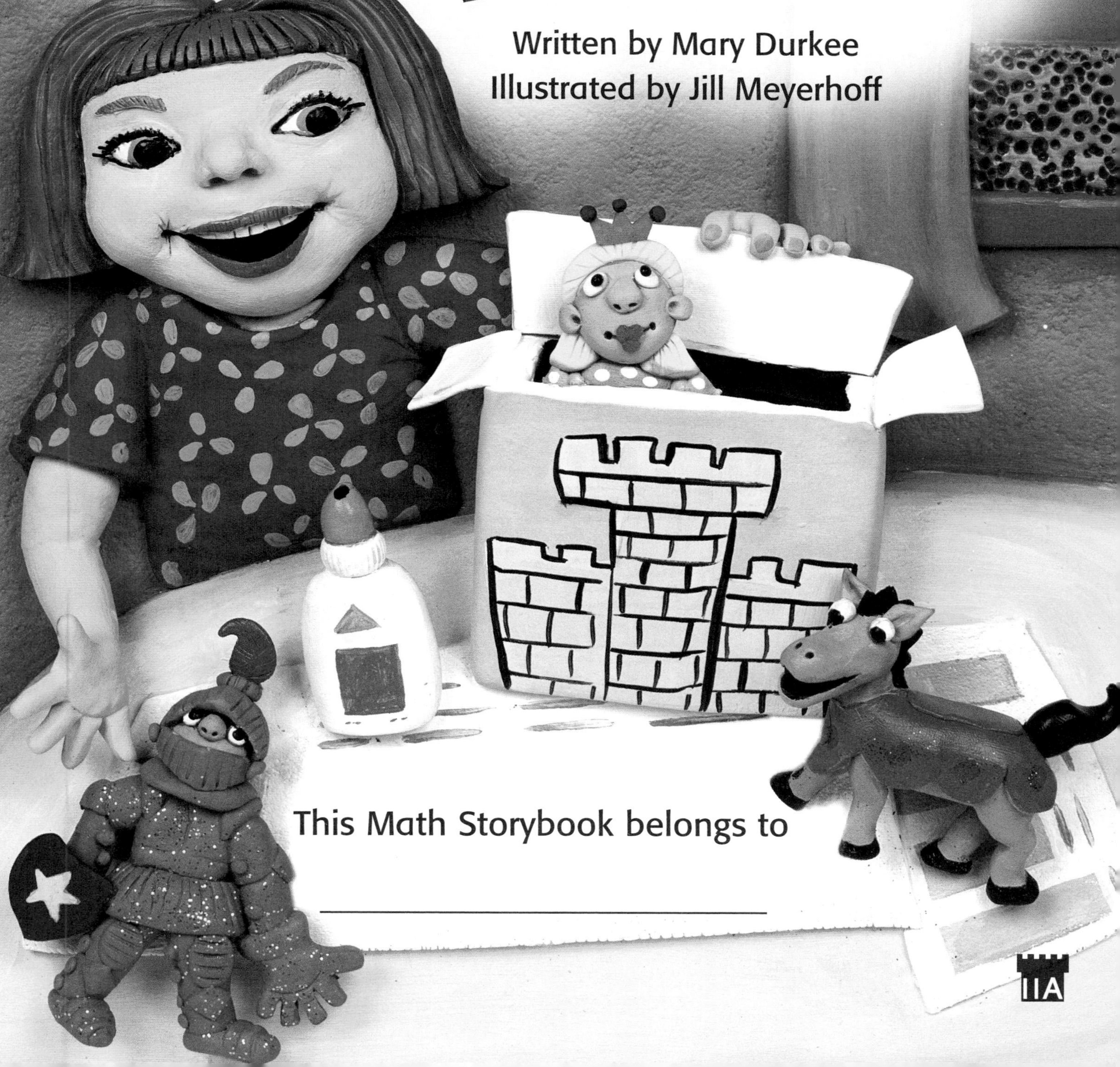

Becky opened her new castle-building kit.

The directions began like this:

You will need about 1,000 toothpicks.

"1,000 toothpicks!" thought Becky.
"Who has that many toothpicks?"

Becky looked on the kitchen shelf.
She found a box of toothpicks, but it wasn't full.

She counted them very carefully.
There were only **225**.

So Becky put them in an empty shoebox
and wrote **225** on the lid.

Then Becky asked her brother, the model airplane king,
if she could have some of his toothpicks.

Fortunately, her brother was feeling very generous that day.
He gave her two brand-new boxes.
Each box had **250** toothpicks in it.
Then he gave her **5** bundles of **25** each.

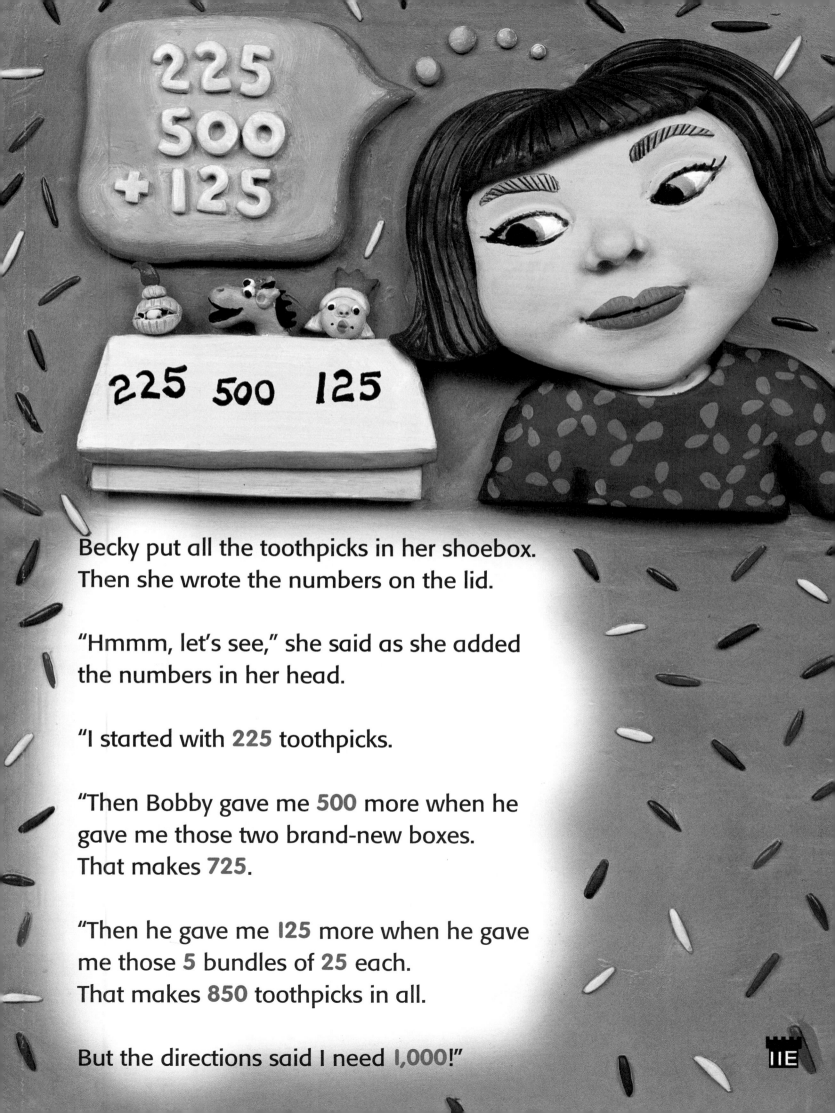

225
500
+ 125

225   500   125

Becky put all the toothpicks in her shoebox.
Then she wrote the numbers on the lid.

"Hmmm, let's see," she said as she added
the numbers in her head.

"I started with **225** toothpicks.

"Then Bobby gave me **500** more when he
gave me those two brand-new boxes.
That makes **725**.

"Then he gave me **125** more when he gave
me those **5** bundles of **25** each.
That makes **850** toothpicks in all.

But the directions said I need **1,000**!"

"1,000 what?" asked her grandpa.

"Toothpicks!" said Becky. "I have **850**, but I need **150** more!"

"Let's see," said Grandpa. "It says here that you need only **750** toothpicks to make the tower. But you should get **1,000** just to be on the safe side."

"Hooray!" said Becky. "That means that I already have **100** more than I need!"

"Then let's build that castle!" said Grandpa.

Dear Family,

Today my class started Chapter 11, **Addition and Subtraction of Three-Digit Numbers.** I will learn how to add and subtract numbers of this size mentally and on paper. I will also learn to estimate sums and differences. Here are some of the math words I will be learning and some things we can do to help me with my math.

Love,

_____

Math Activity to Do at Home

Number nine index cards from 100 to 900. Pick up a 300 card and say, "Help! My full name is 1,000. Part of me is missing! Where is my other part?" Your child then finds your missing part (in this case, 700) to put you back together.

Books to Read Together

Reading math stories reinforces concepts. Look for these titles in your local library:

The 500 Hats of Bartholomew Cubbins
By Dr. Seuss
(Random House, 1989)

So Many Cats!
By Beatrice Schenk de Regniers
(Houghton Mifflin, 1988)

Take It to the NET
More Activities
www.scottforesman.com

My New Math Words

estimate When it's a verb, you say something like this: "I estimate that the answer is about 400." When it's a noun, you say something like this: "My estimate is 400."

mental math It's often a good idea to use this problem-solving strategy when you're estimating and when you're working with numbers that end in one or more zeros or in 5.

regroup If you're adding 469 and 291, you need to regroup the 10 ones as 1 ten 0 ones. And then you need to regroup the 16 tens as 1 hundred 6 tens.

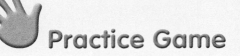

Sum Game!

What You Need

2 paper clips

2 different kinds of small
game markers

How to Play

1. Play with a partner. The first player places the 2 clips on 1 or 2 **addends** on the tower. If that player can find the **sum** of those 2 addends, he or she places a marker on it.

2. The second player moves **only 1** of the clips to a **new** addend. If that player can find the **sum** of those 2 addends, he or she places a marker on it.

3. Partners keep taking turns until one of them has 5 markers in a row, in a column, or on a diagonal.

ADDENDS

125
200
243
260
335
370
442

SUMS

503	884	460	777	460
325	250	705	685	595
520	400	495	578	812
670	486	443	630	385
368	740	613	567	702

To add **three-digit numbers** using mental math, begin with the hundreds.

4 hundreds + 2 hundreds is 6 hundreds.

$$467 + 231 = ?$$

1. Add the hundreds. $400 + 200 = \underline{600}$
2. Add the tens. $60 + 30 = \underline{90}$
3. Add the ones. $7 + 1 = \underline{8}$

so $467 + 231 = \underline{698}$

Word Bank

three-digit number

Check ✓

Add. Use mental math.

1. $236 + 312 = ?$

   ____ + ____ = ____
   ____ + ____ = ____
   ____ + ____ = ____   ____

2. $452 + 323 = ?$

   ____ + ____ = ____
   ____ + ____ = ____
   ____ + ____ = ____   ____

3. $745 + 124 = ?$

   ____ + ____ = ____
   ____ + ____ = ____
   ____ + ____ = ____   ____

Think About It   Number Sense

Find the sum of 324 and 415. Then find two different three-digit numbers with the same sum.

Solve. 620 + 159 = _____

$600 + 100 =$ ___
$20 + 50 =$ ___
$0 + 9 =$ ___

4 402 + 167 = _____

5 517 + 201 = _____   263 + 415 = _____

6 _____ = 714 + 180   305 + 602 = _____

7 _____ = 816 + 111   428 + 350 = _____

8 602 + 184 = _____   522 + 362 = _____

9 703 + 23 = _____   _____ = 425 + 262

10 504 + 205 = _____   421 + 475 = _____

11 222 + 555 = _____   _____ = 331 + 520

Problem Solving   Algebra

Write the missing number that makes
the number sentence true.

12 300 + 300 = 400 + *200*

13 500 + _____ = 400 + 400

14 _____ + 300 = 200 + 700

15 700 + 100 = 300 + _____

16 200 + 600 = _____ + 800

Home Connection Your child added three-digit numbers using
mental math. **Home Activity** Ask your child to explain how to
add 307 and 451, using mental math.

Estimating Sums

Learn!  Algebra

Is 376 + 435 more than or less than 700?
Estimate by adding the closest hundreds.

376 is almost 400.
435 is close to 400.
400 + 400 = 800. So 376 + 435 is __more than__ 700.

Is 121 + 567 more than or less than 750?
Estimate by adding the closest tens.

121 is almost 120.
567 is close to 570.
120 + 570 = 690. So 121 + 567 is __less than__ 750.

Word Bank

estimate

Check ✓

Is the sum more or less than the number given?
Estimate the sum. Then write **more than** or **less than.**

1 Is 279 + 127 more than or
less than 500?   _____ 500

2 Is 312 + 429 more than or
less than 650?   _____ 650

3 Is 417 + 421 more than or
less than 850?   _____ 850

Think About It Reasoning

How do you decide which ten or hundred a number
is closest to?

Is the sum more or less than the number?
Estimate the sum. Write **more than** or **less than.**

4 Is 531 + 284 more than or
less than 700?

_____ 700

5 Is 378 + 109 more than or
less than 550?

_____ 550

6 Is 427 + 214 more than or
less than 600?

_____ 600

7 Is 629 + 309 more than or
less than 950?

_____ 950

8 Is 430 + 299 more than or
less than 800?

_____ 800

9 Is 341 + 349 more than or
less than 700?

_____ 700

Problem Solving   Number Sense

Choose a pair of numbers to give the sum.
Use each number one time.

10 Sum of about 500   _____ and _____

11 Sum of more than 700   _____ and _____

12 Sum of less than 700   _____ and _____

Home Connection Your child estimated whether the sum of
two three-digit numbers was more or less than a given number.
Home Activity Have your child estimate whether the sum of
218 and 395 is more or less than 700.

Adding with Models

Second graders in the library book club read 463 books. Third graders read 275 books. How many books did they read altogether?

You can regroup 10 tens to make another hundred.

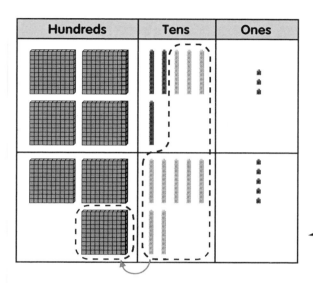

Hundreds	Tens	Ones

$463 + 275 = \underline{738}$

Word Bank

regroup

Check ✓

Use models and Workmat 5.
Show each number. Add to find the sum.

1 $241 + 185 = $ _____

2 $362 + 224 = $ _____

3 $154 + 236 = $ _____

4 _____ $= 670 + 248$

5 $452 + 520 = $ _____

6 _____ $= 350 + 350$

Think About It Number Sense

What do you do when you have 10 or more ones?
What do you do when you have 10 or more tens?

Use models and Workmat 5.
Show each number. Add to find the sum.

7 209 + 715 = _____

8 421 + 333 = _____

9 125 + 250 = _____

10 _____ = 362 + 298

11 600 + 245 = _____

12 _____ = 407 + 392

13 591 + 309 = _____

14 _____ = 777 + 222

Problem Solving   Estimation

Circle the best estimate.

15

Class	Pages Read This Week
Ms. Collins	428
Ms. Stallings	346

About how many pages were read this week?

750   900   600

16

Class	Pages Read This Week
Mr. Grant	204
Ms. Eve	197

About how many pages were read this week?

300   400   500

17 Susie read 2 chapter books last month.
They were both 124 pages.
About how many pages did she read?

150   250   400

 Home Connection Your child added three-digit numbers using models. **Home Activity** Ask your child to tell you how he or she solved Exercise 12, using hundreds, tens, and ones place-value models.

$425 + 137 = ?$

1. Add the ones. Regroup 10 ones as 1 ten.
2. Add the tens.
3. Add the hundreds.

Hundreds	Tens	Ones
☐	1	
4	2	5
+ 1	3	7
5	6	2

$578 + 351 = ?$

1. Add the ones.
2. Add the tens. Regroup 10 tens as 1 hundred.
3. Add the hundreds.

Hundreds	Tens	Ones
1	☐	
5	7	8
+ 3	5	1
9	2	9

Check ✓

Add. Use models and Workmat 5 if you need to.

1

Hundreds	Tens	Ones
☐	☐	
4	5	1
+ 2	9	6

Hundreds	Tens	Ones
☐	☐	
1	0	2
+ 3	5	1

Hundreds	Tens	Ones
☐	☐	
3	1	4
+ 5	4	8

2

Hundreds	Tens	Ones
☐	☐	
3	0	3
+ 4	5	7

Hundreds	Tens	Ones
☐	☐	
2	3	8
+ 1	1	9

Hundreds	Tens	Ones
☐	☐	
2	4	7
+ 1	6	1

Think About It   Reasoning

How do you know when to regroup?

Add. Use models and Workmat 5 if you need to.

3

Hundreds	Tens	Ones
☐	☐	
5	7	0
+ 2	9	3

Hundreds	Tens	Ones
☐	☐	
4	7	6
+ 3	7	2

Hundreds	Tens	Ones
☐	☐	
1	1	5
+ 6	3	7

4

Hundreds	Tens	Ones
☐	☐	
2	8	5
+ 1	3	2

Hundreds	Tens	Ones
☐	☐	
3	4	7
+ 2	2	7

Hundreds	Tens	Ones
☐	☐	
3	0	6
+ 4	7	1

5

$$\begin{array}{r} 415 \\ + 268 \\ \hline \end{array}$$
$$\begin{array}{r} 194 \\ + 532 \\ \hline \end{array}$$
$$\begin{array}{r} 58 \\ + 391 \\ \hline \end{array}$$
$$\begin{array}{r} 503 \\ + 96 \\ \hline \end{array}$$
$$\begin{array}{r} 356 \\ + 128 \\ \hline \end{array}$$

Problem Solving   Number Sense

For each problem, use each number in only one place.

1   3   4   6   7

6 Make the greatest sum.

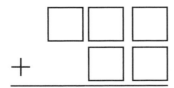

7 Make the least sum.

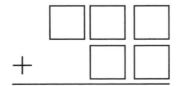

Home Connection Your child added three-digit numbers.
Home Activity Ask your child to show you how to add 218 and 356.

Name _____

245 + 391 = ?

Newspaper Deliveries	
Ted	245
Amanda	391

1 Write the problem.

2 Add. Regroup if needed.

How many newspapers were delivered altogether?

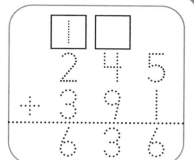

$$\begin{array}{r} 2\ 4\ 5 \\ +\ 3\ 9\ 1 \\ \hline 6\ 3\ 6 \end{array}$$

_636_ newspapers were delivered.

Check ✓

Write the addition problem. Find the sum.

1   519 + 343   183 + 624   235 + 227

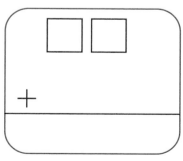 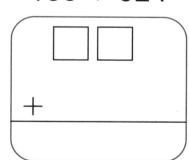 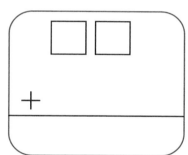

2   380 + 459   192 + 55   68 + 227

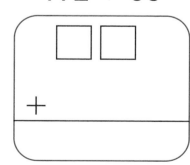 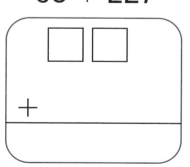

Think About It   Number Sense

How do you find the sum of 251, 102, and 345?

Write the addition problem. Find the sum.

3 620 + 289

$$\begin{array}{r} 620 \\ + 289 \\ \hline 909 \end{array}$$

491 + 243

738 + 55

4 269 + 400

175 + 53

97 + 342

5 205 + 715

263 + 91

556 + 362

Problem Solving   Number Sense

Solve the number riddle.

6 When I am added to 249, the sum is 659. What number am I? _____

7 When I am added to 382, the sum is 597. What number am I? _____

Home Connection Your child wrote and practiced adding three-digit numbers. **Home Activity** Have your child show you how he or she can add 413 and 369.

Understand Graphic Sources: Graphs

1 Look at the chalkboard and check the math.
Circle the problems that have mistakes.

Red Riding Hood

100	212	540
+ 600	+ 102	+ 23
800	314	593

Big Bad Wolf

622	732	569
+ 345	+ 111	+ 430
967	843	999

Grandma

267	623	400
+ 120	+ 105	+ 100
387	739	500

2 Look at the graph. Color a square
for each problem the character got **right**.

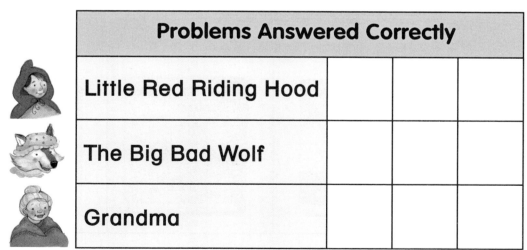

Problems Answered Correctly			
Little Red Riding Hood			
The Big Bad Wolf			
Grandma			

3 Who got the most right? _____

4 Who got the fewest right? _____

Think About It   Reasoning

Why is a graph helpful?

Little Red Riding Hood, the Big Bad Wolf, and Grandma
are characters in a storybook.

5 Make a graph about books.
Ask 6 classmates which one of the following
books they would most like to read.
Write the person's name in a box above that book.
Start with your own name!

	What I Would Most Like to Read		
7			
6			
5			
4			
3			
2			
1			
0			
World of the Dinosaurs	Best Jokes and Riddles	The Haunted Castle Mystery	Great Soccer Players

6 Which book did the most children want to read?

_____

Home Connection Your child used graphs to organize information.
Home Activity Create a graph showing each family member's favorite
meal (out of a choice of 3 or 4). If your family is small, you might help
your child call or e-mail a few relatives to solicit their choices.

Name _____

Make a Graph

Did the second grade sell more tickets to the school carnival than the first grade sold?

Classroom 2A sold 150 tickets.
Classroom 2B sold 250 tickets.

Read and Understand

You need to find out how many tickets the second grade sold.

Plan and Solve

First, add the number of tickets Classrooms 2A and 2B sold.

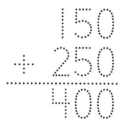

$$150 + 250 = 400$$

_400_ tickets

Then, add this information to the graph.

The second grade sold more tickets than the first grade.

Look Back and Check

How do you know just by looking at the graph that the second grade sold more tickets?

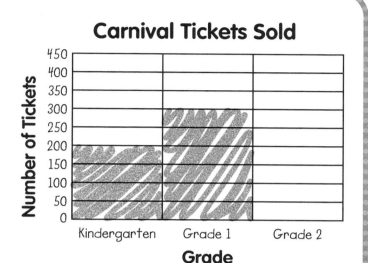

Carnival Tickets Sold

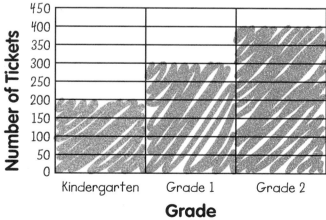

Carnival Tickets Sold

Think About It   Number Sense

Write the number of tickets sold in order from greatest to least.

Use the chart to answer
the questions.

People at the Carnival			
	Friday	Saturday	Sunday
Morning	100	350	250
Afternoon	150	450	400

1. How many people came
to the carnival on Friday?

   _____ people

2. How many came
on Saturday?

   _____ people

3. How many attended
on Sunday?

   _____ people

4. Use your answers from Exercises
1–3 to complete the graph.
Show how many people came
to the carnival each day.

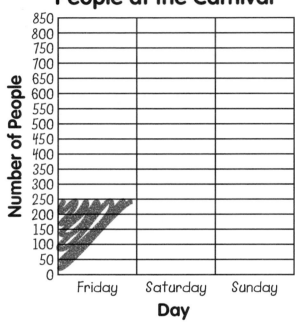

People at the Carnival

Problem Solving Writing in Math

5. Look at the graph. Tell which day the greatest number
of people came to the carnival and which day
the least number of people came.

   _____

   _____

6. Look at the graph and compare Saturday with Sunday.
How many more people needed to come to the carnival
on Sunday to equal the number of people who came
on Saturday?

   _____ more people

Home Connection Your child made graphs to solve problems.
Home Activity Ask your child to use the graph to determine
how many people in all came to the carnival on Friday and Sunday.

Name _____

Add. Use mental math.

1 651 + 238 = _____   402 + 457 = _____

2 115 + 563 = _____   _____ = 710 + 264

Is the sum more than or less than the number given?
Write **more than** or **less than**.

3 Is 382 + 107 more than
or less than 600?   _____ 600

Use models and Workmat 5.
Show each number. Add to find the sum.

4 183 + 725 = _____   **5** 216 + 357 = _____

Add. Use models and Workmat 5
if you need to.

Write the addition problem.
Find the sum.

6

Hundreds	Tens	Ones
☐	☐	
1	4	4
+ 2	9	0

7   538 + 426

Complete the graph.

8 Color the graph to show
that there are 150 books
about animals.

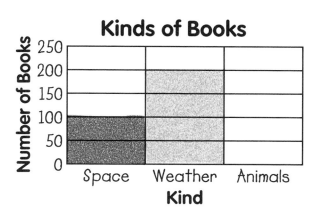

Kinds of Books

Add. Use mental math or cubes.

1

49 and

49 + 17 = ____

Ⓐ 56
Ⓑ 67
Ⓒ 87
Ⓓ 66

2

31 and

31 + 19 = ____

Ⓐ 50
Ⓑ 40
Ⓒ 49
Ⓓ 79

Count on to find the total amount.

3

Ⓐ 62¢
Ⓑ 72¢
Ⓒ 47¢
Ⓓ 80¢

Use the graph to answer the question.

4 How many children wear mittens?

8   7   22   14
Ⓐ   Ⓑ   Ⓒ   Ⓓ

Favorite Hand Warmers	
	웃웃웃웃웃웃웃
	웃웃웃웃

Each 웃 = 2 children.

Mark the one that weighs the most.

5

Ⓐ   Ⓑ   Ⓒ   Ⓓ

Writing in Math

6 Count on to solve the problem.   200 + ____ = 1,000
Write a story using the number sentence.

_____

_____

_____

 **Algebra**

You can count on
or count back to find
missing parts.

670	
460	210

$460 + $ ___?___ $ = 670$

Count on by 100s and 10s.

460 560 660 670
       100   100   10

Or, count back by 100s and 10s.

670 570 470 460
       100   100   10

$460 + 210 = 670$

Check ✓

Count on or count back to find the missing part.
Write the number.

1 $250 + $ _____ $ = 400$

400	
250	_____

2 $360 + $ _____ $ = 600$

600	
360	_____

3 _____ $ + 150 = 300$

300	
_____	150

4 $800 = $ _____ $ + 200$

800	
_____	200

Think About It   Number Sense

How are $4 + 3 = 7$, $40 + 30 = 70$, and $400 + 300 = 700$
the same and how are they different?

Count on or count back to find the missing part.

5 $120 + \underline{\hspace{1cm}} = 500$

6 $340 + \underline{\hspace{1cm}} = 400$

7 $410 + \underline{\hspace{1cm}} = 600$

8 $200 = 80 + \underline{\hspace{1cm}}$

9 $430 + \underline{\hspace{1cm}} = 800$

10 $300 = \underline{\hspace{1cm}} + 160$

11 $700 = \underline{\hspace{1cm}} + 250$

12 $\underline{\hspace{1cm}} + 450 = 900$

13 $500 = 150 + \underline{\hspace{1cm}}$

14 $290 + \underline{\hspace{1cm}} = 800$

Problem Solving Algebra

15 Which side of the scale is lighter, the left side or the right side?

_____

16 How many pounds should you add to the lighter side to balance the scale?

_____

17 Explain how $160 + \underline{\hspace{0.6cm}?\hspace{0.6cm}} = 400$ is like the picture.

_____

_____

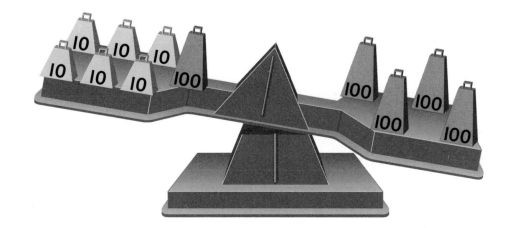

© Pearson Education, Inc.

Home Connection Your child counted on or counted back to find the missing part. **Home Activity** Have your child count on or count back to find the missing part: $250 + \underline{\hspace{1cm}} = 700$. The blank line stands for the amount needed to balance both sides.

Learn! Algebra

Which two numbers have a
difference of about 400? $705 - 193$ or $582 - 217$

Estimate by subtracting the closest hundreds.

$700 - 200 = 500$ $600 - 200 = 400$

$582 - 217$ is about 400.

705 is close to 700.
193 is about 200.

582 is close to 600.
217 is about 200.

Check ✓

Circle the problem that matches the estimate.

1 about 100 $(319 - 187)$ or $875 - 221$

2 about 500 $710 - 218$ or $602 - 369$

3 about 300 $494 - 302$ or $842 - 531$

Think About It   Number Sense

How would you decide which two numbers
have a difference of about 150? $457 - 301$ or $792 - 689$

Circle the problem that matches the estimate.

4 about 200   487 − 230   or   472 − 310

5 about 600   938 − 289   or   694 − 480

6 about 300   923 − 640   or   870 − 307

7 about 200   546 − 210   or   583 − 370

8 about 100   385 − 270   or   672 − 301

9 about 500   831 − 170   or   879 − 360

Problem Solving   Number Sense

Choose a pair of numbers to give the sum or difference.
Use each number one time.

10 Sum of about 500   _____ and _____

11 Difference of about 200   _____ and _____

12 Difference of less than 100 _____ and _____

Home Connection Your child estimated to decide which 2 three-digit numbers had a given difference. **Home Activity** Ask your child to estimate 689 − 207.

$427 - 183 = \underline{\quad ? \quad}$

Show 427 with models.

Take away 183 from 427. First, take away 3 ones.

①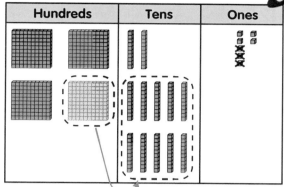

Hundreds	Tens	Ones

Next, regroup 1 hundred as 10 tens.

Then, take away 8 tens and 1 hundred.

②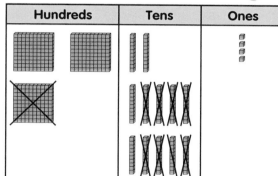

Hundreds	Tens	Ones

$427 - 183 = \underline{244}$

Check ✓

Use models and Workmat 5.
Subtract to find the difference.

① $536 - 174 = \underline{362}$

② $825 - 433 = \underline{\quad}$

③ $642 - 472 = \underline{\quad}$

④ $\underline{\quad} = 486 - 275$

⑤ $\underline{\quad} = 780 - 536$

⑥ $632 - 317 = \underline{\quad}$

Think About It   Number Sense

When you are subtracting and you need more tens,
what do you do?

Subtract. Use models and Workmat 5.

7 508 − 201 = _____

8 729 − 165 = _____

9 413 − 320 = _____

10 _____ = 914 − 652

11 520 − 304 = _____

12 _____ = 693 − 537

13 _____ = 954 − 245

14 881 − 510 = _____

15 391 − 241 = _____

16 _____ = 632 − 321

Problem Solving   Reasoning

17 Write the name of each person with his or her total votes.

Vote for Mayor

Mrs. Jones   Mr. Hare   Ms. Taylor   Mr. Niles

• Mr. Niles had about 200 more votes than Mrs. Jones.

• Ms. Taylor had the most votes.

• Mr. Hare had 100 fewer votes than Mrs. Jones.

_____   _____   _____   _____

610 votes   500 votes   305 votes   205 votes

Home Connection Your child used models to subtract three-digit numbers. **Home Activity** Have your child explain how to subtract 358 from 675.

$342 - 219 = ?$

1. To subtract the ones, regroup 1 ten as 10 ones.

2. Subtract the tens.

3. Subtract the hundreds.

Hundreds	Tens	Ones
[ ]	3	12
3	4	2
− 2	1	9
1	2	3

$458 - 276 = ?$

1. Subtract the ones.

2. To subtract the tens, regroup 1 hundred as 10 tens.

3. Subtract the hundreds.

Hundreds	Tens	Ones
3	15	[ ]
4	5	8
− 2	7	6
1	8	2

Check ✓

Subtract. Use models and Workmat 5 if you need to.

1.

Hundreds	Tens	Ones
[ ]	[ ]	[ ]
7	3	6
− 3	7	2

Hundreds	Tens	Ones
[ ]	[ ]	[ ]
5	6	0
− 1	2	7

Hundreds	Tens	Ones
[ ]	[ ]	[ ]
2	5	7
− 1	0	4

2.

Hundreds	Tens	Ones
[ ]	[ ]	[ ]
4	1	8
− 1	5	2

Hundreds	Tens	Ones
[ ]	[ ]	[ ]
3	2	5
− 2	0	4

Hundreds	Tens	Ones
[ ]	[ ]	[ ]
6	7	8
− 4	5	9

Think About It   Reasoning

Will you regroup to solve $597 - 452$? Why or why not?

Subtract. Use models and Workmat 5 if you need to.

3

Hundreds	Tens	Ones
□	□	□
8	6	5
− 4	9	1

Hundreds	Tens	Ones
□	□	□
5	4	7
− 1	6	0

Hundreds	Tens	Ones
□	□	□
4	3	6
−	8	2

4

Hundreds	Tens	Ones
□	□	□
3	7	2
− 1	3	6

Hundreds	Tens	Ones
□	□	□
8	3	0
− 4	1	5

Hundreds	Tens	Ones
□	□	□
9	1	8
− 3	6	1

5

$$927 - 207$$ $$445 - 380$$ $$526 - 173$$ $$682 - 247$$ $$334 - 106$$

Problem Solving   Visual Thinking

- The sum of each row is at the end of that row.

- The sum of each column is at the bottom of that column.

- Each square stands for the same number.

- Each circle stands for the same number.

6 What number is □ ? _____

7 What number is ◯ ? _____

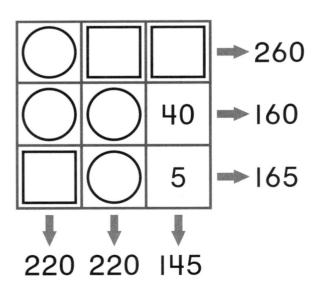

6 What number is □? _____

7 What number is ◯? _____

Home Connection Your child subtracted three-digit numbers.
Home Activity Have your child explain how to solve 758 − 319.

Practice with Three-Digit Subtraction

Lucy counted 716 footsteps around the playground.
Marcus counted 583 footsteps.
How many more footsteps did Lucy count?

$$\begin{array}{r} ^{6}\!\!\not7\;\;^{11}\!\!\not1\;\;6 \\ -\;5\;\;8\;\;3 \\ \hline 1\;3\;3 \end{array}$$

1. Write the problem.

2. Subtract.
   Regroup if needed.

133 more footsteps

Check ✓

Write the subtraction problem. Find the difference.

1   627 − 435   981 − 507   273 − 65

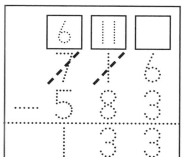   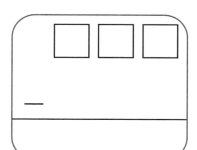   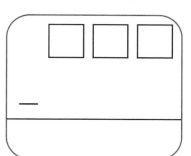

2   185 − 156   821 − 361   704 − 391

   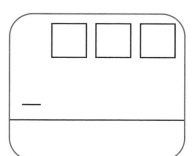   

Think About It   Reasoning

How do you think knowing that $125 + 150 = 275$
can help you solve $275 - 150 = ?$

Write the subtraction problem. Find the difference.

3 749 − 182

$$
\begin{array}{r}
^{6}\!\!\not7\,^{1}\!\!\not4\,9 \\
-\ 1\ 8\ 2 \\
\hline
5\ 6\ 7
\end{array}
$$

463 − 250

382 − 57

4 529 − 109

235 − 140

327 − 309

5 872 − 757

999 − 888

136 − 73

Problem Solving Estimation

Estimate each sum or difference.
Draw a line to match.

	Estimate
6 391 − 205	500
120 + 675	900
593 − 88	200
417 + 498	800

 Home Connection Your child practiced subtracting three-digit numbers.
Home Activity Have your child show you how he or she can subtract
144 from 372.

Exact Answer or Estimate?

Name _____

Alma saw this sign in the gym:

She wondered if all of the first grade and second grade children could fit.

Does she need an exact answer? Can she estimate?

Since she is only wondering, she can estimate.

Capacity

400

Each number is less than 200. So 180 + 171 is less than 400.

Grade	Number of Children
1	180
2	171

Check ✓

Circle **estimate** or **exact answer**. Answer the question.

1 The second grade children collected 152 food labels in January. They collected 194 food labels in February. They need 350 labels. Do they have enough?

estimate   exact answer

_____

Think About It   Reasoning

How do you know when to solve for an exact answer, and when to estimate?

Circle **estimate** or **exact answer.**
Answer the questions.

2 Cory has 112 stamps from the
United States. He has 139 stamps
from other countries. He can fit
275 stamps in a book. Will all of
the stamps fit?

estimate   exact answer

©1990 USPS

_____

3 There are 624 children at Smith
School. About 400 eat school
lunch. About how many children
do not eat the school lunch?

estimate   exact answer

_____

4 Jon's uncle drove his truck
498 miles one day and
375 miles the next day.
About how many miles did he
drive in two days?

estimate   exact answer

_____

Problem Solving Writing in Math

5 Write a math problem in which only an estimate
is needed for the answer.

_____

_____

_____

Home Connection Your child distinguished between problems
needing an exact answer and problems needing only an estimate.
Home Activity Ask your child to explain what an estimate is.

Name_____

Dorling Kindersley

Do You Know...

that a tarantula has 8 legs? And if a leg is lost, it will grow back in about 7 years!

1 This tree frog climbed 120 feet down to the forest floor. Later, it climbed 140 feet back up into a tree. How many feet did it climb altogether?

_____ feet

2 This Blue-and-yellow Macaw flew to a branch that was 102 feet high. Then it flew 100 feet higher than that. How high did it fly in all?

_____ feet

3 Leaf cutter ants live in underground nests. They travel high into the trees to gather leaves. A group of leaf cutter ants left their nest at 8:00 A.M. The ants started crawling up a tall tree 2 hours later. What time was it when the ants started crawling?

_____:_____ A.M.

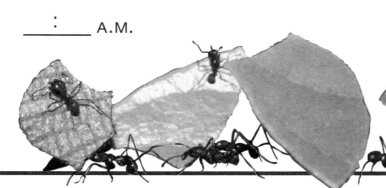

4 A toucan perched on a branch that was 95 feet high.
It flew 20 feet higher to another branch.
Then it flew 30 feet higher to a third branch.
How high was the third branch?

_____ feet

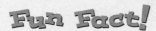

5 A male gorilla can weigh up to 600 pounds.
A female gorilla can weigh up to 300 pounds.
How many more pounds can a male weigh?

_____ more pounds

Fun Fact!

The flying tree snake can flatten its body and glide through the air. It can travel distances up to 165 feet!

6 **Writing in Math**

Write an addition story about flying tree snakes. Use three-digit numbers.

© Pearson Education, Inc.

Name _____

Add on to find the missing part.
Write the number.

1 170 + _____ = 440

440	
170	_____

Count on or count back to find the
missing part. Write the number.

2 90 + _____ = 400

3 500 = _____ + 130

Subtract. Use models and
Workmat 5 if you need to.

 4

Hundreds	Tens	Ones
□	□	□
8	1	7
− 2	5	2

Write the subtraction problem.
Find the difference.

5 964 − 73

Circle the problem that matches the estimate.

6

about 250   564 − 320   or   714 − 193

Circle **estimate** or **exact answer.**
Answer the question.

7 For the school bake sale, the third grade
baked 289 cookies. The first grade baked
112 cookies. 500 cookies are needed
for the sale. Are there enough?

_____

estimate   exact answer

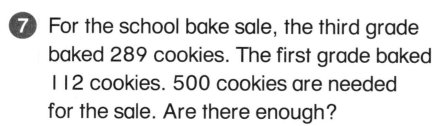

Name _____

Add to find the total amount.

1   71¢
      + 19¢

(A) 90
(B) 80¢
(C) 89
(D) 90¢

2   36¢
      + 25¢

(A) 51¢
(B) 61¢
(C) 62¢
(D) 61

Subtract. Regroup if you need to.

3

Tens	Ones
□	□
8	4
	7

(A) 91
(B) 77
(C) 89
(D) 87

4

Tens	Ones
□	□
6	9
	5

(A) 64
(B) 74
(C) 63
(D) 614

Mark the time that matches the clock face.

5

(A) 1:20
(B) 4:05
(C) 4:20
(D) 9:00

6

(A) 9:30
(B) 9:00
(C) 8:00
(D) 8:30

Mark the length of the marker.

7

CENTIMETERS

(A) 13 cm
(B) 12 cm
(C) 14 cm
(D) 11 cm

8 **Writing in Math**

Write a subtraction story for this problem: **57 – 24**

_____

_____

© Pearson Education, Inc.

 **Enrichment**

Adding and Subtracting Dollars and Cents

Tad's sister Sara earned $5.75 and
$2.40 babysitting. She spent $3.30.

How much did Sara earn?

How much does she have now?

$$\begin{array}{r} \$5.75 \\ +\ \$2.40 \\ \hline \$8.15 \end{array}$$

$$\begin{array}{r} 575¢ \\ +\ 240¢ \end{array}$$

$$\begin{array}{r} 815¢ \\ -\ 330¢ \end{array}$$

$$\begin{array}{r} \$8.15 \\ -\ \$3.30 \\ \hline \$4.85 \end{array}$$

Add or subtract.

1

$$\begin{array}{r} \$1.45 \\ +\ \$2.00 \end{array} \qquad \begin{array}{r} \$1.45 \\ +\ \$2.19 \end{array} \qquad \begin{array}{r} \$7.86 \\ -\ \$2.00 \end{array} \qquad \begin{array}{r} \$2.70 \\ +\ \$4.30 \end{array} \qquad \begin{array}{r} \$5.67 \\ -\ \$1.62 \end{array}$$

2

$$\begin{array}{r} \$3.64 \\ +\ \$3.18 \end{array} \qquad \begin{array}{r} \$2.94 \\ -\ \$2.37 \end{array} \qquad \begin{array}{r} \$4.65 \\ +\ \$0.93 \end{array} \qquad \begin{array}{r} \$6.09 \\ -\ \$4.89 \end{array} \qquad \begin{array}{r} \$0.38 \\ +\ \$1.91 \end{array}$$

3

$$\begin{array}{r} \$5.87 \\ -\ \$1.07 \end{array} \qquad \begin{array}{r} \$5.87 \\ -\ \$2.39 \end{array} \qquad \begin{array}{r} \$5.87 \\ -\ \$2.90 \end{array} \qquad \begin{array}{r} \$5.87 \\ -\ \$3.48 \end{array} \qquad \begin{array}{r} \$5.87 \\ -\ \$4.91 \end{array}$$

Writing in Math

4 Before you subtract in Exercise 3, what do you
know about your answers? Why?

 Home Connection Your child added and subtracted
amounts of money. **Home Activity** Ask your child to
add $2.89 to $4.50 and then subtract $1.07 from $4.50.

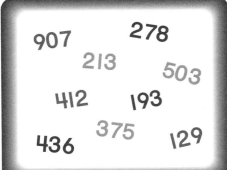

Add and Subtract Three-Digit Numbers Using a Calculator

You can use a calculator to add and subtract three-digit numbers.

Solve each problem. Use your calculator and the numbers in the box.
Press ON/C each time you begin.

907   278
213   503
412   193
375
436   129

1 Find the sum of all of the numbers with a 4 in the hundreds place.   848

2 Subtract the least number from the greatest number.   _____

3 Find the sum of all of the numbers with a 7 in the tens place.   _____

Solve each problem. Do **not** use your calculator for Exercise 4. Use your calculator for Exercise 5.

4 **Estimate** the sum of all of the numbers with a 3 in the ones place.   _____

5 Find the exact sum of all the numbers with a 3 in the ones place.   _____

Think About It   Number Sense

In Exercises 4 and 5, how would you use a calculator to find the difference between your estimated sum and the actual sum?

Home Connection Your child used a calculator to add and subtract three-digit numbers. **Home Activity** Ask your child to explain how he or she used a calculator to find the sum in Exercise 3.

© Pearson Education, Inc.

Name _____

Understand the Question

If you turn a question into a statement, it can help you solve a math problem.

Test-Taking Strategies

Understand the Question

Get Information for the Answer

Plan How to Find the Answer

Make Smart Choices

Use Writing in Math

1. On Friday, 243 people attended the school play. On Saturday, 318 people attended the school play. How many people in all attended the school play?

   Ⓐ 561 people   Ⓒ 574 people

   Ⓑ 575 people   Ⓓ 675 people

First, change the question into a statement:

I need to find how many people in all attended the school play.

Then add to find the answer.

Finally, fill in the answer bubble.

Your Turn

Change the question into a statement.
Solve the problem. Fill in the answer bubble.

2. How many more people attended the play on Saturday than on Friday?

   Ⓐ 65 more people   Ⓒ 75 more people

   Ⓑ 165 more people   Ⓓ 175 more people

Let me see...

 Home Connection Your child prepared for standardized tests by turning a question into a statement to help solve a problem.
Home Activity Ask your child to tell you the statement he or she used to help solve Exercise 2.

Name _____

Big, Bigger, Biggest!

The pyramids in Egypt have been standing for nearly 5,000 years. The biggest one is the **Great Pyramid.** Two smaller ones are named **Menkaure** and **Khafre.** Use addition and subtraction to learn more about these world-famous pyramids.

Powerful Pyramids

1 Menkaure is 216 feet tall.
Khafre is 230 feet taller than that.
How tall is Khafre?

_____ feet tall

2 A long time ago, The Great Pyramid was 481 feet tall. Today it is about 452 feet tall. How many feet shorter is the Great Pyramid now?

About _____ feet shorter

3 The base of each pyramid is a square. One side of Menkaure is 346 feet long. One side of the Great Pyramid is 756 feet long. Find the difference between these two lengths.

_____ feet

Home Connection Your child solved problems about the pyramids in Egypt by adding and subtracting. **Home Activity** Ask your child to estimate whether the perimeter of Menkaure is more than or less than 1,000 feet. *(More than 1,000 feet)*

Chapter Test

Add. Use mental math.

1 531 + 258 = _____

2 702 + 165 = _____

Use models and Workmat 5.
Show each number. Add to find the sum.

3 356 + 172 = _____

4 194 + 222 = _____

Add or subtract. Use models and Workmat 5 if you need to.

5

Hundreds	Tens	Ones
☐	☐	
5	9	4
+ 2	3	5

6

Hundreds	Tens	Ones
☐	☐	☐
9	4	3
− 4	6	1

7

Hundreds	Tens	Ones
☐	☐	☐
4	7	6
−	3	8

Is the sum more than or less than the number?
Estimate the sum. Write **more than** or **less than.**

8 Is 211 + 638 more than or
less than 700?

_____ 700

Complete the graph.

9 There are 200 more homes on
3rd Street than on 1st Street. How
many homes are on 3rd Street?

_____ homes

10 Color the graph to show the
number of homes on 3rd Street.

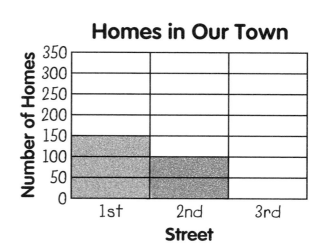

Homes in Our Town

Add on to find the missing part.
Write the number.

 280 + _____ = 660

660	
280	_____

Count on or count back to find the missing part. Write the number.

 90 + _____ = 300

Write the addition or subtraction problem.
Find the sum or the difference.

  634 + 257

(14) 444 + 81

(15) 907 − 726

Circle the problem that matches the estimate.

 about 400   492 − 250   or   921 − 473

Circle **estimate** or **exact answer.**
Answer the question.

(17) Sari spent 187 minutes working on homework last week. She spent 207 minutes this week. How many more minutes did she spend on homework this week?

_____

estimate   exact answer

464   four hundred sixty-four

Goldilocks and the Three Bears Part 2: The Untold Story

Written by Gene Howard   Illustrated by Maryn Roos

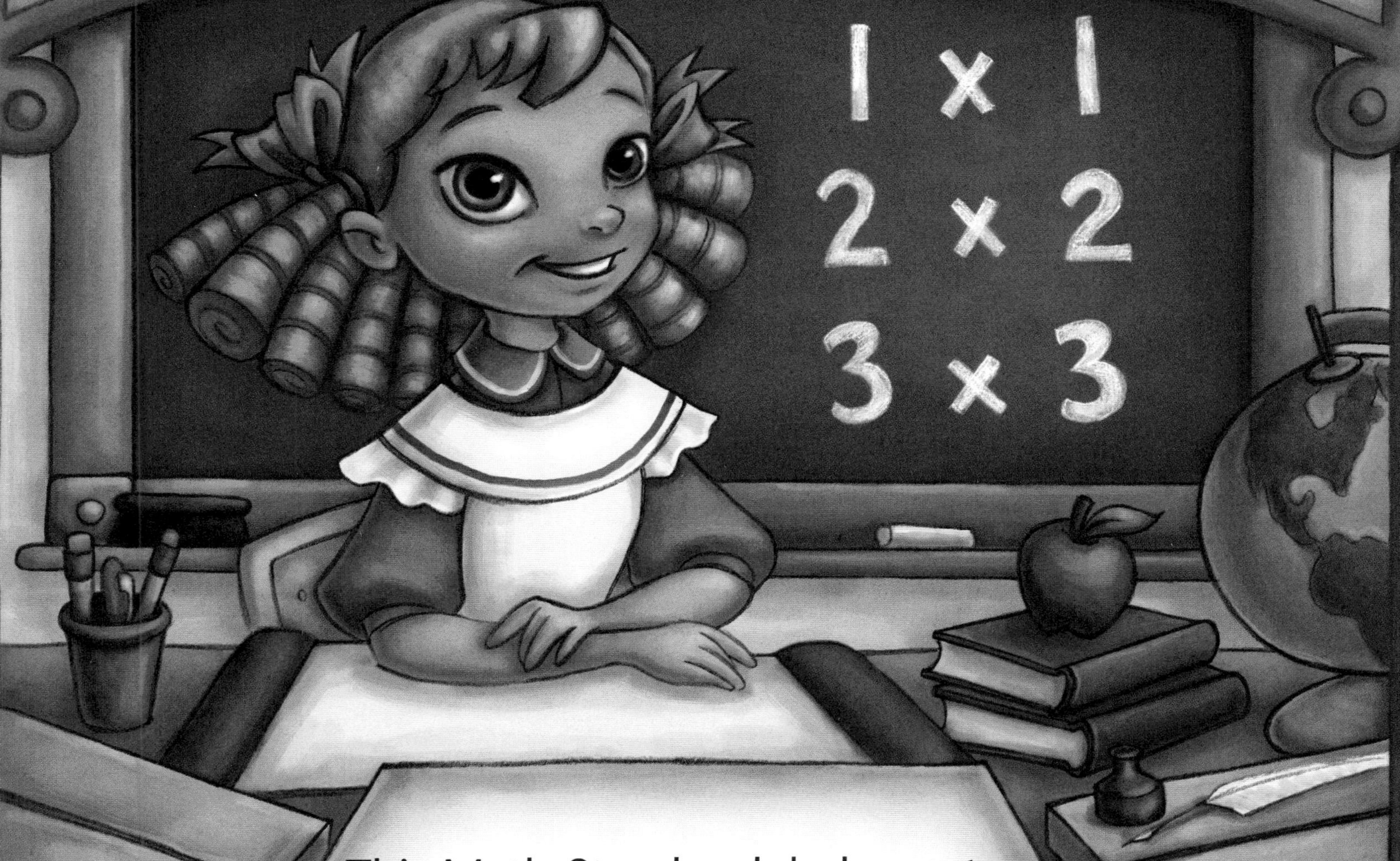

1×1

2×2

3×3

This Math Storybook belongs to

_____

Most people know **Part 1** of the Goldilocks story.

How she ate all of Baby Bear's porridge.
How she broke his chair.
How she fell asleep on his bed.

And how when Baby Bear and his mom and dad found
her there, she had to run all the way back home.

Well, that was not the end of the story.

When Goldilocks got home,
her mom found out what she had done.
And her mom said that she had to do
something nice for the Bear family
to make up for all the trouble she had caused them.

So Goldilocks, who was very good at math, said,
"I know! I will teach Baby Bear and his cousins,
Rodney and Alexis, how to do multiplication!"

"I am a good little girl, and I will be an
excellent teacher," she said.

Goldilocks decided that she needed to take a nap.

In her own house, and in her own bed, this time.

Home-School Connection

Dear Family,

Today my class started Chapter 12, **Understanding Multiplication and Division.** I will learn how to understand these operations and how to write multiplication and division sentences. Here are some of the math words I will be learning and some things we can do to help me with my math.

Love,

_____

Math Activity to Do at Home

Use bottle caps or other small objects to build equal groups—for example, 3 groups of 3 bottle caps each. Add them: 3 + 3 + 3 = 9. Skip count them: 3, 6, 9. Combine the equal groups into one larger group. Then separate the larger group into smaller, equal groups again.

Books to Read Together

Reading math stories reinforces concepts. Look for these titles in your local library:

What Comes in 2's, 3's, & 4's?
By Suzanne Aker (Simon & Schuster, 1992)

Where the Sidewalk Ends: 25th Anniversary Edition
By Shel Silverstein (HarperCollins, 2000)

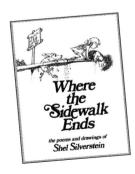

Take It to the NET
More Activities
www.scottforesman.com

My New Math Words

multiply When two numbers are multiplied, the answer is called the product.

$3 \times 3 = 9$ ⟵ **product**

$$\begin{array}{r} 3 \\ \times\ 3 \\ \hline 9 \end{array}$$

A 3-by-3 array that illustrates the multiplication fact $3 \times 3 = 9$

divide When one number is divided into another number, the answer is called the quotient.

$9 \div 3 = 3$

quotient

9 divided into 3 equal groups

Multiplication Pathways

How to Play

1. Play with a partner. Place your markers on START.

2. Toss the cube. Place a marker on the cottage that shows **that number being multiplied by itself.**

3. Read the problem on the cottage. Count the dots to find the answer.

4. Take turns. The first player to cover all five cottages gets to take a nap in the last one!

5. BONUS ACTIVITY: On a separate sheet of paper, draw pictures that show 6×6, 7×7, 8×8, 9×9, and 10×10.

© Pearson Education, Inc.

Name _____

Learn! Algebra

You can skip count to find how many basketballs there are in all.

Count by 2s to find how many in all. 2, 4, 6, 8.

4 groups   2 in each **equal group**   ____ in all

Word Bank

equal group

Check ✓

Use counters to show equal groups.
Skip count to find how many there are in all.

1 3 groups, 5 in each group

_____ in all

2 6 groups, 2 in each group

_____ in all

3 2 groups, 4 in each group

_____ in all

4 5 groups, 2 in each group

_____ in all

Think About It   Number Sense

How many groups of whistles are shown here?
How many whistles are in each group?

Draw to show equal groups. Skip count to find
how many there are in all. Use counters if you need to.

5 3 groups, 3 in each group

_____ in all

6 4 groups, 1 in each group

_____ in all

7 5 groups, 2 in each group

_____ in all

8 3 groups, 5 in each group

_____ in all

Problem Solving *Writing in Math*

Make up your own equal groups.
Skip count to find how many in all.

9 _____ groups,

_____ in each group

_____ in all

10 _____ groups,

_____ in each group

_____ in all

Home Connection Your child made equal groups of objects and skip
counted to find how many in all. **Home Activity** Have your child use
common household objects to show you how to make equal groups.

Name _____

Learn! Algebra

When you have equal groups, you can add or **multiply** to find how many objects there are in all.

There are 3 groups of 4.

Add.

This is the addition sentence.

$$\underline{}4\underline{} + \underline{}4\underline{} + \underline{}4\underline{} = \underline{}12\underline{}$$

3 groups of 4 is 12.

Multiply.

This is the **multiplication sentence**.

$$\underline{}3\underline{} \times \underline{}4\underline{} = \underline{}12\underline{}$$

3 **times** 4 is 12.
The **product** is 12.

Word Bank

multiply
multiplication sentence
times ($\times$)
product

Check ✓

Write an addition sentence and a multiplication sentence that tell how many objects there are in all.

1

___ + ___ + ___ = ___

___ × ___ = ___

2

___ + ___ + ___ + ___ = ___

___ × ___ = ___

3

___ + ___ + ___ + ___ = ___

___ × ___ = ___

4

___ + ___ + ___ = ___

___ × ___ = ___

Think About It   Reasoning

Can you write a multiplication sentence for all three of these groups? Why or why not?

Write an addition sentence and a multiplication sentence
that tell how many there are in all.

5

___ + ___ = ___

___ × ___ = ___

6

___ + ___ = ___

___ × ___ = ___

7

___ + ___ + ___ + ___ = ___

___ × ___ = ___

8

___ + ___ + ___ = ___

___ × ___ = ___

9

___ + ___ + ___ + ___ + ___ = ___

___ × ___ = ___

Problem Solving   Number Sense

Find the sums. Find the products.
Then match addition sentences to multiplication sentences.

10 $2 + 2 + 2 + 2 + 2 =$ __10__

$4 + 4 =$ ___

$6 + 6 + 6 =$ ___

$3 + 3 + 3 + 3 =$ ___

$2 × 4 =$ ___

$3 × 6 =$ ___

$5 × 2 =$ __10__

$4 × 3 =$ ___

Home Connection Your child wrote an addition sentence
and a multiplication sentence to tell how many there are in all.
Home Activity Ask your child to explain how $2 + 2 + 2 = 6$
and $3 × 2 = 6$ are related.

#

A collection of equal groups arranged in rows and columns is called an **array**.

5 and 3 are called **factors**.

5 rows

3 in each row

$5 \times 3 = \underline{15}$

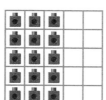

5 rows of 3 is 15.

Word Bank

array

factor

Check ✓

Use cubes to make the arrays.
Color to show your rows.
Write the multiplication sentence.

1 4 rows
4 in each row

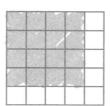

$\underline{4} \times \underline{4} = \underline{16}$

2 2 rows
5 in each row

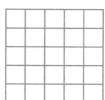

$\underline{} \times \underline{} = \underline{}$

3 5 rows
4 in each row

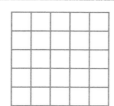

$\underline{} \times \underline{} = \underline{}$

4 1 row
4 in that row

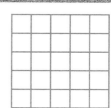

$\underline{} \times \underline{} = \underline{}$

Think About It Reasoning

How are these groups alike?

 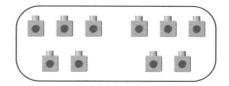

Write a multiplication sentence to describe the array.

5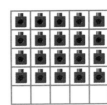

__4__ × __5__ = __20__

rows   in each row   in all

6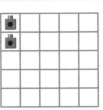

____ × ____ = ____

7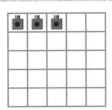

____ × ____ = ____

8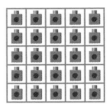

____ × ____ = ____

9

____ × ____ = ____

10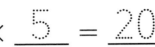

____ × ____ = ____

Problem Solving   Visual Thinking

11 Three second graders drew plans for the school garden. What is the same about each plan?

_____

_____

_____

_____

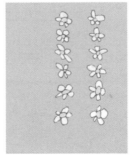
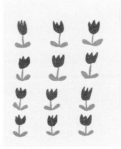

Home Connection Your child made arrays to model multiplication sentences. **Home Activity** Have your child show you an array of 2 rows with 6 objects in each row.

 **Algebra**

You can multiply numbers in any order. The product will be the same.

$2 \times 5 = 10$
$5 \times 2 = 10$

_2_ rows
_5_ in each row

_2_ × _5_ = _10_

_5_ rows
_2_ in each row

_5_ × _2_ = _10_

Check

Write the numbers. Multiply to find the product.

1

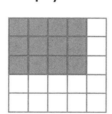

_____ rows

_____ in each row

____ × ____ = ____

_____ rows

_____ in each row

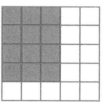

____ × ____ = ____

Think About It   Number Sense

Change the order of the numbers being multiplied in the multiplication sentence. What is the new multiplication sentence? How will the array change?

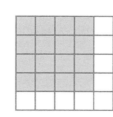

$4 \times 4 = 16$

Write the numbers. Multiply to find the product.

 2

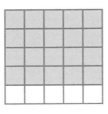

_____ rows

_____ in each row

____ × ____ = ____

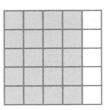

_____ rows

_____ in each row

____ × ____ = ____

 3

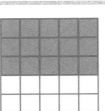

_____ rows

_____ in each row

____ × ____ = ____

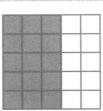

_____ rows

_____ in each row

____ × ____ = ____

 4

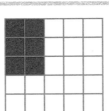

_____ rows

_____ in each row

____ × ____ = ____

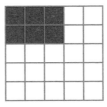

_____ rows

_____ in each row

____ × ____ = ____

Problem Solving **Algebra**

Complete the number sentences.

5

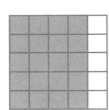

5 × ____ = 20

5 × ____ = 25

6

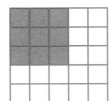

3 × ____ = 9

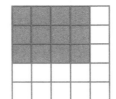

3 × ____ = 12

Home Connection Your child multiplied numbers in any order to get the same product. **Home Activity** Ask your child to use drawings or objects to show that 4 × 5 = 20 and that 5 × 4 = 20.

You can multiply across or down.
A **vertical** problem is down.

There are 2 rows
of 3 bananas.

how many in each group

$$2 \times 3 = 6$$

3
$\times 2$
6

how many groups

Word Bank

vertical

Check ✓

Multiply across and down.

1 2 rows of 4

$2 \times 4 = $ ____

4
$\times 2$

2 3 groups of 5

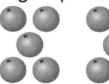

$3 \times 5 = $ ____

5
$\times 3$

3 4 groups of 4

$4 \times 4 = $ ____

4
$\times 4$

4 4 rows of 5

$4 \times 5 = $ ____

5
$\times 4$

Think About It   Number Sense

Look at these multiplication problems.
Why are the products the same?

3
$\times 4$
12

4
$\times 3$
12

Multiply across and down.

5

___4___ × ___5___ = ___20___

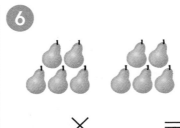

6

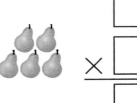

___ × ___ = ___

7

___ × ___ = ___

8

___ × ___ = ___

9

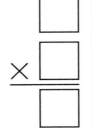

___ × ___ = ___

10

___ × ___ = ___

Problem Solving Reasoning

11   Draw what comes next. Write the multiplication sentence. Describe the pattern.

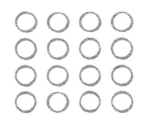  

$2 \times 2 = 4$ $3 \times 3 = 9$ $4 \times 4 = 16$ _____

_____

_____

_____

Home Connection Your child solved multiplication problems across and down. **Home Activity** Have your child show you another way to multiply 2×3.

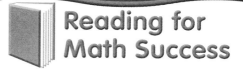

Understand Graphic Sources: Pictures

1 Mrs. Murphy's class is going on a picture hunt.
Each team must find a picture that has at least 10 things with wheels. Can you find 10 things with wheels in this picture?

_____ cars

_____ taxis

_____ buses

_____ bicycle

_____ trucks

_____ cart

_____ **things with wheels**

2 Can you find the one-way street?

Think About It   Number Sense

How much is $5 + 5 + 5 + 5 + 5 + 5$? _____

How do you know?

3 What a mess! Help the vendor put the apples back into the crate. Put an **X** on one of the apples on the ground. Then draw an apple in one of the spaces in the crate. Keep doing this until you have put all of the apples back where they belong.

4 How many rows of apples are there? _____ rows

5 How many apples are in each row? _____ apples

6 How many apples are there altogether? _____ apples

7 Write a number sentence that shows this.

Draw a Picture

Name _____

Learn! Algebra

Read and Understand

There are 3 houses on Lake Street.
Each house has 5 windows.
How many windows are there in all?

Plan and Solve

Draw a picture. Then write a
number sentence and solve.

3 × 5 = 15
windows

$$\underline{} \times \underline{} = \underline{} \text{ windows}$$

$$\underset{\text{number}}{\underline{3}} \times \underset{\text{number}}{\underline{5}} = \underline{15}$$

number   number
of houses   of windows

Look Back and Check

Is your answer reasonable? Explain.

Check ✓

Draw a picture to solve each problem.
Then write the multiplication sentence.

1   There are 4 tables. Each table has
    5 plates. How many plates are
    there in all?

    _____ × _____ = _____ plates

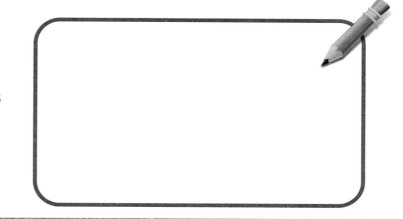

Think About It   Reasoning

Sammy drew 5 tables. Each table had
4 plates. Was he correct?

Practice

Draw a picture to solve each problem.
Then write a multiplication sentence.

2 Benito saw 3 wagons. Each wagon had 4 wheels. How many wheels did Benito see?

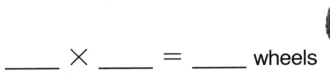

_____ × _____ = _____ wheels

3 Erin has 5 bags. Each bag has 4 pretzels. How many pretzels are there in all?

_____ × _____ = _____ pretzels

4 Nikko saw a plant with 4 leaves. Each leaf had 4 bugs. How many bugs were there?

_____ × _____ = _____ bugs

Estimation

5 The art table has 6 cups on it. There are 5 paintbrushes in each cup. Are there more or fewer than 20 brushes? Explain.

_____

_____

_____

_____

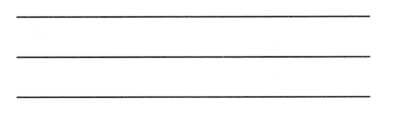

Home Connection Your child drew a picture to solve a problem.
Home Activity Ask your child to draw a picture to help solve this problem: *There are 3 plants with 3 leaves each. How many leaves are there in all?* Then have your child write a multiplication sentence.

Name _____

Draw to show equal groups. Skip count to find how many in all.

1 2 groups, 3 in each group

2 4 groups, 4 in each group

_____ in all

_____ in all

Write an addition sentence and a multiplication sentence
that tell how many objects there are in all.

3

4

____ + ____ + ____ + ____ = ____

____ × ____ = ____

____ + ____ = ____

____ × ____ = ____

Write the number of rows and the number in each row.
Write a multiplication sentence to describe each array.

5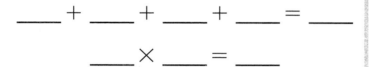

_____ rows

_____ in each row

____ × ____ = ____

6

_____ row

_____ in that row

____ × ____ = ____

Multiply across and down.

7 4 rows of 2

____ × ____ = ____

8 3 rows of 5

____ × ____ = ____

Name _____

What is the end time?

1 Practice the flute.

Starts

4:00

Lasts

30 minutes

Ⓐ 4:00

Ⓑ 3:30

Ⓒ 5:00

Ⓓ 4:30

Mark the object that weighs the most.

2

Ⓐ   Ⓑ   Ⓒ   Ⓓ

Mark the number that comes right before.

3 _____, 500

399	501	499	490
Ⓐ	Ⓑ	Ⓒ	Ⓓ

Mark the number that comes right after.

4 860, _____

861	859	870	960
Ⓐ	Ⓑ	Ⓒ	Ⓓ

Mark the sum.

5
```
  127
+ 348
```

375	475	465	4,715
Ⓐ	Ⓑ	Ⓒ	Ⓓ

Writing in Math

6 Tell something that you do in the A.M. and something that you do in the P.M.

_____

_____

_____

Making Equal Groups

Learn!

15 pennies to share! There are 3 children. How many pennies will each child get?

Each child should get the same amount, or an **equal share**. Each child gets __5__ pennies.

Word Bank

equal share

Check ✓

How many coins will each child get?
Use coins. Draw the answer.

1 12 nickels, 4 children

Each child gets _____ nickels.

2 10 dimes, 5 children

Each child gets _____ dimes.

Think About It   Reasoning

There were 6 coins. Each child got the same amount. If each child got 2 coins, how many children were there?

How many coins will each child get?
Write the answer. Use coins if you need to.

3 16 pennies, 4 children

Each child gets __4__ pennies.

4 12 pennies, 6 children

Each child gets _____ pennies.

5 4 pennies, 4 children

Each child gets _____ penny.

Complete the table.

	Number of pennies:	Number of children:	How many pennies does each child get?
6	12	3	_____
7	25	5	_____
8	10	2	_____
9	8	1	_____
10	6	2	_____

Problem Solving   Number Sense

11 You have 12 pennies. Can you find
6 different ways to show equal groups?

_____ group of _____

_____ groups of _____

_____ groups of _____

_____ groups of _____

_____ groups of _____

_____ groups of _____

Home Connection Your child divided a set of objects into a given number of equal groups. **Home Activity** Have your child show you equal groups of objects.

Name _____

Learn!

To share things equally, you can **divide**.
12 rings are divided among 4 children.
How many rings does each child get?

12 **divided by** 4 is ___3___.
The **division sentence** is:

$$\underline{12} \div \underline{4} = \underline{3}$$

How many   How many   How many in
in all   groups   each group

Each child gets 3 rings.

Word Bank

divide
divided by (÷)
division sentence

Check ✓

Draw to show equal groups.
Write the division sentence.

1 15 balls divided among 5 buckets

_____ ÷ _____ = _____

2 9 marbles divided among 3 bags

_____ ÷ _____ = _____

Think About It   Number Sense

Mr. Carter gave his 2 children 5 tickets to share
equally. How many tickets did each child get?

Draw to show equal groups. Write the division sentence.

3 6 pencils divided among 2 pencil cases

_____ ÷ _____ = _____

4 16 crayons divided among 4 boxes

_____ ÷ _____ = _____

5 5 books divided among 5 desks

_____ ÷ _____ = _____

6 20 lunch trays divided among 4 tables

_____ ÷ _____ = _____

Problem Solving   Reasonableness

Draw a picture to help answer the question.

7 Mila and her friend divided 9 paint bottles between them. They each took 4 bottles and put the last bottle away. Does this solution make sense? Why or why not?

_____

_____

Home Connection Your child wrote division sentences to represent equal groups. **Home Activity** Have your child divide 10 spoons into 5 groups. Then have him or her write a division sentence to tell how many are in each group.

Name_____

Choose an Operation

 **Algebra**

3 children collected 5 leaves each.
How many leaves are there in all?

3 groups with 5 in each group.

Marissa

Annette

George

Circle the number sentence that solves the problem.

$3 + 5 = 8$ $(3 \times 5 = 15)$ $5 - 3 = 2$

There are __15__ leaves in all.

Check ✓

Circle the number sentence that solves the problem.

1 There are 20 balloons. 5 children will share them.
How many balloons will each child get?

$20 - 5 = 15$ $20 + 5 = 25$ $20 \div 5 = 4$

Each child will get _____ balloons.

Think About It   Reasoning

Explain why you chose the number sentence that
you did.

Circle the number sentence that solves the problem.

2 Kara has 2 winter hats and 3 straw hats. How many hats does she have in all?

$$3 + 2 = 5 \qquad 3 - 2 = 1 \qquad 3 \times 2 = 6$$

Kara has _____ hats.

3 4 friends have some bead dolls. Each has 3 bead dolls. How many bead dolls are there in all?

$$4 - 3 = 1 \qquad 4 + 3 = 7 \qquad 4 \times 3 = 12$$

There are _____ bead dolls in all.

4 Sam needs 9 buttons for a puppet. He has 3. How many more buttons does he need?

$$9 - 3 = 6 \qquad 9 + 3 = 12 \qquad 9 \div 3 = 3$$

He needs _____ more buttons.

5 There are 16 pine cones to go in 4 baskets. How many pine cones will be in each basket?

$$16 \div 4 = 4 \qquad 16 + 4 = 20 \qquad 16 - 4 = 12$$

Each basket gets _____ pine cones.

Home Connection Your child chose a number sentence to solve each problem. **Home Activity** Have your child explain to you the meaning of the four operations: $+, -, \times, \div$.

PROBLEM-SOLVING APPLICATIONS
Up, Up, and Away!

 Dorling Kindersley

Mighty Machines
AIRPLANE
And other airport machines

1 A 747 jet has 4 engines. How many engines do three 747 jets have?

_____ × _____ = _____ engines

Do You Know...
that a fully loaded 747 jumbo jet weighs more than 70 elephants? It's true!

A 747 "jumbo jet" is the largest passenger airplane in the world.

2 A 747 jet carried 398 passengers from New York to Los Angeles. Then it carried 402 passengers from Los Angeles back to New York. How many passengers did the jet carry on those two flights?

_____ + _____ = _____ passengers

Fun Fact!
Helicopters can fly forward, sideways, and backward! They can also hover, or stay in one place, in the air.

3 6 passengers on a jumbo jet shared 12 bags of pretzels. How many bags of pretzels did each passenger get?

_____ ÷ _____ = _____ bags per passenger

4 The Concorde flies 1 mile in about 3 seconds.
About how many seconds does it take
the Concorde to fly 4 miles?

_____ miles ✕ _____ seconds per mile = _____ seconds in all

5 The Concorde carried 98 passengers on one trip,
89 passengers on another trip, and 96 passengers
on a third trip. How many passengers in all did
the Concorde carry on those 3 trips?

_____ + _____ + _____ = _____ passengers in all

*The fastest passenger plane
in the world is called
the Concorde.*

6 Some small planes have only 2 seats. They are used as air taxis.
An air taxi made 4 trips a day 5 days in a row.
How many trips did it make in those 5 days?

_____ ✕ _____ = _____ trips

7 **Writing in Math**

*The Citation is
a business jet.*

Write a multiplication story about airplanes.

Home Connection Your child learned how to solve problems by
applying his or her math skills. **Home Activity** Talk to your child
about how he or she solved the problems on these two pages.

Name _____

How many coins will each child get?
Use coins. Draw the answer.

1 12 pennies, 3 children

Each child gets _____ pennies.

2 10 pennies, 2 children

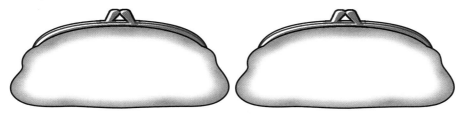

Each child gets _____ pennies.

Draw to show equal groups.
Write the division sentence.

3 16 crackers divided among 4 bags

_____ ÷ _____ = _____

Circle the number sentence that solves the problem.

4 Carly had 8 wind-up animals.
2 animals broke. How many
wind-up animals are left?

$8 \div 2 = 4$　　　$2 \times 8 = 16$　　　$8 - 2 = 6$

_____ wind-up animals are left.

1 You have 50¢. Mark the pair of toys you can buy.

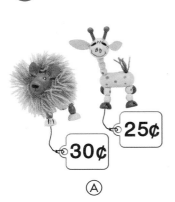
30¢ 25¢

60¢ 15¢

Ⓐ

15¢ 30¢

Ⓑ

Ⓒ

60¢ 25¢

Ⓓ

Find the sum or difference.

2
$$71 + 19$$
Ⓐ 89
Ⓑ 910
Ⓒ 90
Ⓓ 80

3
$$64 - 37$$
Ⓐ 27
Ⓑ 37
Ⓒ 33
Ⓓ 91

Use the graph to answer each question.

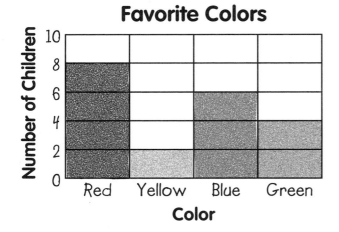

Favorite Colors

Number of Children: 10, 8, 6, 4, 2, 0
Color: Red Yellow Blue Green

4 How many children's favorite color is blue?

2   4   6   8
Ⓐ   Ⓑ   Ⓒ   Ⓓ

5 Which is the favorite color of most children?

red   yellow   blue   green
Ⓐ   Ⓑ   Ⓒ   Ⓓ

Writing in Math

6 Draw the triangle to show a flip.

Name _____

Dividing by Subtracting **Algebra**

If you start at 0 and add 3s,
in 4 jumps you will get to 12.

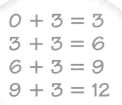
$0 + 3 = 3$
$3 + 3 = 6$
$6 + 3 = 9$
$9 + 3 = 12$

$$4 \times 3 = 12$$

Start at 12. Subtract 3s until you get to 0.

12, 9, 6, 3, 0 _____   __4__ jumps $12 \div 3 = \underline{4}$

Use a number line.
Subtract until you get to 0.

1 Start at 12. Subtract 6s.

_____   ____ jumps $12 \div 6 = \underline{\quad}$

2 Start at 10. Subtract 2s.

_____   ____ jumps $10 \div 2 = \underline{\quad}$

3 Start at 15. Subtract 5s.

_____   ____ jumps $15 \div 5 = \underline{\quad}$

Writing in Math

4 Subtract to find $3 \div 1$, $4 \div 1$, $6 \div 1$, and $10 \div 1$.
What pattern do you see?

 Home Connection Your child used repeated subtraction
to divide. **Home Activity** Ask your child how he or she did
Exercise 2.

Name _____

Multiply Using a Calculator

You can use a calculator to multiply.
Press ON/C each time you begin.
Follow the directions. Use each number once.

1 Cross out two numbers with a product of 9.

2 Circle two numbers with a product of 15.

3 Underline two numbers with a product of 20.

4 Draw squares around two numbers with a product of 28.

5 Put check marks next to two numbers with a product of 100.

6 Draw a star next to the number that is left over.

Think About It   Reasoning

How could you use a calculator to find two numbers with a product of 18?

Home Connection Your child used a calculator to multiply two numbers.
Home Activity Ask your child to explain two ways to find the product of 3 and 2 using a calculator.

Name _____

Use Writing in Math

Some math tests ask you to explain
how you found your answer.
Use math words to help you do this.

Test-Taking Strategies
Understand the Question
Get Information for the Answer
Plan How to Find the Answer
Make Smart Choices
Use Writing in Math

1 For a party, Jay's mom bought
24 balloons for 8 children to share
equally. How many balloons will
each child get? Use counters.
Then explain how you found your answer.

Each child will get 3 balloons. I divided 24 counters

into 8 equal groups. Then I counted the counters in

each group. There were 3 counters in each group.

A boy named Terry used these math words to help him
explain how he found his answer: **divided, equal groups,**
and **counted.**

Your Turn

Solve. Then explain how you found your answer.

2 Jay gave each of the 8 children at his party
2 toy cars. How many toy cars did Jay give away?
Use counters. Explain how you found your answer.

_____

_____

_____

Home Connection Your child prepared for standardized tests by using math terms
correctly to explain how he or she solved a problem. **Home Activity** Have your child
point out math words that he or she used to explain the answer to Exercise 2. *(Possible
response: I used counters to make 8 equal groups of 2. Then I counted by 2s to find
how many counters in all.)*

Name _____

Read Together

Frog or Toad?

Both frogs and toads spend time on land and in the water. But frogs have longer back legs than most toads have. Frogs also have wet and smooth skin, while toads have bumpy and dry skin.

Toad

Frog Facts

Write an addition sentence and a multiplication sentence to solve each problem.

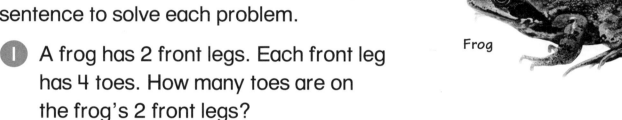
Frog

1 A frog has 2 front legs. Each front leg has 4 toes. How many toes are on the frog's 2 front legs?

____ + ____ = ____ toes   ____ × ____ = ____ toes

2 A frog has 2 hind legs. Each hind leg has 5 toes. How many toes are on the frog's 2 hind legs?

____ + ____ = ____ toes   ____ × ____ = ____ toes

3 The largest frog in the world is the Goliath frog of Africa. It can weigh as much as 7 pounds. How much would 4 Goliath frogs weigh?

____ + ____ + ____ + ____ = ____ lb   ____ × ____ = ____ lb

Take It to the NET
Video and Activities
www.scottforesman.com

Home Connection Your child solved problems about frogs and toads by writing addition sentences and multiplication sentences. **Home Activity** Ask your child to explain how he or she solved one of the problems on this page.

Chapter 12

Name _____

Use counters to show equal groups.
Skip count to find how many there are in all.

1 4 groups, 1 in each group

_____ in all

2 5 groups, 5 in each group

_____ in all

Write an addition sentence and a multiplication sentence
that tell how many objects there are in all.

3

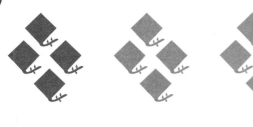

____ + ____ + ____ = ____

____ × ____ = ____

4

____ + ____ + ____ + ____ = ____

____ × ____ = ____

Write a multiplication sentence
to describe the array.

5

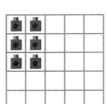

_____ × _____ = _____

Write the number of rows and the
number in each row. Find the product.

6

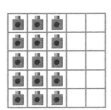

_____ × _____ = _____

How many are there in all?

7

_____ rows

_____ in each row

_____ × _____ = _____

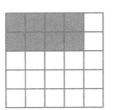

_____ rows

_____ in each row

_____ × _____ = _____

Multiply across and down.

 8

____ × ____ = ____

×

9

____ × ____ = ____

×

Draw a picture to solve the problem.

10 Joey counted 5 grasshoppers in the garden. Each one had 2 feelers. How many feelers were there?

____ × ____ = ____

How many pennies will each child get?
Write the answer. Use coins if you need to.

11 20 pennies, 10 children

Each child gets _____ pennies.

12 8 pennies, 2 children

Each child gets _____ pennies.

Draw to show equal groups.
Write the division sentence.

13 12 apples divided among 2 baskets

_____ ÷ _____ = _____

Circle the number sentence that solves the problem.

14 3 rings will fit in a box. How many boxes are needed for 15 rings?

_____ boxes are needed.

$$15 - 3 = 12$$
$$3 + 15 = 18$$
$$15 \div 3 = 5$$

Name _____

Cumulative Review and Test Prep

Mark the number that makes the statement true.

1   ___ < 27

30	25	44	29
Ⓐ	Ⓑ	Ⓒ	Ⓓ

2   63 > ___

65	78	63	61
Ⓐ	Ⓑ	Ⓒ	Ⓓ

Mark the doubles fact that helps you solve the problem.

3
```
  20
- 10
```

6 + 5 ――― 11	9 + 9 ――― 18	10 + 10 ――― 20	5 + 5 ――― 10
Ⓐ	Ⓑ	Ⓒ	Ⓓ

Mark the plane shape you could show by tracing the solid figure.

4

◯	▢	△	▭
Ⓐ	Ⓑ	Ⓒ	Ⓓ

Mark how many. Use models if you need to.

5

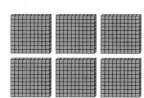   **100 more is _____.**

- Ⓐ 500
- Ⓑ 600
- Ⓒ 700
- Ⓓ 800

Mark the object that holds the least.

6

| Ⓐ | Ⓑ | Ⓒ | Ⓓ |

Estimate. Circle **more** or **less** to answer the question.

You have:	You buy:	Answer:
⑦ 70¢	 51¢	Will you have more or less than 30¢ left? more less

Cross out the extra information. Then solve the problem.

⑧ There are 18 boys and 23 girls playing in the park. There are 6 swings. How many children are playing in all?

_____ children

Write the ordered pair where each ball is located.

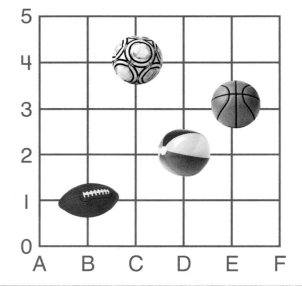

⑨  _____

⑩  _____

⑪  _____

Writing in Math

⑫ Write a math story in which the numbers 34 and 65 are added together. Then solve.

_____

_____

_____

Picture Glossary

addition sentence

$$3 + 2 = 5$$

addends

area

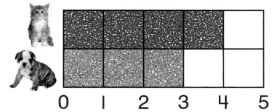

The **area** of the shape
is 12 square units.

bar graph

Favorite Pets

0　1　2　3　4　5

calendar

January								← month
S	M	T	W	T	F	S		← days
		1	2	3	4	5		
6	7	8	9	10	11	(12)		← date
13	14	15	16	17	18	19		
(20	21	22	23	24	25	26)		← week
27	28	29	30	31				

cent (¢)

A penny is 1 **cent** (1¢).

centimeter (cm)

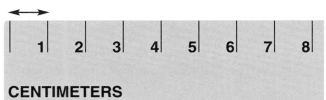

CENTIMETERS

count back

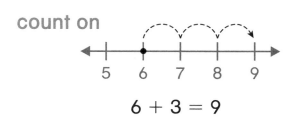

$$8 - 2 = 6$$

count on

6　7　8　9

$$6 + 3 = 9$$

cup (c)

difference

$$9 - 3 = 6$$

$$\begin{array}{r} 9 \\ -\ 3 \\ \hline 6 \end{array}$$

difference

digit

5 3

digits

53 has two **digits.**

dime

10¢ or 10 cents

divide

$$10 \div 2 = 5$$

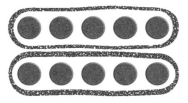

division sentence

$18 \div 3 = 6$

dollar ($)

$1.00 or 100¢

estimate

$38 + 19$ is about 60.

even numbers

2, 4, 6, 8, 10, ...

fact family

$9 + 3 = 12$ $12 - 9 = 3$
$3 + 9 = 12$ $12 - 3 = 9$

foot (ft)

A **foot** is 12 inches.

fraction

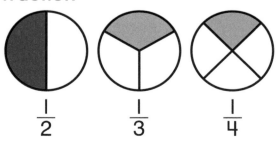

$\frac{1}{2}$ $\frac{1}{3}$ $\frac{1}{4}$

greater than (>)

68 is **greater than** 49.

68 > 49

half-dollar

50¢, $0.50, or 50 cents

half hour

A **half hour** is 30 minutes.

hour

An **hour** is 60 minutes.   **hour
It is 7 o'clock.**   **hand**

inch (in.)

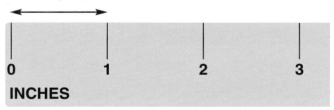

kilogram (kg)

This book measures about
1 **kilogram**.

less than (<)

32 is **less than** 48.

32 < 48

line of symmetry

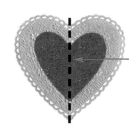 **line of symmetry**

liter (L)

meter

A golf club is about 1 **meter** long.

minute

minutes   **minute hand**

There are 60 **minutes** in 1 hour.

multiplication sentence

$7 \times 3 = 21$

multiply

$3 \times 4 = 12$

nickel

5¢ or 5 cents

odd numbers

1, 3, 5, 7, 9, ...

ordinal numbers

fifth shelf
fourth shelf
third shelf
second shelf
first shelf

penny

1¢ or 1 cent

perimeter

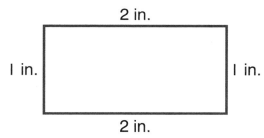

2 in.

1 in.   1 in.

2 in.

The distance around is the **perimeter.**
perimeter = 6 inches

pictograph

Rock Collections	
Kayla	
Tyler	

Each = 2 rocks.

pint (pt)  =

place value

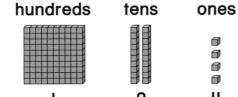

hundreds	tens	ones
1	2	4

There are 1 hundred, 2 tens, and 4 ones in 124.

plane shapes

circle   rectangle   square   triangle

pound (lb)

The bread weighs about 1 **pound.**

product

$3 \times 4 = 12$

$$\begin{array}{r} 3 \\ \times\ 4 \\ \hline 12 \end{array}$$

times ⌐   ⌐ **product** ⌐

quart (qt)

 =

quarter

25¢ or 25 cents

regroup

13 ones =
1 ten 3 ones

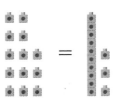 =

solid figures

cone   cube   cylinder

pyramid   rectangular   sphere
              prism

subtraction sentence

$12 - 4 = 8$

sum

$2 + 3 = 5$

$$\begin{array}{r} 2 \\ +\ 3 \\ \hline 5 \end{array}$$

⌐ **sum** ⌐

Venn diagram

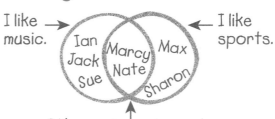

I like music. →   ← I like sports.

Ian Jack Sue   Marcy Nate   Max   Sharon

↑
I like music and sports.

yard (yd)

A baseball bat is about 1 **yard** long.